DATE DUE

HARVARD TERCENTENARY PUBLICATIONS

———

FACTORS DETERMINING HUMAN BEHAVIOR

AUTHORITY AND THE INDIVIDUAL

INDEPENDENCE, CONVERGENCE, AND BORROWING IN INSTITUTIONS, THOUGHT, AND ART

The foregoing volumes embody the papers presented at three symposia of the Harvard Tercentenary Conference of Arts and Sciences (August 31–September 12, 1936)

———

THE FUTURE OF THE COMMON LAW

This volume comprises the principal addresses at the Conference on the Future of the Common Law (August 19–21, 1936)

———

HARVARD TERCENTENARY CELEBRATION

A chronicle of the Tercentenary Year, this volume includes the proceedings of the Tercentenary Days, September 16, 17, and 18, 1936.

HARVARD TERCENTENARY PUBLICATIONS

AUTHORITY AND THE INDIVIDUAL

LONDON : HUMPHREY MILFORD

OXFORD UNIVERSITY PRESS

AUTHORITY AND THE INDIVIDUAL

CAMBRIDGE, MASSACHUSETTS

HARVARD UNIVERSITY PRESS

1937

PRINTED AT THE HARVARD UNIVERSITY PRESS

CAMBRIDGE, MASS., U.S.A.

PREFACE

THE Harvard Tercentenary Conference was a part of the University's corporate expression of gratitude to all who have built and enriched her life. Harvard men have always been proud of the high courage which marked their Puritan forebears. They may be equally proud of the intellectual level of that little band. In 1643 the graduates of Cambridge and Oxford who had migrated to New England numbered 130, and constituted in the population a higher proportion of university-trained men than was again seen until the twentieth century. If we turn to the English counterpart, we find that the Royal Society germinated in Oxford during the period of Puritan domination and that the brother-in-law of Oliver Cromwell was a leader of that scientific movement. Another leader, and one of the strongest forces in what he called the "invisible college," was Robert Boyle, who has left on record significant and weighty statements of his ideals as a scholar and experimenter. He speaks of "that noble and improvable faculty which enables an Ingenious man to pry into the innermost Recesses of Mysterious Nature," and goes on to a memorable phrase, "that noble and improvable faculty whereby an Inquisitive Soul may expatiate itself through the whole Immensity of the Universe." Thereby Boyle takes his stand with his master Bacon, points clearly to the common basis of all our knowledge, and upholds its unity.

From these developments we may divine something of what must have been in the minds of the men who founded Harvard. They were concerned with learning as a whole, and the committee charged with the organization of the Tercentenary Conference was faced with the obligation of trying to do something which should in a measure correspond to their ideals. Accordingly, while providing to the best of their facilities for those aspects of knowledge which did not seem to admit of being grouped, they planned three symposia: Factors Determining Human Behavior; Authority and the Individual; Independence, Convergence, and Borrowing in Institutions, Thought, and Art. These symposia, unlike the rest of the Conference, called for the collaboration of scholars working in diverse fields of science and learning and thereby cut across conventional academic disciplines. Thus we had on one platform three groups of eminent men who contributed, each from the standpoint of his own special experience, with his own characteristic way of thought and his own method of study, to a common understanding of the vast problems of human behavior. The first symposium thus begins with our inner makeup and treats the forces which condition or impel human conduct; the second proceeds to the consideration of the economic, social, political, and intellectual factors in the structure of society which act upon the individual through social institutions and through accepted ideas; the third traces the yet broader interrelations and approximations observable in peoples separated by time or space.

In these days many delight in taunting the scholarly world with the charge of specialization and in repeating against our universities the old quip of "Knowing more and more about less and less." However, the men within academic walls know that the essential unity of the learned world is manifested by a common origin, a common history, and a common tradition preserved for nearly a thousand years in the universities. Scaliger, Casaubon, Grotius; Harvey, Descartes, Newton — they are our heroes just as they were the heroes of an earlier age. To use the words of a writer of the twelfth century, "We are like dwarfs, sitting on the shoulders of giants, in order that we may see things more numerous and more distant than they could see, not, certainly, by reason of the sharpness of our own vision or the tallness of our bodies, but because we are lifted and raised on high by the greatness of giants."

The great men of the past could survey all or a great part of the domain of knowledge as then understood. The expansion of that domain has of necessity entailed specialization: but only a superficial observer will hold that specialization leads mainly to sterility. Hitherto, in the whole history of our race, it has in fact had a beneficial influence upon the progress of general knowledge. Specialization gives rise to skill and to method. These in turn lead to the formation of a new department of knowledge. Then interactions are set up between this department and other departments, new or old, and thereby the cycle is completed and still another special field of study comes in view. Meanwhile, the interactions continue. With the multiplication of specialties they become more numerous, and general knowledge increases. The symposia reported in the present book and in the two companion volumes are presented as illustrations of such interaction: *sed nondum finis.*

CONTENTS

IV. CLASSICISM AND ROMANTICISM

I
THE STATE AND ECONOMIC ENTERPRISE

INTELLIGENCE AND THE GUIDANCE OF ECONOMIC EVOLUTION

Wesley Clair Mitchell, Ph.D., LL.D., Litt.D.

Professor of Economics, Columbia University

IN THE confident days of its youth, political economy believed that it had solved the important and timely problem put before this session. It was ready to dispense advice on public policies, and its admonitions concerning the duties of the state toward economic enterprise were especially clear and urgent. Current economics, the off-spring of this authoritative discipline, is a more cautious creature. When asked for practical advice it reveals an inferiority complex; but in compensation it claims to have a stricter scientific conscience than troubled its philosophic forebear. Economic theory now seldom forgets that its conclusions rest upon assumptions expressly designed to simplify its problems sufficiently to make them amenable to analysis. When asked for advice it answers primly: "That is not a proper request to make of a science. My task is merely to examine the functional relations among certain processes under a variety of carefully specified conditions. What I have to say is the truth and nothing but the truth; it is not the whole truth. In practical affairs," economics goes on, "it is necessary to take account of many factors that I purposely exclude. You should indeed pay heed to my findings, they are highly important. But you should not expect me to tell you what to do in this messy world, so unlike the orderly realm I create for scientific ends. If some of my alleged representatives desire to dictate your policies, don't suppose that they speak with my authority. Of course an economist is also a citizen, and like his fellows must reach decisions on current issues of all sorts; but if he remembers what I have taught him he won't try to pass off his notions about policy as my deliverances. You do well to seek scientific understanding as a basis for action; but please note that I have several sister sciences of human behavior whose business it is to study the numerous factors that I pass over. You should consult the whole family, though I am sorry to say that my younger sisters are so immature that you cannot expect much help from them." On which ungracious note, economics resumes the irreproachable attitude it has learned to strike when asked to make itself useful.

Needless to say, the planners of this symposium on "Authority and the Individual" would not express themselves in this wise. They have proposed collaboration among the social sciences and humanities "with a view to breaking down traditionally specialized lines of approach to an important and timely problem and to make its solution the object of a common attack." My whimsical version of the methodological position of current economics indicates that its votaries are logically bound to accept this program. For us in particular collaboration should be a wholesome experience, for it should correct our attitude toward the other social sciences and put us in our proper place. The "purer" we make economics the more generously must our findings be supplemented before they can be relied upon as a trustworthy guide, and the keener should we be to work with men of other disciplines.

But collaboration may take two courses. First, representatives of different disciplines may bring each his own contribution to the understanding of a problem in as perfect a form as his technique makes possible, leaving to others the responsibility of fitting together the several contributions. Conscientious specialists who realize how likely they are to go wrong when they wander outside their familiar boundaries may well prefer this course. But who can vouch that the several contributions worked out by independent specialists will make a whole? And what group is ready to assume the difficult and responsible task of putting the results together so far as they will fit? If there is no such group at present, can one be formed? That is a question for the future and I shall come back to it later. But as matters now stand, cannot the representatives of the social sciences and humanities collaborate with one another in a more direct fashion? If we wish to break down our traditionally specialized lines of approach and join in a common attack upon social problems, must not each of us strive to effect some such change in his own thinking? This second mode of collaboration involves not merely following one another's work but also making use of one another's approaches to our own problems. It is a difficult course and beset by dangers; yet in so far as we can pursue it each of us can make his work as a specialist more interesting to himself, more valuable to his colleagues in other sciences, and more effective in a common attack upon the problems we hope to solve.

Believing that we should construe in this sense the invitation of Harvard University to collaborate with one another, I shall discuss the formidable topic assigned to me, "Intelligence and the Guidance of Economic Evolution," not as a problem in pure economics but as realistically as I can, making use of what notions I possess about human behavior at large. Doubtless I shall make mistakes that economic historians, psychologists, sociologists, or political scientists would avoid. And I know that some men of my own craft will think my whole procedure ill-advised. But genuine efforts at collaboration involve such risks, and each of us is justified in running them.

I

Let me start with the solution of the problem set me that was given by Adam Smith in 1776. His *Wealth of Nations* was devoted in large part to criticizing the Mercantilist doctrine that it is the statesman's duty to regulate the economic activities of private people as much as it is his duty to provide for the common defense. Adam Smith's critique centered on the proposition that the wealth of a nation is the aggregate of the wealth of its citizens, and that each citizen in his local situation is a better judge of how to augment his wealth than a distant statesman can be. Restated in terms of my topic, this argument runs: Nations prosper more when they leave the guidance of their economic evolution to individuals than when governments attempt to guide. No distrust of intelligence as a guide is implied; the contention is that in the industrial army planning by a central staff is worse than futile; the planning should be done by the private soldiers, individually or in such companies as they voluntarily form under captains who rise from the ranks. All that the staff need do for industry is to see that the privates and officers treat one another fairly, and to perform a few necessary tasks that no private or company would find it profitable to undertake.

Had this symposium been held on the hundredth anniversary of the *Wealth of Nations*, I fancy that the economists invited to participate in it would have felt competent to treat this problem without the collaboration of authorities in the other social sciences. And they would have endorsed Adam Smith's solution of the problem, some with more, perhaps some with less, reservations than the Father of Political Economy had made. It is true that the last of the great classical trinity, John Stuart Mill, had avowed himself a socialist; but he built his temperate hopes for the betterment of economic conditions, not upon a recrudescence of governmental planning, but primarily upon the cumulative growth of producers' co-operation. Gradually the employees of business enterprises would take over the functions of ownership and management; for workers expecting a share in the profits would be more industrious and more intelligent than mere wage-earners, and so co-operative concerns would prevail in the competitive struggle for survival. Of course this speculation posits the continuance of what Adam Smith fondly called "the obvious and simple system of natural liberty." Since the most respected socialist of the time accepted the general principle of *laissez faire* that doctrine seemed secure.

But 1876 marks as well as any date we could select the culmination of faith in the guidance of economic evolution by individual intelligence. Today the problem that Adam Smith thought he had solved is as timely as it was in 1776. I doubt whether any economist attending the present symposium feels as competent as Adam Smith did to tell governments just how far they should carry their intervention in economic activities. For within the past one-hundred-and-sixty years economists have made progress toward grasping the complexities of social problems, if not toward agreement upon solutions. Numerous developments have combined to change their attitude toward governmental regulation of economic enterprise, of which the most important has been the world's experiences with different types of economic organization.

Great Britain was far better prepared than Adam Smith

realized to accept his teaching. Private enterprise, often in defiance of mercantilist regulations, had become a mass phenomenon before the *Wealth of Nations* was published. The new doctrine was a philosopher's rationalization of practices engaged in by enterprising men because they were profitable. Negatively it eased the consciences of technical lawbreakers by assuring them that their actions promoted the public welfare; constructively it gave them a logical argument for demanding the repeal of hampering regulations. Of course, beneficiaries of the old system were not deterred by any theorizing from striving to maintain their legal rights. But technical developments that Adam Smith could not foresee kept weakening the defenders of the old order, swelling the number and increasing the power of those who profited by *laissez faire*. A growing volume of trade, domestic and foreign, stimulated men with initiative to try new forms of business organization, some of which proved highly efficient. The same factor created a lively interest in finding cheaper methods of producing, processing, and transporting materials in bulk. This alliance of mechanical invention and business enterprise proved irresistible. The classes that had vested interests in the old order could neither meet the commercial competition of their rivals who were introducing new methods, nor make effective answer to Adam Smith's logic. Statesmen of a speculative turn of mind readily accepted the *Wealth of Nations* as their guide in commercial policy; statesmen who waited for the teachings of experience followed more hesitantly but in increasing number; politicians who accepted the dominant opinion of the day slowly fell into line. Partly by allowing mercantilist statutes to become dead letters, partly by formal action, the country dropped the policy of mercantilist planning and deemed the results good on the whole. By the 1860's or

'70's most Britons who thought about such matters believed that practical experience had demonstrated the soundness of Adam Smith's doctrine, and that other countries would gradually learn the great lesson that theory and practice combined to teach. A glowing vision was cherished by liberal spirits of freedom for all men in their economic, political, and social relations, a vision of peace among the nations securely based upon recognition that peace is the best policy, a vision of cumulative progress in the conquest of nature assuring not merely a higher standard of comfort for all mankind but also a nobler life. What Carlyle had dubbed the "dismal science" appeared to many as the brightest hope of the race.

II

But decades before this stage was reached, certain emendations had proved necessary in "the obvious and simple system of natural liberty" as presented by Adam Smith. The horrible treatment of "pauper apprentices" in some cotton mills and of climbing boys apprenticed to chimney sweeps early convinced the public that these unfortunate children were not able to judge or to defend their own interests. They seemed to need and they were granted the protection of the state. Later revelations of the exploitation of child workers at large, of young persons, and also of women, led to further protective legislation justified by the same argument. Only adult males were credited with knowing better than Parliament what was good for them and with being able to look out for themselves. But even that amended proposition was challenged with success. Seamen would sail on overloaded ships, colliers would go down ill-ventilated mines, factory hands would take foolish risks with unfenced machinery, men would expose themselves to occupational diseases. Indeed the new industry, imperfectly controlling the powerful natural forces it was putting to work, was full of hazards that men underrated, and government felt constrained to exercise its superior intelligence for their benefit. It appeared also that many investors were quite incapable of judging where to place their capital safely, that consumers would buy impure foods and drugs, that town dwellers endangered one another by their ignorance of sanitation. In short, the assumption that the individual is a better judge of his own interests than a distant statesman was found to be subject to many exceptions. These exceptions became more numerous and more important as social organization became more complex. Hence governmental intervention was gradually extended in many directions of which Adam Smith had not thought, but of which perhaps he would have approved could he have revisited Great Britain in 1876.

Interwoven with the problem presented by those who seemed not to know their own interests was a cognate problem presented by persons who claimed that they could not protect interests of which they were painfully conscious. The argument for *laissez faire* assumed that in pursuing his own interest every individual would be prevented from charging unduly high prices for his goods or services by the competition of rival sellers and also protected against having to accept unduly low prices by competition among buyers. This competitive regime promised to work out a rough sort of justice and also to stimulate efficiency in serving the public. Business men who did not measure up to current standards would be reduced to the status of workmen, taking orders from abler captains of industry. Thus inefficiency would be penalized, merit rewarded, and the country assured that its economic

energies were directed by the ablest available leaders —
the ablest because they were continually being subjected to
the infallible test of ability to survive in a competitive
struggle. It is no wonder that this view captivated many
philosophic minds and suited successful men of affairs; nor
is it any wonder that other classes were less satisfied.
Wage-earners in particular protested that the conditions of
the labor market did not assure them a fair price for their
services. For in this market the sellers were a crowd of
individuals ill-informed about current conditions and future prospects, unskilled in bargaining, forced by pressing
need to underbid one another. On the other side of the
market stood the employers, each one a combination in
himself, able to merge into larger combinations when they
saw fit, the best judges of commercial conditions, keen bar-
gainers, able to wait. How valid was this distressful picture
of the workingman's plight in the early decades of the
nineteenth century admitted of argument. The point
that concerns us is that disciples of Adam Smith persuaded
Parliaments that were moving toward *laissez faire* to repeal the Anti-Combination Acts and to legalize trade
unions. Some advocates of these measures believed that
wage-earners would learn that combinations were expensive
and futile, but they were bad prophets. Trade unions grew
in strength after the fluctuating fashion of human institutions, and later Parliaments confirmed the policy of coun-
tenancing voluntary restriction of competition among
sellers in the labor market.

Meanwhile cases were becoming prominent in which
competition among business enterprises themselves seemed
plainly detrimental to the public interest. The classic illustration was provided by the gas industry. If two competing companies sought to serve the same town each would
have to lay mains and provide connections. The total in-

vestment would be needlessly large. If both companies received the going rate of return upon their capital the consumers would be overcharged. If neither company made money, or if one succeeded and the other failed, part of the country's precious capital would be wasted. Thus what were often called "natural monopolies" seemed to be exceptions to the rule that prices would be kept reasonable by competition. They were also recognized as exceptions to the rule that government should let business alone. For the only way to protect the customers of monopolies from extortion seemed to be governmental regulation of rates or governmental ownership. British municipalities that were strongholds of *laissez faire* became strongholds also of "municipal socialism," while the central government experimented with various plans for controlling the railways and took the telegraph and telephone systems into the post office.

The continued progress of the Industrial Revolution and the concomitant development of large-scale business kept raising new problems of this type. Were all public utilities best treated as monopolies and subjected to special controls? Should the production of electrical current, perhaps coal mining and even housing be added to the list of public utilities? Was not the progress of engineering with its trend toward more elaborate and specialized machinery threatening to put many industries into a position where cut-throat competition among independent concerns would be almost as wasteful as competition between two gas companies? And if business managers stopped short of cut-throat competition, how far short would they stop? Left to themselves, would they compete actively enough to protect consumers?

The theoretical difficulty underlying this practical danger had been pointed out by Adam Smith's younger contemporary, the Earl of Lauderdale, who challenged the assumption that the wealth of a nation is the aggregate of the wealth of its citizens. On the contrary, said Lauderdale, public wealth consists in an abundance of useful goods, while scarcity enhances the value of private property. The individual pursuing his own gain seeks to limit his output to the volume most profitable to himself, and that aim is antagonistic to the public's interest in abundance. Where active competition prevails, the individual who seeks to increase his profits by limiting the supply will lose customers to his rivals; there the pursuit of self-interest leads every producer to sell as much as he can so long as prices exceed his costs of production. But this "artificial harmony of interests" established by competition is precarious. For the pursuit of self-interest gives every man a strong incentive to escape from the pressure of competition into the ampler freedom of monopoly; that is, to destroy the one great safeguard of the public's interest in abundance. Every class engages in this destructive practice so far as it can, and blames other classes that succeed in so doing. Employers charge that labor unions limit the number of apprentices, working hours, and output per man-hour; that they seek to limit employment to union members, and limit admission to their own ranks by high initiation fees. Business men are popularly assumed to be the most successful sinners. Thorstein Veblen could picture the modern captain of industry as a strategist concerned mainly with the practice of "capitalistic sabotage"; that is, with the effort to limit the inordinate abundance of goods that modern engineering would provide to those modest supplies that will yield the maximum net revenues.

Another type of difficulty, business interference in government, had been pointed out by Adam Smith himself. In his eloquent plea for "the simple and obvious system of natural liberty," Smith tacitly assumed that government aimed to increase the wealth of the nation as a whole. But in a much earlier passage, not often recalled by his disciples, he had pointed out how unscrupulously clever are men of business in persuading the government that measures profitable only to their selfish interests will be advantageous to the public. A wise administration would be suspicious of advice from that quarter. Of course the laboring classes were too ignorant to form opinions upon public policy; but the country gentlemen, though often stupid about commercial matters, might be trusted, for their interests coincided broadly with those of the nation. Ricardo reversed this dictum: The interests of the landlords were opposed to those of every other class in the community, and a government controlled by them was selfishly misused to restrict foreign competition in foodstuffs in order to keep up rents — a policy that made food dear and money wages high, thereby reducing profits and impeding the accumulation of capital, on which progress depended. Later generations found reason for believing both Smith and Ricardo, or rather for believing that every class, the wage-earners included when they attain political influence, is eager to use the power of government for selfish ends. If any class has a bad eminence in this respect it is because circumstances enable that class to exercise more pressure upon government for the time being. And the more developments of one sort or another forced government to concern itself with economic affairs, the more private parties strove to control government. This development attracted more attention in the United States than in Great Britain; but it is naïve to think that in any country the problem of the state and economic enterprise can be treated realistically without considering economic enterprise in politics. We economists have been so prone to chide governments for interfering in business that we have often overlooked the extent to which these interferences are dictated by particular groups of business men. We usually think of government as Adam Smith did when he was expounding the policy of *laissez faire*, forgetting what we know of politics, just as Adam Smith for the moment forgot his warnings about the machinations of the commercial interest.

III

Not only did private enterprise produce various unfortunate results, it also failed to produce some good results that were expected by its champions. One bitter disappointment came in international relations. As noted before, during the heyday of *laissez faire* it was predicted that the mutual gains from free trade, demonstrated so convincingly by political economy, would bind the peoples of the world in an economic league of peace. Unhappily that was not the outcome. The volume of international trade did increase enormously as applications of science reduced the costs of transportation. But even the great commercial nations did not raise their foreign policies to the level of enlightened self-interest. They continued as in the age of mercantilism to waste their economic energies and to prostitute their intelligence in waging intermittent wars, though all sensible men knew that the chief outcome of wars is mutual impoverishment and frustration. Competition among the nations for economic gains kept degenerating into wrangles, and wrangles into fights — as would competition among individuals if there were no authority in the background to enforce peace. The economic theorists of *laissez faire* had committed a sin of omission that John R. Commons is helping this generation tardily to repair. They had failed to realize the implications of the role played by courts in economic transactions. Where there is no court to decide disputes, backed by power to enforce its decisions, enlightened self-interest has but a feeble control over human passions.

Nor was that the whole or the worst of the psychological error. Even in individual dealings regulated by courts, enlightened self-interest did not dominate behavior so much as the logic of *laissez faire* required. The most disconcerting discovery, or rather rediscovery, made by the social sciences in the nineteenth century was that man is a less rational animal than he thinks himself. He is prone to commit the "intellectualist fallacy" in giving accounts of his own behavior; that is one of his subtle ways of maintaining his self-esteem. Systematic thinkers are especially subject to this fallacy because the easiest way to give an intelligible account of what men do is to suppose that they are guided by calculations that the theorizer can repeat and foretell. Thus, as Walter Bagehot happily remarked, Adam Smith tacitly assumed that "there is a Scotsman inside every man." The literal-minded closet philosopher Jeremy Bentham made the assumption explicit. He crystallized the conception of functional psychology current among British thinkers of his time in the "felicific calculus" — a scheme so congenial to minds formed by a money-making age that diluted versions of it still dominate many of our speculations about economic behavior. Even the Malthusian "principle of population," with its modern-sounding emphasis upon instincts and habits, could be interpreted in terms of the felicific calculus by disciples of Bentham. The working classes, like their betters, were controlled by the two sovereign masters, pain and pleasure; but their lamentably defective education prevented them from foreseeing the pains that large families would bring upon them. The obvious remedy was to teach these un-

fortunates to associate low wages with premature mar-
riages. Thus political economy had a great civilizing
mission to perform for the most wretched part of humanity as well as for the more fortunate; it should help all
mankind to calculate correctly, that is, to find the real way
of maximizing net pleasures. But Darwin's teaching that
man is an animal fundamentally ruled by instincts changed
the perspective in which the social sciences saw problems
of human behavior. Psychologists revealed the artificiality
of the hedonistic analysis. Thinking appeared to be at best
an intermittent process, concerned with the humble task
of finding ways toward ends set by more fundamental
forces, and engaged in typically when routine modes of
action encounter obstacles. Bentham's clarity gave way to
confusion. Men are moved by fears and angers, vanity
and curiosity, longings for adventure and longings for security, sympathy with others and delight in making in-
vidious comparisons to their own advantage, by obsessions,
prejudices, visions, by forces conscious and unconscious to
which we give a hundred names but cannot delimit, describe, and classify in any way on which we can agree.

The rediscovery of man's irrationality helps us to understand why Adam Smith's "obvious and simple system of
natural liberty" was never given a full trial. Perhaps a
race evenly endowed with enlightened self-interest might
have made an earthly paradise of the sort they would have
liked by practicing *laissez faire*. Certainly the very unevenly endowed men that populate this planet, short-
sighted, quarrelsome, sentimental, did not do so. When
individual enterprise produced results they did not like
they would not wait for the evils to correct themselves in
the long run. Each generation has realized the force of
Mr. Keynes' remark that in the long run we shall all be
dead. Nor do all economic evils tend to cure themselves;

human nature being what it is, there are social processes
of degeneration that work cumulatively. The actual outcome was a mixed system of control by the imperfect
intelligence of individuals and control by the imperfect
intelligence of governments. And toward the end of the
nineteenth century the factor of governmental control was
gaining ground even in Great Britain. Just as individual
enterprise had become a mass phenomenon in a nation that
accepted mercantilism in principle, so governmental planning was becoming a mass phenomenon within a nation
that accepted the principle of *laissez faire*.

IV

While dwelling upon the difficulties encountered as the
system of free enterprise unfolded, we should not forget
how that form of economic organization stimulated men to
apply scientific discoveries to the work of the world, how
industry in turn aided scientific research, how standards of
living rose, death rates declined, and population increased,
how the Europeans spread over the earth exploiting natural resources and backward peoples, or how mightily the
leading commercial nations gained in power and prestige.
Those are highlights in the dazzling picture of progress in
the nineteenth century, as seen by people of our culture.
But the economic progress, so powerfully promoted by
individualism, produced consequences that led the successful nations to tinker further with their economic organization. If the earlier stages in the resurgence of national
economic planning were due primarily to incidental defects in the workings of *laissez faire*, the later stages were
due primarily to results produced by the major successes of
that system.

The growing economic prosperity of the nineteenth
century pushed men closer together while it also widened

the areas from which they drew supplies and over which they marketed products. Increasing density of population makes what one man does more important in numberless ways to the health and happiness of his neighbors. Men feel the need of more common rules concerning what no one shall do and also concerning more things that everyone must do for the commonweal. Government is the great agency for setting minimum standards of conduct that must be enforced upon the recalcitrant, and so finds its functions multiplying as the interdependence of individuals becomes more intimate and intricate. So also the wider geographic scope of economic organization exposes the modern man to more and more hazards that he cannot control, and he calls stridently upon his government for aid. Local regulations that served well enough in an earlier day are replaced by national rules, supplemented by international conventions.

This trend appears most clearly in American experience. "Rugged individualism" flourished upon the frontier. Laws were of slight help to the trapper and the squatter; they wanted little from the government. But the farmers who followed soon began demanding that the government aid them in getting facilities for shipping their produce to market; when these facilities had been provided they demanded that government regulate railroad rates; that government provide "cheap money"; later that government make grants to improve roads, set up land banks, subsidize exports of surplus produce, extend protective duties to agriculture, and so on. When we tell the story of American prosperity, we stress the westward expansion as one of the brightest episodes and celebrate the sturdy enterprise of the pioneers that made it possible. But when we study the record in detail, we find the conquerors of the continent full of complaints concerning their economic plight, and insistent with the full force of their rugged personalities that government come to their aid.

In other ways also the prosperity of the nineteenth century turned men's minds toward governmental planning. The extraordinary increase in the physical volume of production made unprecedented inroads upon the resources provided by nature. So far as I know, Stanley Jevons was the first economist to call attention to this danger. In the 1860's he showed that British industry and commerce rested on a foundation of cheap coal, and that if the extraction of coal continued to grow as rapidly in the future as it had been growing in the recent past the commercially accessible deposits would be exhausted in no long time. Mineral deposits were irreplaceable by man, and the race might wreck its career by looting Mother Nature's cupboard. Even abundantly endowed America took alarm over the destruction of its timber resources, the drain on its reserves of anthracite, the waste of its natural gas and petroleum, and, most menacing of all in the long run, the depletion of its soils through reckless cropping and erosion. The time span taken into account by individual enterprise was but as a day in the life of a nation. In manufacturing, transportation, commerce, and finance this difference might give rise to no grave troubles; but in the extractive industries a few generations of ruthless individuals might destroy the nation's heritage to get a mess of pottage for themselves. To prevent that irremediable disaster the conservationists saw no other remedy than governmental regulation based upon long-range planning.

Finally, the more completely any country organized its economic life on the basis of making and spending money incomes, the more effectively it developed its natural resources, but the more did it suffer from recurrent business depressions. It seemed that the equilibrium among economic activities directed toward the making of profits was essentially unstable. Periods of rapid expansion never lasted more than three or four years. Some parts of the economic mechanism always expanded faster than others, and when the resulting stresses exceeded the limit of tolerance prosperity ended in a crisis followed by a period of contraction, from which business recovered only to repeat the same disillusioning round. Men learned some devices for mitigating the violence of crises and alleviating the sufferings of depression; there were times when some nations fondly believed that they had mastered the disease; but further experience corrected that optimistic error. And these rhythmical alternations in the fortunes of commercial nations produced cyclical fluctuations about the secular trends of *laissez faire* and of governmental planning. During the prosperous phases of business cycles men were minded to demand that government let business alone; during depressions they demanded governmental interventions of the most diverse kinds. In this way also governments have been led to assume heavier responsibilities for stimulating, repressing, and supplementing private enterprise.

Another concomitant of economic progress that caused grave apprehension in many minds was the increasing disparity in the size of individual fortunes and in the magnitude of business enterprises. The poor did not grow poorer, but the rich certainly grew richer. The one-man business did not disappear, but the billion-dollar corporation came into existence. Those who feared these trends invoked governmental action to moderate them. Inheritance taxes, steeply-progressive income taxes, and anti-trust legislation of numerous sorts were in large part efforts to check the inequalities in economic success which a system of individual enterprise breeds.

V

No other people had gone so far as the British toward accepting the doctrine of *laissez faire*, and, to the best of my knowledge, in no other country was the reversal of the trend in the latter part of the nineteenth century so clear. But a change of the same type can be discerned in the economic speculation and the practical policy of other nations, among them the United States.

From the outset, American policy had been an unstable mixture of national planning and reliance on the play of private enterprise. The severing of relations with Great Britain forced our ancestors to devise a formal plan for governing themselves. When their first plan, the Articles of Confederation, had proved itself inefficient, they drew a second plan providing for a stronger central government, and that worked better. The first Secretary of the Treasury under the Constitution plunged at once into national economic planning and scored a series of notable successes. Among other measures he induced Congress to adopt a mild protective tariff to stimulate domestic manufactures. After decades of acrimonious struggles over this issue, we built a high wall of tariffs around our borders, while practicing free trade within them. The more powerful our industries grew the higher the duties rose; for this is one form of government planning that was guided substantially by private enterprise itself. Early in our history we sought to develop a national transportation system of highways and waterways; later we put our trust in privately owned railroads, to which we made lavish grants of public lands; later still we subjected the railroads to a complex set of state and federal regulations. We devised plans that promoted the settlement of the public domain by independent farmers, and allowed our timber and mineral lands to be plundered in wasteful fashion. First as farmers clearing fields for the plow, then as lumbermen supplying a market, we slaughtered our forests; now perhaps the most carefully devised of our national plans aims to conserve what remains of our timber resources. For decades we complacently watched the tide of immigration rise; then we began excluding those whom we held to be undesirable aliens; recently we have adopted a systematic plan for limiting the number and supposedly improving the quality of those whom we admit. We lagged behind European countries in social legislation and in governmental ownership of public utilities, but we led in efforts to check the growth of monopolies and to compel business men to compete with one another. We have evinced a childlike faith in what we can accomplish by passing laws and a childlike vanity in our sturdy individualism. But more and more our individualism has expressed itself in efforts to use the government as an agency for attaining what we severally desire.

This secular trend toward bolder and more varied economic planning by governments that prevailed in the western world during the closing decades of the nineteenth and the opening decade of the twentieth century was suddenly and enormously stimulated by the World War. Each of the belligerents felt compelled to mobilize its economic resources in order to maximize its military efficiency. Governments endeavored to control production and consumption, imports and exports, railroads and shipping, employment and investment, prices and finance. Vexatious as these schemes were felt to be, they were approved by the citizens at large as essential to success. No combatant dared trust to the free play of individual enterprise when threatened by invasion.

Though most of the governmental controls were released

more or less promptly after the return of peace, there has been no such trend toward *laissez faire* as followed the Napoleonic Wars. The collapse of the Czarist regime in Russia under the stress of war made it possible for a communist party to seize control and initiate the most ambitious experiment in national planning ever tried by a great country. Italy has accepted Fascism and its plan of a "corporative state." Germany has entrusted her fortunes to a party that is trying to remold both the economic organization of the nation and its spirit. The new states set up in Europe by the treaty of Versailles for the most part have followed a policy of extreme economic nationalism. For a time Great Britain and the United States seemed to be working back toward pre-War conditions as rapidly as the unsettled state of world affairs allowed; but the grave economic errors perpetrated by private economic planning during the 1920's combined with the after-effects of the War to bring on the Great Depression of the early 1930's, and with it a marked recrudescence of national planning. Great Britain gave up her historic gold standard for a managed currency and free trade for moderate protection. In the United States, discouraged by three years of ineffectual efforts to stem the growth of unemployment by an administration that believed in "rugged individualism," the electorate put in power a party whose leader promised a New Deal in economic affairs. Even France, which had withstood the earlier stages of the world depression most stubbornly, has installed a radical ministry pledged to sweeping economic reforms.

VI

To my mind, this cursory survey of the relations between the state and economic enterprise in the western world since 1776 suggests that we are in for more rather than for less governmental planning in the calculable future. Economic forecasting is a notoriously hazardous enterprise, and political forecasting is perhaps even more risky. But the chances of forming approximately correct anticipations are best when we are dealing with a secular trend; when we can ascertain the more potent forces that have shaped this trend in the recent past, and when we have reason to believe that these forces will retain their character and their potency during the limited future of which we are thinking. We expect technological progress to continue; for it rests upon scientific discovery, which does not seem to be approaching a limit, and upon man's desire to get larger returns for his economic efforts, which shows no signs of failing. Presumably, technological progress will continue to throw men out of work, to depreciate old investments, to shift sources of supply, to introduce novel products. The growth of very large business enterprises has not been checked; the economic, political, and social problems to which their operations give rise have not been solved. In nations that retain a capitalistic organization these changes will bear heavily upon numerous individuals, while they benefit others largely. Economic life will continue to be full of uncertainties, and those who suffer mischances will follow the precedents our generation is setting and make even larger demands for government aid. Social security legislation is more likely to expand than to contract in the great democracies, and dictatorial governments will practice paternalism. Business enterprisers will increase their efforts to limit or suppress competition; for the more we mechanize industry and specialize machinery, the heavier will be overhead costs and the more dangerous competition will become to vested interests. The problems that the courts and the legislatures face in devising and enforcing rules of fair competition will grow more subtle and difficult. It will not be surprising if investors in great industries that are threatened with loss by technological progress organize campaigns for government purchase and operation. The draft upon exhaustible natural resources will grow greater and the movement for conservation through government regulation will wax stronger. Communities will become increasingly interdependent and the task of planning water supplies, sewage disposal, protection of streams against pollution, highway systems, power lines, and the like will be one in which the central governments will be forced to take a larger share. Nor can we leave out of account the probability of future wars and the practical certainty that, if they occur between great nations, each belligerent government will seek to effect a more drastic economic mobilization than was effected in the latest world war. It is most unlikely that this trend toward national economic planning will rise steadily. Its course will be diversified by accelerations and retardations, perhaps by some vigorous reactions toward *laissez faire*. But the indications seem to me fairly clear that in the long run men will try increasingly to use the power and resources of their governments to solve their economic problems even in those nations that escape social revolutions. And, if it should turn out that Communism, or the corporative state, or some as yet unchristened form of economic organization makes a stronger appeal to the mass of people than does the complicated mixture of private enterprise and governmental regulation that is evolving in the capitalistic nations, then social revolutions may sweep the world, presumably carrying with them drastic governmental control over economic activities.

VII

Whether we fear or welcome these prospects of an evolutionary trend or a revolutionary shift toward governmental regulation, we must all agree that the relations of the state to private enterprise is a problem which the social sciences should join in attacking.

No scientifically minded man nowadays will assume that the immediate aim of this attack should be to pronounce a verdict that *laissez faire* is better than governmental regulation, or that governmental regulation is better than *laissez faire*. It is not the business of the social sciences to say what is good and what bad; all they can do is to trace functional relationships among social processes, and so elucidate the most effective means of attaining whatever ends men set themselves. Nor should anyone expect a demonstration that private enterprise always begets one set of results, that governmental planning always begets a different set, and that as citizens we have merely to choose which of the two sets we prefer. The problem is not so simple as that. On the contrary, it is a problem of numerous variables that may combine with one another in an indefinite number of ways, and a given combination may produce very different results when applied to different processes. Our choice does not lie between two sharply contrasted systems, private enterprise and governmental regulation; the real choices that we shall be making more or less deliberately are choices among the indefinitely numerous possible mixtures of private enterprise and governmental regulation, as applied to this, that, or the other type of activity, under different conditions of time and place. Hence the common attack of the social sciences upon this problem should aim, not at finding "a solution," but at finding methods by which communities can carry

on intelligently the process of working out the endless
series of detailed solutions with which they must keep
experimenting.

In dealing with this problem the social sciences are not
confined to speculation. They have before them for
analysis the experience of several autocratic governments
that are professing to guide the economic evolution of their
nations according to some system and the experience of
several democratic peoples that are fumbling with the
problem in different ways. On paper, the methods of
autocratic governments look the more imposing to an outsider; but how plans are really made in present-day Russia,
Italy, and Germany I do not know. Perhaps the processes
that go on behind the scenes are admirably organized to
make use of the best intelligence available. Perhaps the
critically important decisions are made on an inspirational
basis by a leader whose genius is trusted as the guiding
star of the state. Or the controlling group may believe
that it is applying in practice rules deduced from a scientifically established body of principles. Or there may be a
confused and shifting struggle among ambitious cliques,
each seeking the favor of the powers that be. Probably a
mixture of these various elements prevails in all autocratic
governments, one element preponderating here, another
there, one last year, another this year. Of course, it is part
of the task of the social sciences to penetrate behind the
stage sets painted by official propagandists, to find out as
much as they can about how the national planning is actually done, and to trace its consequences, direct and indirect, immediate and delayed, in social and political as well
as in economic affairs. The rapidly growing literature
about these experiments will become increasingly instruc-
tive if they are continued long enough to let their cumulative effects mature. But anyone who glimpses the vastness

and complexities of the researches called for will pardon me for considering only the processes of the democratic peoples, and primarily the people of this country.

As I said before, American methods of applying intelligence to the guidance of economic evolution have run the gamut from a rather extreme reliance upon individual enterprise under some circumstances to a rather extreme reliance upon the federal government under other circumstances. However, one simple generalization may be ventured: we have seldom tried to work out national plans except when some considerable group among us has become seriously dissatisfied with the results of private enterprise, or of private enterprise as regulated by local or state governments. In the life of the nation planning plays the role that thinking plays in individual life. Both processes are resorted to typically to find ways of surmounting difficulties that occur in the course of routine behavior. And just as our individual thinking is commonly directed toward an immediate, specific difficulty, so most of our efforts at national planning have dealt with some single need that has been keenly felt by groups sufficiently numerous or sufficiently powerful to command attention. Let me call this "piecemeal planning." Examples are campaigns for federal aid to develop turnpikes and canals in our early days, for protective duties on imports, for the abolition of slavery, for free silver, for reduction of railroad rates, for curbing the "trusts," for "prohibition," for old-age pensions, and so on almost without end. The groups pushing these plans have been animated at times by philanthropic zeal and at times by sordid interests; some groups have relied upon fervid appeals to the moral conscience, some upon frank presentation of economic claims; some have resorted to bribery. What they have in common is advocacy of a measure designed to accomplish some one change in social organization, with slight regard to its collateral and long-run effects upon other social interests.

Of course piecemeal planning is defective in principle, however high its aims and however generous the spirit that inspires it. Each of the social sciences has its own way of demonstrating that all social processes are inter-related. When we alter the conditions under which one process operates we are certain to affect other processes. Many of these unplanned effects are negligible, but some are important; among the latter effects some may be pleasant surprises but others are likely to be unpleasant. Also we know when we stop to think that the long-run effects of our reforms often differ widely from the immediate effects that we intended to produce. However heartily we approve the abolition of slavery we must admit that emancipation as we managed it without regard to the cultural status of the slaves was attended by grievous results not only for the former masters but also for the freedmen and for the relations between the northern and the southern states. No measure is so good in itself that its advocates are justified in thinking only of its direct and immediate effects. In short, we are not making the best use of what limited intelligence we possess when we plan on a piecemeal basis.

Though piecemeal planning is our common method of attempting to use the powers of government, on occasions we devise programs dealing with many matters at the same time. Party platforms make pretensions of being programs of this sort; but we have learned not to take them seriously. Outstanding instances in our history are the adoption of the Articles of Confederation and the Constitution, the economic planning of Alexander Hamilton, the economic mobilization during the World War, and the attempt of our present administration to inaugurate a New Deal. In each instance, the country faced a grave emergency — only under such pressure have we ever set ourselves vigorously to the task of thinking out and putting into practice a comprehensive scheme of national policies. Two of these emergencies were produced by war, one by the inefficiency of existing political organization, two by economic troubles. When times are good, we let well enough alone. As yet we have not risen to the point of continuous systematic efforts to think out co-ordinated policies that will make what we deem satisfactory better still.

Planning in the face of national emergencies is commonly handicapped by the need for quick action. There is not time enough to bring the nation's full intelligence to bear upon the problem. The more intense the pressure the less the chance of doing a good job. The framers of the Constitution set an admirable precedent by taking time for deliberation; but our later emergency plans have been hastily concocted. Of course the inspirations of a desperate moment are sometimes fortunate; but we do not trust to luck in our most rational activities. To design an efficient National Industrial Recovery Act is vastly more difficult than to design an efficient bridge across the Golden Gate. The one task we essayed in a fine frenzy of good intentions and rushed it through in short order; the other we performed deliberately after elaborate study of the geological as well as the mechanical factors involved.

One reason why we act less rationally in devising national plans than in building bridges is that the sciences of social behavior lag far behind the natural sciences in certainty. If economists, political scientists, and sociologists could tell us how certain proposals would work in practice with as much assurance as engineers can give, we would leave technical matters largely to them. The layman is naturally disinclined to trust professions whose members seem to be continually disagreeing with one another. That is a justifiable hesitation as matters stand. We might, however, if we chose, so alter the present status of affairs that we could make fuller use of the social sciences and, what is not less important, of the practical sagacity possessed by experienced citizens in many walks of life.

What I have in mind is an attempt to organize ourselves for deliberate, systematic study of social problems as a step toward devising solutions that can be applied in practice. Organization is often a critically important factor in determining the efficiency of group action. The same men who made a mess of national government under the Articles of Confederation made a success of national government under the Constitution. It is conceivable that we of the present generation who flounder so in public policy might reach a decidedly higher level of efficiency by following the example of reorganization set by the Fathers of the Republic.

Precisely what form an organization for the study of social problems should assume and how it should operate are delicate questions, but experience suggests some simple answers. First, the organization should be a continuing one, not like a constitutional convention that draws up a plan of government and adjourns *sine die*; for social problems are ever assuming new forms and the task of dealing with them is never finished. Second, to be effective the organization should center in a small board, responsible not for making technical studies and formulating plans — that task calls for more technical knowledge and more insight than any small group possesses — but for seeing that studies are made and that plans are formulated. It would be the Board's task to make sure that in this work available knowledge is utilized to the full — not merely such contributions as social scientists could make, but also the contributions of experienced men of affairs, and the contributions of natural scientists, which are fundamental to many social problems. Also it would be the Board's particular care to see that before measures were proposed for dealing with one issue the collateral effects, direct and indirect, immediate and delayed, were considered. The Board should endeavor to take up problems before they reach the emergency stage, while there is time for full consideration before reaching a decision. To enable it thus to focus the intelligence of the nation upon social problems of a wide and shifting range, the Board should have a technical staff including men of many qualifications, means for obtaining professional assistance from anyone whose counsel is needed, and close contacts with government agencies, federal, state and local. It should foster the planning attitude toward public problems, co-operating with the state, regional, and municipal planning organizations in all parts of the country. Finally, it should give all the interests affected by the issues under consideration an opportunity to present their views before it formulates proposals.

Sharing in the staff work of a National Planning Board would give representatives of the various social sciences a continuing opportunity of the sort that this Tercentenary Conference seeks to provide for a few days. As the organizers of the present program have implied, the most effective way to secure genuine co-operation among specialists is to get them to join in attacking common problems. The men who shared in seeking solutions for the problems that came before a Planning Board would have facilities for extensive and intensive investigations, and they would have time to absorb in as large a measure as human limitations permit the significance of one another's contributions. While serving the Board they would also be fostering the increase of knowledge that the world needs desperately — knowledge of human behavior.

An organization such as I am sketching would have the best chances of rendering service if it were accepted by public opinion as an agency of the federal government, but an agency empowered merely to draw up plans for consideration by the constituted authorities or the voters. No doubt the outcome of the deliberations upon many issues would be a recommendation to take no public action. In the many-faceted problem of how best to combine governmental regulation with private enterprise it might as often counsel a policy of *laissez faire* as a policy of intervention. If I am right in forecasting a multitude of demands that the federal government extend its activities vigorously in the future, I may be right also in thinking that a planning organization charged to study the collateral and the long-run effects of public policies would be the best safeguard against ill-considered measures. Only the careless will jump to the conclusion that systematic study of national problems by a federal agency would accelerate the trend toward government regulation. It might have the opposite effect.

Needless to say, the most wisely guided organization for national planning would encounter opposition. Every attempt to extend the role of intelligence over new areas seems to many persons presumptuous or silly. Despite the plainest explanations that the central board was merely a device for focussing the practical wisdom and scientific knowledge of the whole community upon problems that have to be dealt with in some fashion, there would be misunderstandings aplenty. Of course interests that thought themselves threatened would attack the organization with the weapons of prejudice, misrepresentation, and ridicule.

Reformers in a hurry would wax indignant over the deliberate methods of a board that tried to foresee consequences before it recommended action. Early friends who expected the prompt formulation of sweeping plans embodying their own predilections might be turned by disappointment into enemies. Unless public opinion is convinced that it is worth while to think carefully about social problems, no planning organization worthy of the name can last long in a democracy.

Even if given a fair trial, the organization would find its technical tasks exceedingly difficult. Experienced men of affairs and social scientists know how hard it is to foresee the indirect and cumulative consequences of public policies, to approximate social gains and social costs, to find the most efficient ways of accomplishing given ends. And the ends to be aimed at are not given; they must be chosen. There have been occasions in American history when public opinion accepted a definite end as paramount; but these occasions have been rare and of brief duration. They vastly simplify the problem of national planning. For example, economic mobilization during the World War was facilitated by the fact that a large majority of the people were ready to sacrifice comfort, property, and life for military success. But seldom is the national scale of values thus crystallized in a single dominant pattern. As a rule numerous limited ends command wide support, but no one end is predominant. To make matters more puzzling, the widely popular ends are likely to conflict with one another. I suppose that at present most people think it desirable to balance the federal budget, to reduce taxation, to increase employment, and to keep the unemployed from suffering hunger and cold. Most of the time a national planning organization would have to work amidst confusion of this sort. That condition makes planning difficult, but not impossible. It is the condition that most individuals habitually face in their private planning. Somehow they manage to reach decisions despite the incompatibility among their desires. Presumably a wisely conducted planning organization could achieve a similar qualified success. In a democratic country, national planners would have to serve as an agency for accomplishing what the majority desired. But by throwing light upon the consequences that different lines of action would produce, they could contribute much toward making social valuations more rational. In the long run one of the greatest gains from trying to plan national policies in the light of their probable consequences would be the attainment of a more valid scale of social values than now prevails among us.

Whether this country is ready to organize its intelligence, practical and scientific, in an effort to guide the evolution of its institutions more wisely, I do not know. But a bill creating a National Planning Board along the lines that I have followed is now pending in Congress. We may prefer to continue for years our past policy of piecemeal planning, supplemented in grave emergencies by sweeping changes made in a hurry. Or we may follow the example of those nations that have made a sudden plunge into Fascism or Communism. Our best chance of avoiding a dictatorship of some sort, with its compulsory regimentation of our lives, lies in infusing a larger measure of intelligence into our public policy.

THE STATE AND ECONOMIC FLUCTUATION

DENNIS HOLME ROBERTSON, M.A., D.COM., D.LITT.

Reader in Economics, University of Cambridge

IT SEEMS a little mad to attempt to discuss in half an hour the vast theme of the role of the state in the control of economic fluctuation. Madder still to make the attempt on one's first visit to the great country which has been the scene of the boldest and most enormous experiments in this field. Maddest of all, perhaps, to speak on this subject in the presence of Professor Copland, that skillful designer of cunningly mixed cordials for depressed economic systems. But I must fulfill my promise.

Let me state in a few words what I shall try to maintain. It seems to me that the problem consists, in theory, of an easy half and a difficult half; that the difficult half would be difficult even in a world in which fluctuation was the only significant kind of economic movement: and that its difficulty is increased by the circumstance that fluctuations in fact occur against a background of secular and structural change, from which they are not always easy to disentangle.

The easy half of the problem concerns the role of the state in the face of pronounced economic depression. When I say that it is easy, I do not mean of course that it is easy to handle in practice: on the contrary its solution is attended with the most formidable practical difficulties. I do not even mean that, in most countries, there is any close agreement, either among economists or among practical persons, as to the particular measures which would be effective towards the end sought, still less as to the degree to which each of them can be usefully applied. But I do mean that there is a measure of general agreement — a much greater measure, I think, than prevailed only a few years ago — both in the diagnosis of what, in this phase of the story, has gone wrong and consequently also as to the ends which public action should seek to promote. Whatever the cause of the original recession of trade, and whether or no it has been an inevitable or even a salutary occurrence, it seems evident that after a certain stage it is apt to degenerate into a purposeless and obscene orgy of destruction, like a snake eating its own tail — a process "devoid," as Professor Röpke has recently put it, "of every necessary function and therefore without sense." It seems clear that in such circumstances it is right and reasonable to use the manifold powers of the state to reverse the evil process of cumulation, and to restore what I will call for the moment by the question-begging name of a normal level of activity. Nor, under such conditions, is there necessary opposition between measures helpful to consumption and measures helpful to the formation of capital equipment. For re-employed bricklayers and engineers will buy boots; and rehabilitated bootmakers will, eventually, buy buildings and machines. We can usefully start at either end, or at both.

The difficulties in the way of framing effective action along these lines are well known: it would take me the rest of my half-hour even to catalogue them. I must content myself with posing — alas! not answering — two questions under which a great many of them are subsumed. That they are questions, ultimately, not only of economics but also of ethics and psychology only illustrates the hard lot of the economist, masquerading as a man of science in a universe not of cells and atoms but of passions and volitions.

The recovery measures open to a national state may be classified broadly into those which, if successful, will benefit the world at large, and those whose direct effects, at all events, are merely to enable the country which applies them to hoist itself up on the shoulders of its neighbors. A successful public-works campaign by a large creditor country is an example of the former, the introduction or elevation of a protective tariff of the latter. How far — this is my first question — can a given country wisely or decently go with measures of this second class? The question is complicated by the fact that attention cannot always be fairly confined to the direct effects of such measures, apart from their setting in a whole complex situation. Take for instance what is, from some points of view, the deadliest card in the whole pack with which the game of international beggar-my-neighbor is played — the card of currency devaluation. To many Continental observers the depreciation of the pound in 1931 seemed, and I think still seems, an unforgivable stab in the back, a prime cause of the final agonies of the depression in Europe, with all that they have involved of economic disintegration and political menace: to most Englishmen it appears in retrospect as an inevitable preliminary to the creation of a center of recovery whose healing influence has spread far beyond the confines of England and even of the British Commonwealth. Again, the freeing of the dollar in 1933 was condemned as a wanton act by many who had found excuse in *force majeure* for the depreciation of the pound: but a good case can be made for the view that the freedom of maneuver so obtained was essential to give a fair chance to America's great constructive and world-assisting experiment. Finally, almost everyone outside the

European gold countries has agreed for some years that
the writing-down of their monetary units, however incon-
venient to special interests elsewhere, would amply pay its
way from the world point of view in the release of confidence and the removal of fear.

Thus selfishness is not always as selfish as it seems.
Nevertheless if we are concerned rather with prescription
for the future than appraisal of the past, there can be no
doubt, I think, of the general lines of the answer to my
first question. It seems clear that the combating of depression could be made immensely more effective in the future
than it has been in recent years if nations were more concerned to defeat the common enemy and less concerned to
steal a march on one another, less anxious about their
balances of payments, less ready to be shocked at one
another's budgetary difficulties. And evidently this is a
matter where *noblesse oblige*: acts of self-denial and self-
restraint which would be useless quixotry on the part of
weak and isolated and indebted nations may not be too
much to demand from the concerted wisdom of powerful
creditor states.

I turn to my second question — remember I am still
dealing with the easy half of my subject! How far is the
taking of effective action against developed depression
compatible with popular government on the one hand and
private capitalism on the other, or how far must it always
come to grief against the rocks of loss of public confidence,
especially the giant rock of the distrust of the organizers of
employment and the owners of wealth? In particular,
what type and degree of disequilibrium in the public
finances will popular opinion stand? Will it permit local
governments to incur debt, as long as the national budget balances? Or will it acquiesce in the existence of an
extraordinary national budget which does not balance, as

long as there is also an ordinary budget which does? Will it
countenance a large volume of public loan expenditure as
long as there are bricks and mortar to show for it, but
stick at the financing of pensions or unemployment relief
by similar methods? Will its wealth-owners suffer the
government to borrow almost gratis from the banks with
nothing worse than a shaking of heads, but, at the very
mention of an expansion in the issue of legal tender money,
will they, like the sea-blooms in Shelley's poem,

> . . . suddenly grow gray with fear
> And tremble and despoil themselves?

Who can tell? The problem would seem to be one for the
psychoanalyst rather than the economist: yet the economist if he wishes to be listened to, no less than the statesman if he wishes to be re-elected, will neglect it at his
peril. There are said to be, in the far north and the far
south, happy lands where economists all give the same
advice, where the government listens to it, where the
public understands why the government has listened —
and where, the cynic might add, the very prices of timber
and wool play, as though by magic, their appointed part in
the harmonious scheme. But we cannot all live in Sweden
or Australia. Perhaps in darker but nevertheless not
yet totalitarian lands the solution for the present lies in
the rigid separation of professional economists into two
classes — a class of economic advisers, who must subdue
their hand to the material it works in, and never forget that
there is nothing either good or bad but thinking makes
it so; and a class of pure economists, who are licensed to
think what the Japanese call dangerous thoughts and even
to think them aloud, but who in return must suffer themselves to be burnt at the stake rather than ever be trapped
into giving advice to anybody about anything.

In England of late years the thinker of dangerous thoughts has looked out upon a varied scene. He has watched, with a sort of melancholy and negative satisfaction, some foreign governments which have made "Sound Finance" their prime objective find themselves ever further and further from their aim, like Alice in the garden of live flowers, when she tried so obstinately to reach the Red Queen by the old-fashioned method of walking towards her. He has watched with mixed feelings the rulers of his own country handling with extreme skill some of the weapons of recovery, and condemned by the aftermath of their own somewhat misty economy propaganda to leave others rusting and unused. He has watched, as through a glass darkly, the dictatorships wielding those rejected weapons with apparent effect, but at a cost in freedom which seems to him too high to pay. And finally he has watched a government which the laws of hospitality forbid me to name, lengthening its own journey, perhaps, by straying into strange and gaily colored flower beds, but destined, as he hopes, through turning its back so firmly on the Red Queen of "Sound Finance," in time once more to meet her face to face.

I must hurry on to the second, or difficult, part of my subject, or I shall never reach it. Granted that the state, working through its control of the public finances as well as its ultimate authority over the mechanisms of money and banking, should initiate measures of recovery, how far should it press them, and when if ever should it reverse the engines? Is there an evil symmetry between boom and slump, and virtue in the middle course? or does the symmetry stand revealed as illusion, the golden mediocrity as cowardice and defeatism, when we reflect that the mean level between boom and slump is a mean level not merely of prices and profits or even of output but also of employment, and that to stop short at any but the highest possible level of activity means to turn a deaf ear to the claims of individuals for reabsorption into the economic machine? It is here, I think, that a real cleavage of opinion still persists.

Let me try to summarize the opposing viewpoints. So long, one party urges, as there are men who can be drawn back into employment by an enlargement of the stream of money demand, drawn back they ought to be. That prices may rise substantially in the process is no argument against its legitimacy, in the later any more than in the earlier phases of expansion: it is merely the consequence of living in a world where certain elements of equipment are limited, temporarily or permanently, in supply. Not until unemployment is conquered can inflation in any damaging sense be said to begin.

"Yes," say the other side, "but consider the character of the employment created in the high boom. We do not, most of us, maintain, as some of us did a few years ago, that all the capital equipment then called into existence is doomed to melt away irretrievably like the snow. On the contrary we admit that in the main it contributes in the long run to the permanent enrichment of the world. But we still think that to press on so rapidly with its formation is a mistake, because it sets before the economic system problems in digestion and readjustment which it cannot possibly solve. And we still think that the process by which you propose to achieve your ends, namely the unreasonable enrichment of the entrepreneur class, is fairly and illuminatingly described as the infliction of a system of forced levies on the rest of the community, including the working class as a whole, and that sooner or later their effort to react against this system will play its part in inducing crisis and collapse. This way of looking at things does not, as you seem to suppose, depend on an unfounded assumption that there is no unemployment left. For by attempting to abolish the residuum of unemployment to-day you are making it worse for tomorrow; whereas by acquiescing in its temporary continuance you would be promoting a tempo of industrial progress, and an eventual distribution of labor between industries, more appropriate to the modern world — a world which has no need to be in such a hurry since, as you admit yourselves, the devil which Malthus unchained has been hooked up again."

"You are a defeatist!" cries Party A.

"You are a Communist," replies Party B, "or if you aren't you ought to be. For nothing short of a completely authoritarian state could cope with the immense problems of transfer and readjustment, let alone fiscal embarrassment, in which your policy will land you if you carry it out to the bitter end."

I must not attempt to carry the debate further, or I should have to make the parties fall at loggerheads over the nature of that central mystery of the economic scheme — a theme too intricate for the closing minutes of my half-hour, the theory of the rate of interest. But I have said enough, perhaps, to indicate what seems to be emerging, with increasing clearness, especially since the publication of my colleague Mr. Keynes' latest book, as the true issue. It is not so much a conflict between different views of the most effective method of controlling cyclical fluctuation. It is rather a conflict of view between those who still believe that cyclical fluctuation is the worst enemy which controlled capitalism has yet to subdue, and those who think that they detect, lurking beneath the coils of the cyclical snake, a more insidious enemy still. This alleged enemy is a chronic and endemic tendency towards the stifling of enterprise, the leakage of thrift, and a consequent

running-down of the whole system — a sort of worm
seated at the very heart of the institutional and psychological bases of our society, and battening on the very growth
of wealth which he strives unavailingly to prevent. Is he a
real worm, or is he the figment of generous imaginations
tortured by the tragedies of the worst and deepest slump
of history?

I dare not swear he is an unreal worm; but I may conclude by offering one or two reasons why he might be
thought to exist even if he does not — in more prosaic
language, why the problem of the control of cyclical fluctuation may be complicated by the fact that such fluctuations are apt to occur against a background of structural
change. If it is always hard to know where to stop in a
policy of expansion, it is hardest of all in a country in which
large numbers of persons have lost their employment
through a permanent decline in the demand for their
labor. And if, as was the case in Britain, these persons
happen to be found partly in the instrumental trades which
are liable anyhow to be specially affected by cyclical depression, the difficulty becomes acute of distinguishing between unemployment which it is sensible to try to remove
by expansionist measures, and unemployment which, in so
far as it can be removed at all and not merely relieved,
calls for the less spectacular but more difficult treatment
of gradual industrial and local transfer. It is not surprising that, in recent months, Rearmament should have seemed
to come as a *deus ex machina* to solve, or rather postpone
the solution of, the dilemma. Neither is it surprising that,
in the years preceding 1929, Restriction, the paradoxical
twin brother of Expansion (for Boost and Bolster are the
father and mother of them both), should have been invoked to ease the problem of excess capacity in a number
of leading raw materials. Yet it can hardly be doubted

that those attempts, in high boom, to resist the process of structural change contributed to the violence of the ensuing collapse: and the spectacle of governments—in order to implement what is, let us pray, a temporary and gluttable demand—unbalancing gaily in the boom of 1936-37 those budgets so meticulously balanced in the slump of 1931-32, may well make us uneasy about what is to follow.

Finally, I must mention very briefly another type of secular change which may confuse the course of cyclical policy. It may be — there are signs of it, I think, in England as well as in the United States — that, with the growth in the average size and strength of individual firms, there occurs a decline in the demand for that type of service which the virtuously brought up banker is most ready to render — the provision of working capital by short-term loans. In this event the banking system may lose efficiency as a conduit for the transmission of thrift into industry, and a super-cyclical tendency towards deflation and the waste of saving may develop, bearing a certain resemblance to the phenomena of epidemic slump and even suggesting the presence of endemic worm. Yet it does not follow, I think, that anti-slump measures of the regular kind — cheap money, open market purchases, budget deficits — are an adequate or appropriate response. Structural faults call rather for structural remedies — in this instance, perhaps, for the devising of new types of financial institution to fill the gap left by the old.

I have left you, I am afraid, with a picture somewhat negative and confused. Perhaps if I were to attempt to sum up in two sentences what I have tried to suggest it would be thus. The advocates of energetic state action against developed depression have had in all countries a hard fight to wage against the forces of apathy and despair. Let us salute them everywhere, in their victories or in their honorable defeats: but let us beg them, whether flushed with success or saddened with failure, to think again before concluding that cheap money and government deficits, still less trade restriction and exchange manipulation, are the right diet for all phases of the trade cycle or the right remedy for all the economic ills of the world.

THE STATE AND THE ENTREPRENEUR

Douglas Berry Copland, M.A., D.Sc., Litt.D.

Professor of Commerce, University of Melbourne

THIS subject is on the frontier between economics and political philosophy. It contains problems that cannot be solved by economic analysis or abstract philosophy alone. There is still much unknown territory in which no one can speak with the authority of the scientist. Judgment and belief have a wide influence. In what I say this morning I am influenced by my judgments of what has happened in many countries in the recent past and by my belief that in the immediate future important developments will occur in the relation of the state to the entrepreneur.

Let me summarize my thesis.[1] The function of the entrepreneur must continue to be performed in any community that desires to make progress. The qualities of imagination, leadership, and adventure necessary for great constructive work were exercised by the entrepreneur under free capitalism. During a large part of the nineteenth century he was left free in most countries to pursue his objective of maximum profit without serious interference by the state. This was true especially of the United States, where even in the post-war period (1919–1929) capitalism flourished and its virtues were extolled as never before in the history of man. Then came the great depression to ex-

---

[1] As Mr. Dennis Robertson has preceded me with a paper on *The State and Economic Fluctuation* I have omitted any but passing references to the problem.

pose the grave defects of an economic order that had no solution for economic fluctuations and no means of ameliorating the burdens of depression. Capitalism under the control of the entrepreneur guided mainly by considerations of maximum profit is now completely discredited. It does not give economic security to the masses of the people; it does not provide the administrative machinery whereby increased technical efficiency is transformed easily into a generally higher standard of living; it does not furnish society with the social institutions required to meet the strains imposed by economic fluctuations and rapid technical progress; it does not provide the increasing range of free or collective goods that enter more and more into the standard of living. Countries have been able to absorb the shocks of depression and improved technique in inverse proportion to their dominance by the capitalistic entrepreneur. The contrast between the experiences of the United States and Australia in the depression is significant. Australia got out of the depression quickly by taking unorthodox action through state and banking control; the United States got deeper into the depression by holding firmly to an orthodox course. This, I admit, is a sweeping generalization that requires close examination of the differing circumstances of the two countries. I point the contrast to emphasize a fundamental fact in recent economic evolution — namely, the increasing need for state action if capitalism is to continue to yield its best fruits.

The Private Entrepreneur not as Important as We Think

There is one point on which we should clear our minds at the outset. The capitalistic entrepreneur occupies much less territory than we think. In all European countries and in some British dominions the state is entrepreneur over a large field of industry — water-supply, communication, some forms of transport, lighting services, education, public health, certain forms of banking and the supply of credit, housing of the poor, road construction.

Every rise in the standard of living, every increase in the complexity of economic organization sooner or later forces the state to assume control or ownership of natural monopolies, of the supply of collective goods (such as education, health services, libraries), of the provision of services that would cause ruinous competition under free enterprise. The principles underlying this extension of state control are well understood and accepted in most countries. To a visitor from a country which had long ago gone far in this direction, the controversies over state control in the United States appear a little unreal. They show that unfettered capitalism will die hard in the United States, as it did elsewhere. I believe that it must die if the United States is to build up an industrial structure that will provide both social security and economic well-being. The problem is one of reconciling the authority of the state with the free play of individual enterprise in a wide though diminishing field of industry. The early enthusiasm of the New Dealers has perhaps obscured the view of this fundamental problem. It is well to start a steep climb in low gear. You have been in high gear for three years, and you may feel the need of relief from machine-gun legislation.

In a reaction against state interference it is tempting to think of the entrepreneur as being the driving force in economic progress. In all countries, even in the United States, governmental or semi-governmental bodies plan and carry out a substantial proportion of new development. In Australia it is much more than 50 per cent, and in Great Britain it is about 50 per cent. Public investment accounts for half the total new development. In some

European countries the proportion is higher, culminating in nearly the whole of investment in Russia being under the direct control of the state. This is highly significant. The state has devised administrative machinery with which, in an increasing range of industries and services, it can and does perform the functions of the entrepreneur. This is perhaps the most striking change that has taken place in the economic system in the present century. It has been accompanied by the development of administrative machinery by the state and by an increasing emphasis upon the social responsibilities of the entrepreneur. The rise of the state as entrepreneur is a direct challenge to individual enterprise and its methods.

Under undiluted capitalism the typical industrial entrepreneur works through the joint stock company. This is a form of group control which has its own bureaucracy and its own administrative methods of reconciling initiative and authority. But in its extreme form it recognizes few social responsibilities and no fixed obligations to labor or capital. "I owe the public nothing," recently declared a great American entrepreneur. This is an extreme example of individualism. Many cases of entrepreneurs taking the opposite view could be given, but it is well to remember that joint stock enterprise by its very organization may, and frequently does, take its social responsibilities lightly. In times of depression the lower rate of profit becomes the standard rate of dividend throughout industry; the reduced volume of employment, the accepted rule. By devising the principle of the equity share and by assuming the right to "hire and fire" labor, joint stock enterprise gets the maximum freedom of action with the minimum social responsibility. This must be summarily rejected as an unsatisfying ideal, though many economists have sought in the past to rationalize and justify the behavior of the entrepreneur when he acts in his own right to pursue his objective of maximum profitable output without regard to the social effects of his action.

The State Commission as Good as the Joint Stock Company

The state as entrepreneur has found difficulty in devising an appropriate administration. Where, as in the United States, it had limited its intervention largely to control, it devised the regulating commission, which left the entrepreneur free to manage and develop his enterprise within certain broad limits. In a country that retains its faith in individual enterprise, even in public utilities, there is great scope for the development of this form of control. Perhaps this will be the distinctive contribution of the United States to the problem. In countries where the state or public authority has assumed ownership of an increasing range of industries, it has devised administrative machinery not unlike joint stock. The state now hands over the enterprise to a board or commission with complete powers in internal management and the right of initiative in development, though not necessarily full financial powers. There are many examples already of this machinery, e.g., the Port of London Authority or the State Electricity Commission in my own State of Victoria. There is no reason why the state should choose its board less wisely than the average joint stock company which is controlled by directors selected from the heirarchy of finance found in every modern industrial center. If the commission has full powers and the untrammeled right of initiative, it should give results not less satisfactory than those of the joint stock enterprise. But where, as in many cases of state enterprise in Australia, Parliament retains the right to plan and develop the enterprise, there is wide scope for mistakes and financial losses. Parliament must delegate its authority, retaining the right to lay down general policy and to call upon its commission for guidance and information. The fear of parliamentary control, itself often irresponsible in industrial enterprises, competes with the social irresponsibility of the entrepreneur in deciding whether an industry shall be state-owned or not.

The state as entrepreneur encounters two obstacles which do not beset the path of the capitalistic entrepreneur in his pursuit of maximum profit. The first is publicity. The state enterprise must do much of its ordinary work and all of its planning and development in the full light of day. It must give information when asked and offer explanations that hamper both expedition of decision and effectiveness of action. But this is, on the whole, a good thing. The capitalistic entrepreneur would often pause if he were forced to explain his action and to discuss the social disturbances caused by rapid changes in technique initiated by him. Many do hesitate before plunging whole areas into distress, but many are powerless against the new processes or new industries created by a young and enterprising generation of competing entrepreneurs. In a world where, as Professor A. N. Whitehead has remarked, the changes of generations are now concentrated in a single lifetime, anything which reduces the rate of change of scientific technique until social administration makes up some of the leeway is probably a net economic benefit. But this would not be the case if our social administration were inspired by the fire and imagination of the inventor and the successful entrepreneur. The world is richer in material things than it thinks, and it will be richer still. Its progress is retarded by timidity, by confusion of ideas, and by conflict of interests in social administration. Nothing is more striking in the modern world than the contrast between the entrepreneur's devotion to the material benefits of scientific progress and his distrust of improved methods of social administration. The one appeals to his idea of progress; the other offends his sense of freedom. Yet it is clear that the entrepreneur cannot himself utilize the rapidly improving technique science holds out for him unless the state provides the administrative machinery through which social organization can be adjusted to improved processes of production. The state as entrepreneur must reconcile its social responsibilities with its desire to adopt more efficient processes. The individual entrepreneur cannot do this if his competitor takes immediate advantage of the improvement.

The control of finance in state enterprise gives rise to the second obstacle which the state as entrepreneur encounters. Experience shows that an increase in public investment is inevitable. The proportion of public to private investment will increase. This means that the proportion of fixed to equity debt[2] will increase. The state raises its funds on fixed interest-bearing bonds. So does the local body or the semi-governmental authority. The state is expected to meet the interest on the whole of the debt in season and out of season. The joint stock company, on the other hand, has an equity debt to deal with and can vary dividends according to the prosperity of the company or the general prosperity of the country. There is, moreover, much capital lost in joint stock enterprise; no one knows how much, and no one knows what is the average rate of interest earned on the total capital laid out in joint stock enterprise. I can only raise the doubt whether it is 4 per cent, which we may accept as the average rate of interest

[2] Fixed debt is a fixed capital sum, often with fixed interest, such as debentures, government securities. Equity debt is a debt which fluctuates in amount and interest with the fortunes of the enterprise. Shares are the common examples.

that the state may have to pay on its debt. If the state extends its functions as entrepreneur and fails to earn 4 per cent, as I think it inevitably will, the balance has to be made good from taxation. This is a levy on the community in order to maintain a certain rate of interest which may be out of harmony with the real earning capacity of industry.

The problem is likely to become very important. The state will be encouraged to borrow and to extend the proportion of fixed interest-bearing debt. With the increased demand for economic security and the greater capacity to save, more and more savings will pass into the hands of institutions like insurance companies, trustee companies, and savings banks that invest predominantly in the gilt-edged bond. As the demand for this form of investment expands, and the scope for it is enlarged with the extension of state enterprise, it becomes less and less a sound investment. Unless the state is prepared to tax its people for the benefit of the *rentier* the investment loses its gilt. The alternative is to establish some form of equity in a portion of the debt, so that the interest varies according to the prosperity of the country. This change will be resisted by financial entrepreneurs, but short of a periodic scaling-down of the interest burden, or its counterpart in a moderate dose of inflation, some extension of the principle of the equity-debt to state enterprise appears to me inevitable. Widespread demand for economic security through savings and investment in fixed interesting-bearing bonds creates a new financial problem. It is not possible for the whole community to insure itself against risks. The greater risks are those of contraction of enterprise and deflation. No country since 1928 has suffered from taking a modest dose of inflation. Countries that have administered it have prospered most. The fear of inflation is a confession of inability to control banking and financial policy. Without this control sound administration of the modern economic system is impossible, if only for the reason that fixed debts become too burdensome.

Supplanting Price as the Regulator in Primary Production

Thus far I have assumed that the state was supplanting the entrepreneur in large-scale industries and that there was very little change in the organization of the industry. It is surprising how state enterprises have copied the capitalistic technique, even to the practice of advertising a virtual state monopoly. There are essential differences in finance, social responsibility, and publicity, but not in the technique of management. State enterprise is relatively easy in these fields, and its logical extension may take place in transport, insurance, banking, supply of standard goods.

But in recent years the state has been driven into another field where the difficulties are very much greater and the conflict between the state and the entrepreneur likely to be much more drastic. I refer to the intrusion of the state into the regulation of output, prices, and finance in primary industry. The impelling motive here is the increasing pressure from the primary producers for economic security. There is, on the one hand, their desire to be protected from normal cyclical fluctuations in prices. No system of insurance against this risk has been effectively designed by individual enterprise. The elimination of the risk of "normal" fluctuations in prices, normal in the sense that they represent the ordinary business cycle, would rather strengthen the primary producer in his discharge of the entrepreneur's function. But control does not stop at the reduction of these price fluctuations. It goes much further and has derived great stimulus from the depression, which has emphasized the effects of "the pace of progress" in commercial farming in the new world. We have seen in the last five years the long-period decline in prices of certain primary products caused by improved technique and increased acreage in new countries. To benefit by this capacity to produce primary products at lower cost, the world must allow prices to fall until a new equilibrium has been established between prices and production of primary and other products, with consequent writing-down of capital values. The state is justified in attempting to regulate conditions so that the adjustment will be less disturbing. But it has everywhere in the world gone much further than this. It has sought in the Old World to protect peasant agriculture by duties and prohibitions against imports of cheap products, or by establishing elaborate machinery for controlling marketing and prices, as in the British schemes. In the New World many experiments are being tried — the "domestic" price, direct bounties, destruction of some output, elimination of some areas of production, adjustment of farm debts. Some of these measures may merely retard adjustment, and this is quite a reasonable protective action against sudden and disturbing change. But many of the measures, if successful, would deny the world the benefits of cheaper goods, maintain effete methods of production, establish a cramping form of control, and destroy the initiative of the entrepreneur. Primary industry is in the hands of numerous small entrepreneurs. Control schemes must reach down into the intimate life and thought of these *paysans*, and limit the scope for the exercise by the individual of skill and initiative. They thus have the double disadvantage of keeping prices higher than is really necessary and impairing the efficiency of the entrepreneur.

The state may act as entrepreneur, it may compel the entrepreneur to observe certain conditions when discharg-

ing his own functions, but it cannot reconcile rigid control
of market conditions with free exercise by the entrepreneur
of his own functions. The state through its marketing
board dismisses market price as an agency of control in
favor of its own price. The individual entrepreneur will
adjust his activities to this price, and soon production and
price will be out of balance. The state must then abandon
its control of price or set up control of output. This is the
present dilemma of control schemes, but the state usually
shrinks from the task of rigid regulation of output. It is
difficult to secure the co-operation and acquiescence of the
farmers necessary to push it far enough. It will be easy
enough to establish and protect a monopoly in importing
countries and to give the local farmer a favorable price.
But this means stopping progress, not merely retarding it,
and it throws the weight of adjustment upon the new
countries where the entrepreneur has pioneered the way in
commercial farming at relatively low costs. This is an
alignment of economic forces that cannot endure. The
state is not something external to the people comprising
the state. It cannot permanently deny a benefit to its consumers or thwart the efforts of the successful entrepreneur.
It cannot impose the necessary discipline on thousands of
individual producers.

Unfortunately, the primary producers in new countries
have not grasped the significance of the lower costs of commercial farming. Like the farmers in the Old World, they
too sigh for pre-depression prices and resist the contraction
of the frontier necessary to restrict output to the profitable
areas. For the time being they join with producers in the
importing countries in a fruitless effort to combine maximum output and maximum price and to get the best of all
possible worlds. Such striving after the unattainable must
end in failure. There will be protection of agriculture in

Europe and higher prices and increased production; there will be co-operation and control of producers in new countries for grading products, research, and reducing the costs of marketing; but if farming is to be carried on by the individual entrepreneur the rigorous marketing schemes and price controls will be preserved in name only. We have not yet devised a satisfactory halfway house between the state or collective farm and the individual entrepreneur in agriculture.

It is of interest to note that the schemes of state control of agriculture have in the main drawn upon the experience of the cartel. On account of the number and the dispersion of the entrepreneurs, the state has been used as the agency of control. In Australia we have for a long time used the device of "the home price" behind import duties against foreign supplies. Butter is our classic example. We subsidise butter producers by this device to the extent of about £4000 per annum. New Zealand is experimenting with a system of guaranteed prices in the same industry and is using the power of the central bank to inflate credit to pay the guaranteed price when world prices are low. Later, when the world price rises, it will be possible to deflate credit. This is a workable device, provided the datum price is not higher than costs on the average farm and there is a rigid observance of the scheme when the market price exceeds the datum price. The United States has gone further in the cartelization of agriculture by its scheme of compensating producers for reducing output and its long range plan of shifting or eliminating the marginal producer. But every country is alarmed at the reduction of the proportion of its people engaged in agriculture, when it should in fact welcome such a change. There is a common resistance to the cheapening of primary products, though a general welcoming of lower prices for finished products.

Apart from the resistance of the farmer to change and the general rigidity of the structure of rural industry, there is an additional influence at work retarding adjustment to new conditions. This is the method of financing agriculture. During times of depression there is a constant conflict between the mortgagee and the mortgagor. The former struggles to maintain the value of his fixed interest-bearing loan, the latter to preserve some of his equity in the enterprise. There is no automatic adjustment of debt burden to the varying fortunes of agriculture as there is in industry where the equity debt prevails. In times of major reorganization the resistance of the debt structure to change can only be overcome by somewhat drastic moratoria and state schemes to adjust the burden of farm debts. It is all very cumbersome and disturbing. Perhaps the best way the state can help the entrepreneur in agriculture to perform his functions satisfactorily and to respond to technical changes is to devise some more elastic system of financing agriculture. Doubtless the state could develop a form of equity debt for the large number of producers under its control at present, leaving private enterprise to follow its example or evacuate the field in favor of the state.

The State a Bad Loser

The state has been forced to enter the field of agriculture and to attempt some form of regulation of the entrepreneur largely for the same reasons that it has entered other fields, for example, the control of monopoly. It must provide reasonable economic security and preserve the economic order against the ravages of rapid technical change. These are largely negative actions. The negative aspect of state control or supplanting of the entrepreneur may be pushed too far. On the one hand, the state may be left to deal with the social problems created by the entrepreneur; on the other hand, the state may attempt too vigorously to retard progress. The entrepreneur should be encouraged to assume greater social responsibility for his own actions; the state must endeavor to promote the rapid and easy absorption of improved technique and efficiency in industry into a higher standard of living and a greater consumption of collective goods of the higher order. I believe there is wide scope for fruitful state action along both lines, and that the state of the future will spend more and more of its energy in positive action to promote a flexible economic and social structure. But the state can do only what its citizens want it to do, and the average citizen dislikes being disturbed.

The extension of state control and ownership is not, however, to be contemplated lightly. The state is a bad loser and by no means a good employer. It easily falls into the bad habits it deplores among entrepreneurs. Thus it is ready to use its powers to protect a monopoly, when it has one, to support high prices, and to use freely the weapon of price discrimination. All these were formerly regarded as cardinal sins of monopoly. Examples of these lapses into despised capitalist ways are numerous — e.g., where the state owns railways and has sought to cramp new forms of transport, where the state has acted in the interests of a special group of producers, such as coal owners or agricultural producers or highly protected manufacturers. As an employer we have had many examples in Australia of the state's seeking to deny its employees the facilities of wage-fixing tribunals which have complete control over industrial relations in private enterprise. Again, the state has not scrupled to use its sovereign powers to push nationalistic aims, just as the individual entrepreneur will exercise to the full his powers to push his individual interests. Much of the economic nationalism of the modern world is made possible because the state has used its powers regardless of the international complications that follow the pursuit of narrow national policy. Finally, I repeat that the state is a bad loser in the sense that its capacity to cut its losses is usually much lower than that of private enterprise. State enterprises when unsuccessful are politically hard to liquidate. Their position is allowed to drift, as we in Australia know to have been the case with some costly experiments in land settlement and irrigation. If the enterprise should be stopped when failure is apparent there would remain a debt to meet. This unhappy prospect deters a firm and prompt withdrawal, and so allows the experiment to be continued in spite of cumulative losses. The net result is a greater burden of debt and a discrediting of state enterprise.

Social Responsibilities of the Entrepreneur

With these strictures upon state enterprise in mind we must proceed cautiously in recommending any extension of it. What are the grounds upon which the state should assume greater control? If the individual entrepreneur meets his social responsibilities with reasonable efficiency it is better that he be left in occupation of his present industrial territory. He will then be fairly free to allow his imagination to conceive new plans and methods, to indulge his spirit for adventure to his own satisfaction and to the benefit of the community, and to contribute to the advancement of thought and culture in his own individual way, as in the past. What are the social responsibilities he should recognize in the performance of his economic function? He should be able to offer reasonable security of employment to his men, or regard the provision for unemployment caused by industrial change as one of the costs of industry. He should establish, under control or otherwise, reasonable working standards. Wages should move up with improved efficiency and technical progress. Investment should not be recklessly pursued in industries already fully capitalized. The entrepreneur should be willing to continue to assume risks when depression threatens to supervene on prosperity, and he should be prepared to pioneer the way in the production of new goods made possible by improved technique and a higher standard of living. The dismissal of labor and the race for liquidity that mark the conduct of the average entrepreneur in times of doubt and impending depression are the negation of his social responsibility. They throw heavy burdens upon the state and discredit an economic system. In these days when men are massed in great industrial cities, the state is forced to assume the responsibilities that the entrepreneur has evaded, or to establish forms of control, such as industrial tribunals or national insurance, that will enable the entrepreneur to discharge his responsibilities. In the end the entrepreneur will be superseded unless he devises a technique for dealing with such a situation. Capitalism's lament may become a posthumous dirge.

This means that the entrepreneur of the future will perform his function within a framework of control that has been developing rapidly in many countries over the past three decades. Where the entrepreneur plays an important role his thinking dominates society. Much, therefore, depends upon how he thinks. But there is a conflict in the entrepreneur class as between the *rentier* and *entrepreneur* (enterpriser) proper. The latter deals with economic enterprises requiring planning and constructive administration. He comes closely into contact with human interests, and his social responsibilities are likely to be more present to his mind. The *rentier*, on the other hand, must constantly think of the liquidity of his assets and the necessity for meeting his fixed obligations (bank deposits, insurance claims). He forces the pace in times of difficulty and relaxes control when things are easy. It is against him that a revolt in thought has occurred in the United States. He has lost much of his authority in Great Britain, where the industrial entrepreneur has come to dominate the stage since the mistake in monetary policy in 1925. The Premiers' Plan in Australia was, as much as anything else, an effort, and a successful one at the time, to force the *rentier* to accept his social responsibilities. Much of the agitation against banking under private enterprise is a protest against the failure of the *rentier* to discharge his social functions. Those banking systems will endure which recognize social obligations and submit readily to some form of control. But this is only one of the examples of the increasing scope of economic control in the future.

What form will this control take? The insistence on minimum standards of working conditions and wages is now familiar in most countries and is accepted as a general rule of industry. In the United States there is now proceeding a great controversy over this development of state action. I cannot comment in detail on this controversy and shall merely remark in passing that regulation of minimum standards in industry is on the whole in the best interests of the entrepreneur in countries that have developed a system of regulation. True, regulation of industrial conditions reduces the flexibility of costs, but it establishes a norm about which there is little dispute save in times of emergency or increasing productivity. In Australia the leading wage-fixing tribunal, the Commonwealth Arbitration Court, revised the basic wage downward in the depression, but only after lengthy inquiry. It has since raised it, but not yet to the pre-depression level. Where confidence in a tribunal is established, its findings are accepted and much controversy and conflict avoided. The establishment of some form of control of industrial conditions is a major controversy in the United States. You may work out a voluntary system typical of your industrial genius, but whatever form it takes, control will reduce the sovereignty of the entrepreneur, and in his own interests.

I pass to consider other aspects of control that raise questions less settled in theory or practice. They are (a) the claim for economic security, (b) the regulation of investment, and (c) the provision of collective goods and services not possible by private enterprise. All these may be shown to be essential to the building of an economic order that will use to the full, progress in science and invention without causing social disturbance, while at the same time providing the conditions that will enable the entrepreneur to continue his work in the more restricted field in which he now operates. In a word, they imply that the capitalism of the future will be preserved by social controls. We are justified in making the old aphorism run: He who is not a "socialist" at twenty has no heart; he who is *not* a "socialist" at forty has no head.

The Claims of Economic Security

Take first the question of economic security. Even if the economic system were freed of the losses and disturbances of periodic depressions, unemployment caused by industrial change, sickness, and old age must be insured against. Much has been done in many countries to provide through private or state schemes for security against these risks of unemployment. The experiment of national insurance and old-age pensions in Great Britain is now perhaps the classic example. This is almost certain to be followed in other countries; some have already partial schemes in operation. But these schemes require state action, and they demand on the part of the entrepreneur a readiness to recognize the risks of unemployment and to contribute towards a solution. It is true that in the long run industrial progress benefits all the people. It is equally true, as the classical economists insisted, that invention in machinery will ultimately increase the demand for labor, perhaps at higher wage rates and shorter working hours. But this "long run" means a relatively long period of unemployment for many workers directly affected by the decay of old methods of production. No scheme of insurance against this unemployment is practicable unless it covers a wide area, so that the costs of liquidating the old methods can be charged to the new. This is indeed one of the costs of progress. The entrepreneur must be prepared to assist in meeting these costs, whether he does it through a direct contribution to the unemployment fund in England, or an indirect contribution through special taxation, as in some states in Australia, or again as a special levy for public works, as in some European countries. I need not labor the main point. It is sufficient to draw attention to the failure of free enterprise to meet the situation. It is one of the situations that must be met in the future if the entrepreneur is to survive the criticism that will be leveled against him. We were forced to meet it in Australia by special measures during the depression; and we are now being forced to meet it by devising measures of a more permanent character.

Controlling Investment

I pass to the second main field of control. Free investment was regarded as the undisputed right of the entrepreneur under the old regime and is still so regarded as his right over a considerable field of enterprise. I have deliberately refrained from dealing with problems associated with economic fluctuations, which are also problems directly related to the flow of investment. But assuming that periodic economic fluctuations are eliminated, there is still an unsolved problem of investment. Progress means continuous investment in new enterprises. It means the devising of new methods, the production of new commodities, the provision of new services for consumers. All this requires the expansion of investment into new fields. Is there any guarantee that this will take place automatically under free enterprise? Is there any reason to suppose that old industries will not be grossly over-capitalized or that they will be organized on the most efficient plan? I think not. In Australia the tariff board in its survey of protected industries has revealed very disturbing examples of over-capitalized industries — boots and shoes, textiles, cement. We have recently had a survey of the flour and bread industries by a royal commission. This survey shows how costly unrestricted private enterprise is in these two industries. Inefficiency in these industries and over-capitalization in other industries would be avoided or greatly reduced by some collective effort to provide information, and to eliminate overlapping of effort and plant. The industries themselves apparently will not make the effort on their own account. It will be necessary for the state sooner or later to insist upon the effort's being made. But it will be necessary to avoid action that will preserve old technique because of the fear of over-capitalization. The right of the entrepreneur to duplicate plant and equipment in an industry already fully capitalized will doubtless be denied the entrepreneur in the future, unless he satisfies a constituted authority that he can make a real contribution to the efficiency of the industry. This development will be resisted because the entrepreneur is impatient of any restriction upon his freedom. He has to be reminded of the words of a great Harvard philosopher: "A great society is a society in which its men of business think greatly of their functions." If saving is a virtue, investment becomes the cardinal economic achievement. Society has everything to gain by increasing its stock of capital and improving its social equipment. To suggest that the motive of private profit is the best guide and inspiration to this development is childish folly. We want to maintain the driving force of the profit motive, but to avoid the wastes and errors of competitive investment.

Collective Goods and Services

Lastly we come to the role of the state in providing, or ensuring the provision of, an increasing flow of goods and services that will not normally be provided by private enterprise. This is partly a problem of investment and partly a problem of transforming increased technical efficiency into a higher standard of living. Without this action by the state the world will be denied some of the best fruits of the application of science to industry. Political economy was nurtured in the cradle of physiocratic doctrine, which taught that wealth came directly from the soil, and made a foolish but far-reaching distinction between productive and unproductive labor. Economics has not yet emancipated itself fully from this doctrine, which has also cast its spell over the entrepreneur and is a firmly rooted belief of the primary producer, who has a greater influence on political policy than he thinks. It is at the root of the popular complaints against so-called rural depopulation. It is responsible more than anything else for the survival of a Calvinistic fear that the world is deteriorating because it enjoys the fruits of its labors. Yet a moment's reflection will show how great has been the progress, in all countries that enjoy a high standard of living, of the provision of what I have called collective goods and services — education, public health services, libraries, parks and playing grounds, roads, municipal and government buildings, museums and picture galleries, better housing of the poor, broadcasting. This is state control of consumption. Without state action these services would have been provided for a few who could afford them. The world would have been poorer. As the economic system, exploiting the resources of science, yields its fruit more abundantly, these services and goods will be provided in greater quantities. We are richer than we allow ourselves to think, and we could be richer still if we extended these services even by reducing our consumption of the alluring but illusory products dangled before our eyes because they can be produced and sold at a profit. The services and goods I have in mind are what one of my colleagues has called "tertiary" products, but they require some form of collective action for their production. They account in some measure for the increasing proportion of modern investment that is controlled by or directly made by the state. They take an increasing proportion of the productive effort of the community out of the hands of the entrepreneur. They involve the deliberate and compulsory transfer of part of the national income from private to public control.

I have said nothing of large-scale planning, which has become more important in every country. It necessarily must become so. We have it in the British Empire in migration and settlement. You in the United States have it in the Boulder Dam, the much disputed Tennessee Valley Authority, and the gigantic problems of shifting soil and erosion in the prairies. England has it in the grid system in electricity and in transport. These are problems that can only be faced by concerted community effort. Their solution is quite impossible by the entre-

preneur alone. They involve long-range effort in which
the scope for error is very great; and many errors are made.
These errors are quoted again and again as an example of
the inevitable inefficiency of state enterprise, when for the
most part they are the results of political interference in the
conception and administration of the enterprise. I have
discussed this point already, but it must be repeated that
the state will be compelled to devise a system of planning
independent of the politician, whose business it is to debate
large problems of policy after hearing expert opinion and
attempting to reconcile it with lay opinion. This can be
done best by the commission or board, working subject to
general policy laid down by Parliament, but possessing
initiative in planning and independence in management.
It is only fair to the advocate of state enterprise to insist
that the state gets the difficult jobs — those in which the
planning must be at very long range and the margin of
profit, if any, small. The entrepreneur, like the pirate
tramp ship and the motor carrier, skims the cream of the
trade and leaves the rest to the state. It is thus all the
more important that the state should take extreme care in
providing itself with expert administrators.

The Future of the Entrepreneur

There is ample evidence in the trend of social policy in
many countries to support the main conclusions of this
paper. The state is assuming more and more the functions
of the entrepreneur or exercising more and more control
over the entrepreneur. This I believe to be the inevitable
result of the rise of capitalism, with its enlarged scale of
operations, increased complexity of organization, and
greater productivity. There is a fundamental change in the
attitude of the entrepreneur; more and more enlightened
entrepreneurs preach the gospel of the social responsibility

of their class. But it cannot be left to the class as a whole to discharge these responsibilities without state intervention; nor can it be left to the entrepreneur class to supply all the goods and services of modern industry and undertake all the long-range planning of modern communities. The transformation to controlled economy and the state as entrepreneur in many fields of enterprise has gone far in most countries. There is a danger that it may go too far, as perhaps it has under dictatorships. In the English-speaking world democracy still prevails; its continuance depends in no small part upon the future of the entrepreneur. We in Australia have inherited some of the British capacity for compromise. We are not logical, but we can improvise a solution of a problem when we have to face one. In 1931 we acted on the impulse of fair treatment to all, and we invoked the power of the state to enforce it. But having provided a basis upon which to reconstruct our impaired fortunes, through a liberal banking policy and public works expenditure, we encouraged the entrepreneur to make his own effort to recovery unimpeded by restrictive state action. Much the same comment is true of Britain, the other British dominions, and the Scandinavian democracies. Here we have what I think is the sound conception of the relation of the state to the entrepreneur. You aim at getting the best of both possible worlds, and you succeed if your entrepreneur recognizes the justice and sound economic sense of some degree of control, while your democracy recognizes on its part that the entrepreneur should be encouraged to make his great contribution to economic and social progress. In this way we reconcile authority and the individual — the combination of control, where that is necessary, with the exercise of initiative and responsibility by the individual in his own sphere.

I am not extolling the virtues of the British system, but

merely drawing attention to a trend of industrial evolution which I think will exercise great influence upon our central problem. It is your greatest problem in the United States, and your future democratic system will in large measure depend upon its solution. If the people come to distrust the entrepreneur he will after years of bitter conflict be eliminated. If the entrepreneur kicks against the pricks he may maintain a privileged position, and eventually impose some authoritarian system upon the country. Neither solution appeals to me, if I may be permitted to say so, as rational for the United States, or in keeping with the democratic tradition of the country. You must build a bridge between them so that you will allow your native genius for rapid development under individual enterprise to flourish. After the state has entered fully into its new sphere as entrepreneur or as an agency for control, there will still remain wide scope for the exercise by the entrepreneur of those gifts of imagination, courage, and initiative which have done more than anything else to build up your industrial system. But the gifts will at last yield their full fruits because they will not be offset by the entrepreneur's neglect of his high social function.

In this hall of learning in the oldest university in the United States I have been all too conscious of my limitations to deal with a central problem in economics, and one that is daily engaging the attention of many respected economists in this and other great American universities. My only claim to speak is that I come from a country which knows the failures and the successes of state enterprise. I belong to a small band of economists who have had the opportunity of participating in discussions upon the formulation of economic policy and the devising of appropriate administrative machinery. Our problems are simple, compared with yours, and we are able perhaps to measure our economic forces with a little more precision, and to educate our masters a little more effectively. But I have no wish to draw from our limited experience conclusions of wide application. We, in common with other British countries, have problems enough yet to solve, and I am happy to be among my fellow economists in the United States once more to learn from them what lessons your own experience has to offer in developing forms of economic control that will improve the efficiency of the entrepreneur and reconcile his interests with those of the state.

ECONOMIC NATIONALISM

WILLIAM EMANUEL RAPPARD, DR. EN DROIT, LITT.D.

Professor of Public Finance, University of Geneva

Introduction

THE reasons which led the organizers of this scientific symposium to do me the great honor of asking me to discuss the subject of economic nationalism are unknown to me.

It does not, however, take much imagination to discover the probable explanation of their choice of the topic. Economic nationalism — whatever the term may mean, and our first endeavor will be to define it correctly — reigns supreme in the world today. It is preached as an ideal by some in many countries and by all in some countries. More important still, it is practiced as a policy with enthusiasm, reluctance, resignation, or rancor by all governments in all countries. The North and the South, the East and the West, America, Europe, Asia, and Africa, democracies and dictatorships, be they reactionary or conservative, socialistic or communistic, everyone everywhere is today carried away by the all-overpowering torrent of economic nationalism. Some are eagerly, although hardly ever happily, paddling downstream. Others are frantically, but never successfully, struggling against the current. All are carried away. It is indeed a sadly significant commentary on the present state of the international community that one of the few points on which its members are unanimous is in the practice of a policy which necessarily opposes them one to another.

The choice of the topic is therefore as readily explicable as it is well justified by the circumstances of the times. There is no social phenomenon more universal in its incidence, nor, as we hope to show, more far-reaching for the future of mankind in its consequences, than economic nationalism today. The reasons for the choice of the speaker are more conjectural. By calling upon one whom economists would repudiate as a deserter to political science and whom political science could welcome only as an intruding or refugee economist, our hosts have seemed to imply that, in their eyes, economic nationalism is a fact germane to both disciplines, but one of which neither should seek to monopolize the analysis.

Were they further influenced in their personal selection by the nationality and city of residence of the speaker? Let us hope not. For to ask a Swiss from Geneva to discuss, as a Swiss and as a citizen of the seat of the League of Nations, a policy of which the League and his small, landlocked country are perhaps the most obvious victims, would be to display a regrettable form of intellectual cruelty!

However that may be, my prime purpose is not to enlarge on the dangers of economic nationalism from the point of view of any one nation or even of the League of Nations. It is rather, in all intellectual independence, to seek first to define it as a scientific notion, then to understand it as an historical fact, and finally to assess its possible consequences for the human race.

In this threefold aspect of my task, I shall endeavor to limit my observations to what should strike everyone as rational and objectively true. Should any of my statements fail to commend themselves as such, either to the friends or to the foes of economic nationalism, it would be a disappointment, but hardly a surprise. Experience in the at least attempted practice of impartiality has taught me that, in the field of the social sciences, it is not at all sufficient to mean to be fair, nor even to be fair, in order to seem fair to those whose prejudices one does not share. This is particularly the case when one ventures on the discussion of a topic such as that of economic nationalism.

Between economic nationalism on the one hand and political and economic liberalism on the other, there is an obvious antithesis, which often gives rise to passionate controversies. Between political and economic liberalism on the one hand and intellectual liberalism on the other, there are on the contrary deep psychological affinities. It is therefore not surprising that any impartial analysis of economic nationalism should expose its author to the onslaughts of those who repudiate liberalism in all its forms and for whom impartiality itself is but the surviving failing of a bygone liberal age.

On the merits and demerits of political and economic liberalism, everyone of course has, and is entitled to have,

League of Nations?" their answer, as often as not, is to the effect that it is not a super-state. May we, for a moment, adopt the same cautious approach?

On January 26, 1770, the French economist Turgot wrote to Mlle. de l'Espinasse:

... No one will ever deal adequately with any question of political economy unless he forgets the existence of states politically separated one from another and variously constituted. . . .[1]

However one may interpret this statement, characteristic of the extreme liberalism of pre-revolutionary French thought, it is certainly not the expression of economic nationalism. To assert that, in order to understand economics, one should forget the existence of separate and different political states, is to imply that their existence is irrelevant to economic analysis. This strange view could be cleared of its apparent absurdity only if there were in fact no separate states, diversely interfering with the processes of economic life. But that assumption is precisely the one on which all the economics of Turgot and his school is based. As a theoretical doctrine, their economics was an attempted explanation of what would happen if these factors, disturbing the natural course of events, were removed. As a policy, Turgot, as well as his liberal English contemporaries, recommended the realization of this assumption as the best means of promoting human welfare.

Now it is obvious that economic nationalism is not an economic theory in the above sense, but an economic policy. It is equally obvious that, as an economic policy defined by its aims, it is far from identical with eighteenth-century liberalism. Could we then define economic nationalism as a policy tending to promote to the utmost the material welfare, not of the human community, but of the national state?

Plausible as it might seem at first glance, such a definition would be no less misleading. It would be misleading,
first because it would not distinguish economic nationalism
from other economic policies and particularly from that of
its most ardent opponents, and secondly because it would
fail to place the emphasis on what is most characteristic.
To imagine that the advocates of economic nationalism are
the only defenders of the material welfare of the national
state is as mistaken as to assume that it is material welfare
in which they are most interested.

Let us briefly consider these two points in turn.

The opponents of economic nationalism attack it, not
because they would subordinate the welfare of the nation
to that of the world community, but because they hold
that, the two being inseparable and interdependent, the
former is best served by measures which also favor the latter. Thus Adam Smith, who may be regarded as the greatest enemy of mercantilism, the economic nationalism of
his day, did not hesitate to declare approvingly: "The
great object of the political economy of every country, is
to increase the riches and power of that country." [2] He
combated, however, the maxims by which, as he wrote,
"nations have been taught that their interest consisted in
beggaring all their neighbors." [3]

He combated these maxims not only as ungenerous, but
as unwise, not as contrary to the interests of the neighbors
merely, but as ruinous for the nations themselves. His
purpose was as truly, if not as exclusively, national as that
of the economic nationalists, whom he denounced as being
not only mistaken in their economics, but also misguided
in their patriotism.

What was true of Adam Smith and his mercantilist opponents of the eighteenth century, is not less true of the
surviving liberals of the twentieth and of contemporary

economic nationalism. In spite of Friedrich List, who never tired of accusing economic liberalism of sacrificing the state to the individual and to mankind, we know of no liberal economists today who base their case on the interests of the world, as opposed to those of the nation. We are not concerned here with the relative merits of the two schools of thought, but only with their fundamental aims. To define economic nationalism as the policy best calculated, in the eyes of its advocates, to promote the material welfare of the nation, would therefore be to adopt the very definition claimed for the contrary views by its opponents.

Nor would such a definition do justice to economic nationalism and to the intelligence of its advocates. If the pursuit of national wealth were their true purpose, one could not help wondering how they could hope to achieve that purpose by preventing the nations from purchasing in the cheapest markets and selling in the dearest, by urging them to concentrate their productive energies on industries for which geography had least fitted them, and by recommending that they abandon those in which they enjoyed the greatest natural advantages. It is economic nationalism which has led the United States government to subsidize the reduction of grain acreage in the American corn belt and the Swiss government to subsidize the growth of wheat in the heart of the Alps. It would be a gratuitous insult to the intelligence of our two governments and of their advisers to believe that it was the desire to increase the national wealth that prompted these peculiar measures.

If we wished to define economic nationalism by its underlying purpose, we should say that it was a doctrine destined to serve the nation by making it not richer, but freer, by promoting not its material welfare, but its inde-

pendence of foreign influences. Economic nationalism is
the policy of national self-sufficiency. In a world divided
into states which differ in their natural resources much
more than in their fundamental needs, economic nationalism, therefore, is not, cannot be, and its most enlightened
advocates have never claimed that it was, the policy of
national wealth.

Our definition of economic nationalism as a policy destined to promote national self-sufficiency may be justified
both by the pronouncements of its leading exponents and
by the analysis of the measures taken to attain its aims.

To collect and to reproduce quotations from contemporary speeches and writings would be as easy as it would be
fastidious and unnecessary. Two recent statements may
suffice as particularly significant examples of the autarchic
ideals of economic nationalism.

The first we extract from Herr Alfred Rosenberg's *Der
Mythus des 20. Jahrhunderts*, in which, as in Herr Hitler's
Mein Kampf, the underlying strategy of German foreign
policy is clearly revealed. It is therefore more enlightening and more convincing than the fiery speeches in which
Der Führer from time to time defines his immediate tacti-
cal aims. Rosenberg, the philosopher of National Socialism, writes:

> The great catastrophe of our intellectual life consisted in the
> gradual distortion of the German conception of liberty. As a
> fruit of this sinful distortion, for which the blood poisoning of
> our race was partly responsible, freedom came to be identified
> with economic individualism. . . . Thus an apparently slight
> change in our philosophical conceptions brought tremendous
> material misfortunes upon the world. Implacable nature is hav-
> ing its revenge from day to day until the coming catastrophe,
> when the so-called world economy, with all its artificial and un-
> natural substructure, will collapse with a violence comparable to
> that of the end of the world.[4]

Today we can no longer play hide and seek, "internal colonization" can no longer be suggested as a saving solution. Such measures can hardly be expected to change the total destiny of the nation. Today there is but one solution: the act engendering the will to gain space for millions of coming Germans.[5]

The other extract is taken from one of Signor Mussolini's recent speeches. On March 23rd, 1936, he declared in a public statement made on the Capitol:

The question of raw materials shall be raised once for all, but not in the terms in which it was raised by a defeatist liberalism resigned to the acceptance of an eternal inferiority of Italy, a conception which was summed up in the phrase, which has become an abusive commonplace, that Italy was poor in raw materials.

We must say, on the contrary, that Italy does not possess certain raw materials and that is one of the fundamental reasons of its colonial claims, that Italy possesses other raw materials in sufficient quantities, that Italy is rich in many other raw materials.

That is an accurate description of the reality of the situation and that is the basis of our conviction that Italy can and must attain the highest useful level of self-sufficient economy for peace times and especially for times of war. The whole economic life of Italy must be organized with a view to this supreme necessity. The future of the Italian people is at stake.[6]

Both these statements show the real basis of economic nationalism, with which we shall deal presently.

Although the technical devices employed to render the nations independent of each other's resources, or at least of each other's goodwill, are almost infinitely numerous and varied, they may conveniently be summarized under the following four headings.

First, economic nationalism seeks to limit the nation's consumption to those goods which are the fruit of its own soil and labor. By appeals to patriotism, as well as by the more drastic and effective means of tariffs, quotas, exchange controls, and outright prohibitions, nations are urged to prefer national products and constrained to forego the enjoyment of foreign commodities and services.

Secondly, economic nationalism seeks to promote the domestic production of all those commodities for which the national needs are imperative. When, in spite of all government protection and assistance, such production proves technically impossible or economically impracticable, the scientific and industrial talent of the country is mustered and set to discover and manufacture substitute goods, honors and bounties being showered upon successful inventors and venturesome enterprises.

Thirdly, when these efforts also prove vain, as has heretofore been the case for certain mineral and vegetable raw materials, economic nationalism is apt to raise the cry for more space, that is for annexations of neighboring or colonial territories. It is not always clear whether such claims are based primarily on material considerations or whether economics is not made subservient to political motives. Two significant facts cannot fail to strike the impartial observer in this connection. On the one hand, the demands for territorial expansion are commensurate not with the economic needs of the states that formulate them, but rather with their actual or potential military power. On the other hand, far from wishing to adapt the size of the population to the resources of the country, economic nationalism, as expounded by all its most fervent nationalistic advocates, does not encourage emigration and actually spurns birth control. These two facts could hardly be understood if such economic nationalism was not, in its vital impulses, more national — that is political — than economic.

As no measure of restriction of imports, of stimulation of home products, and of territorial expansion, can possibly make any state entirely self-sufficient under modern conditions, economic nationalism seeks, fourthly, to secure a favorable balance of payments, and thereby to promote an influx of gold. In this, as in all other respects, present-day economic nationalists show themselves to be the legitimate offspring of their mercantilist ancestry. The first three policies we have just mentioned tend to make the state independent of foreign resources. The fourth tends to make it independent of foreign goodwill. For there is no foreign treasure, be it ever so jealously guarded by national envy and hatred, of which the vaults cannot be unlocked by him who possesses the key of gold. To forge this key, that is to obtain the wherewithal to purchase abroad what one cannot produce at home, is thus the subsidiary, but none the less a necessary, aim of economic nationalism.

It is here that the policy becomes internally self-contradictory.[7] It is here also that rival economic nationalisms must necessarily clash. In order to secure for itself a favorable balance of payments, a state dominated by this doctrine must inevitably seek to inflict on its neighbors the very treatment against which it seeks to protect itself. If all countries endeavor to develop their exports while restricting their imports, to attract foreign capital and foreign tourists while prohibiting external loans and discouraging travel abroad, to expand their shipping, banking, and insurance services beyond their frontiers while monopolizing them at home, general failure, strife, and chaos cannot fail to be the result. The simple logic of these deductions is but too generally confirmed by the present tragic state of the world.

It is this fourth characteristic of economic nationalism also that explains why its contagion has spread even to the least nationalistic of states. If its exponents were content to preach and to practice the limitation of imports and the promotion of domestic production, there would doubtless be a general contraction of foreign trade and a consequent lowering of the standards of living in the world. Liberal states, however, would remain free to pursue their own policies and to maintain among themselves at least a normal exchange of goods and services. But since economic nationalism is as aggressive as it is defensive in its commercial policies, it imposes itself and all its methods even on those who are least inclined to accept its underlying philosophy.

No statesman today, however convinced he might be of the advantages of commercial *laisser faire*, *laisser passer*, under conditions of at least partial reciprocity, could submit to the economic aggression of ruthless neighbors who, while closing their own doors to all imports and to all immigration, insisted on dumping abroad their entire surplus of goods and services. His markets would be swamped by commodities sold below their net cost, his industrial population reduced to unemployment, and his gold reserves rapidly depleted. The ensuing fall in the domestic price level would be a meager consolation indeed for the general economic dislocation and consequent social upheavals which such a statesman would have to face, if he did not protect himself by imitating his aggressor. Adam Smith himself, were he made responsible for the economic policy of a state in the world of today, would doubtless resort to the very measures on the denunciation and repudiation of which his reputation and the prosperity of nineteenth-century England were based. How could he who, in 1776, declared retaliation to be "a matter of deliberation . . . when some foreign nation restrains by high duties or prohibitions the importation of some of our manufactures into their country," refrain from retaliation in 1936 when not "some manufactures" but all imports were not only "restrained by high duties" but expressly excluded by quotas, depreciated currencies, or direct exchange controls? [8]

To be sure, retaliation alone does not account for all the restrictive commercial policies practiced today by those states whose economic nationalism is not inspired by political nationalism. But it explains many of them. The other factors we shall examine presently. Having seen what economic nationalism is, let us now consider why it is.

II. *Why is Economic Nationalism?*

The origins and universal practice of economic nationalism today undoubtedly call for an explanation. It is not as if the policy were in the obvious material interests of the world community or even in that of the states which pursue it. This is manifestly not the case.

To show it, no economic analysis is necessary. It is sufficient to note the repeated declarations of the statesmen who recommend the policy. They are of two types, whom we may characterize as the apologetic and the defiant.

The apologetic are those, by far the most numerous, who feel reluctantly driven to propose measures of economic nationalism, much as military authorities in certain contingencies are driven to prescribe the use of gas masks or of bombing planes. They prescribe these measures as means of self-protection and of retaliation, recognizing them to be unfortunate in themselves, but deeming them unfortunately necessary. Now what is the danger which, in the eyes of its apologetic exponents, justifies the resort to economic nationalism by the state for which they are responsible? Purely and simply the economic nationalism of their neighbors. Far from being a justification, that is of course the most devastating condemnation of economic nationalism as a general policy.

The defiant nationalists, it is true, follow another line of argument and one which is far more enlightening to him who seeks the real *raison d'être* of economic nationalism.

In the Spring of the present year, during the months which preceded the occupation of the demilitarized Rhineland, there was a shortage of butter in Germany. The shortage — which, so far as the discipline imposed on the German people allowed one to judge from without, seems to have aroused some discontent — was due not to diminished domestic production but to reduced imports from Denmark and Holland. The German government, whose restrictive policies had thus determined this shortage, justified its action by the campaign cry: "We can do without butter, but we must have iron!" It was explained to the impatient housewives on the town markets that, as the limited foreign exchange available did not allow for sufficient imports of both butter and iron, the former had to be sacrificed to the latter.

A brief analysis of this cry, "We can do without butter, but we must have iron!" will, we believe, explain the fundamentals of economic nationalism far more revealingly than any learned disquisition. First, who is "we" in the above-quoted phrase? It is the German individual who consumes, or who is deprived of, the butter. But it is the state that requires the iron. As the state takes precedence over the individual, under German National Socialism as under all other forms of nationalism and of socialism, iron takes precedence over butter. Secondly, why does the individual want butter and the state want iron? The individual wants butter to improve his material well-being. The state wants iron to enhance its military power. As military power is held to be more essential than material well-being, iron again is imported to the exclusion of butter.

The individual subordinated to the state — that is, as

we have seen, an aspect of nationalism. The material interests of the individual subordinated to the state's preparations for war — that is militarism. Now, in the field of economics, nationalism combined with militarism almost necessarily makes for economic nationalism.

If that is, as we believe, the true explanation of the origins of this policy in the world today, it is of course not by itself a sufficient explanation.

Why, one may ask, is the welfare of the individual subordinated to the power of the state? Moreover, why are the material interests of the individual sacrificed to military considerations? And, finally, how is it that economic nationalism flourishes today even in countries where the individual is not deliberately subordinated to the state and where the state is not obsessed with warlike ambitions?

Fully to consider these three further questions would take us very far afield. We can therefore but outline the answers as they appear to us.

The subordination of the individual to the state is one of the most significant characteristics of contemporary civilization. In those countries which still pride themselves on the freedom of their political institutions it is but a partial subordination, grudgingly endured or reluctantly accepted as a regrettable but inevitable reaction against the conquests of the popular revolutions of the eighteenth and nineteenth centuries. In the dictatorships, on the contrary, which expressly repudiate these conquests, it is acclaimed as a new ideal and ruthlessly applied as a fundamental principle of the post-liberal order.

In order to understand this present subordination of the individual to the state, it is well to remember how recent and how imperfect was his previous emancipation. Political liberty has never been either general or lasting in the world. In its modern forms it is an achievement won, over a very limited part of the globe, in the course of the last one hundred and fifty years. The Russian people have never tasted of it. For the Germans, it became a recognized institution only after the World War and then only as an import from abroad and as a by-product of defeat, national humiliation, and material distress. In Italy, its history is perhaps somewhat longer, but how could it have been a true reality for a people largely poor and ignorant, who had reached the stage of manhood suffrage only in 1919?

For those countries in which the individual enjoyed a large measure of emancipation throughout the nineteenth century — the Anglo-Saxon world and Northwestern Europe — his gradual resubordination to the state is, as I have recently sought to show in detail for Switzerland,[9] the indirect result of democracy, technical progress, and the increasing complexity and cumbersomeness of the machinery of government. In all these countries, the individual, having freed himself from the state in the latter half of the eighteenth and in the former half of the nineteenth century, has since become its master. However, exercising his authority over the state in the interests of his personal comfort and security, he has entrusted his newly won servant with ever more onerous duties and has thereby inevitably been led to forfeit ever more of his former freedom. In these so-called liberal countries, the individual is to the state in much the same semi-tyrannical and semi-tyrannized position as a pampered old bachelor to his faithful cook. She dutifully obeys all his commands, to be sure, but, having become indispensable to his well-being, she has gained an ascendancy over him which leaves but little play for his former masterly independence.

So it has come about that the state has everywhere subordinated the individual to its will, suddenly, brutally, and

completely in the dictatorships — be they of the prole-
tariat, of *Il Duce*, or of *Der Führer* — gradually, insinu-
atingly, and still only partly in the surviving democracies.

But why, to recall our second question, should the state
sacrifice the material interests of the community to its own
military power? The universal reply will be: security.
And for many nations this reply is entirely convincing.
Many nations, too weak or too obviously pacific to be
threatening themselves, are, or at least genuinely feel,
threatened by their neighbors. Without expressing any
opinion that has not been expressed by the omnipotent
leaders of the nationalistic states themselves, one cannot
but note their professedly aggressive designs. In order to
declare that Japan, Italy, or Germany, for instance, were
today as amorous of peace as the United States, France,
or the United Kingdom, one would have to be blind and
deaf to the events and to the warnings of yesterday and
unheedful of the most patent signs of the times.

Impartiality does not demand, and indeed forbids, that
form of intellectual neutrality for which all states are at all
stages of their development equally dangerous or equally
inoffensive. However, whether it be for purposes of aggression, of intimidation, of prestige, of collective security,
or of defense, all states are arming heavily. Their motives
are manifestly different, but their policies are the same.
And these policies all tend to sacrifice the material interests
of the community to national military power.

These statements, which cannot reasonably be challenged by any independent observer, give us the answer
not only to our second, but also to our third, question. The
same anticipation of war, be it through fear or through
premeditation of aggression, which leads states to increase
their armaments, also inspires their economic policies.
Self-sufficiency is lauded as a condition of national inde-

pendence and security. That is doubtless the prime reason for the universality of economic nationalism in the world today.

It is not, however, the only reason. Over ten years ago an economic conference had been summoned to Geneva under the auspices of the League of Nations. Its purpose was already to improve international economic relations, in other words to combat economic nationalism. Still, in 1927, the Manchurian, the Ethiopian, and the Rhineland ventures had not yet revealed the temper of the governments responsible for them.

The economic nationalism of 1927 was the product not so much of the wars one feared for the future, but of the war from which one had but recently emerged. Directly and indirectly, that war had bred economic nationalism. While it was being waged, belligerents and neutrals alike had thoroughly learned the lessons of national self-sufficiency and of generalized state control. When it was over, vested interests everywhere were clamoring for increased protection or rather for the continuance by peaceful measures of the unheard-of protection which they had enjoyed under the conditions of war. In the industrial West of Europe as well as overseas, agriculture demanded that war prices be at least partly maintained. In the agrarian East and especially in the newly created states, the cry was for industrial protection. A universal fever of economic nationalism, exasperated by the claims and recriminations to which an unwieldy volume of international indebtedness gave rise, was the result.

The world had not yet overcome this post-war fever when, in the autumn of 1929, an economic crisis occurred which was to be as unprecedented in its incidence and in its gravity as in its duration. Generated in part by economic nationalism, this crisis has led to an aggravation of the very disease of which it was a symptom. As in all previous periods of depression, governments and parliaments everywhere sought to protect their people against the evils of falling prices, growing unemployment, and collapsing currencies, by restricting imports and immigration and by artificially promoting domestic production. And, as ever before, these remedies, universally but anarchically applied, have delayed instead of hastening recovery.

Furthermore the impotence of contemporary capitalism, too hemmed in by the state to cure itself by the normal processes of economic competition and yet too unbridled to be susceptible of effective control from without, gave rise to new theories of economic reform. Under the generic name of planning, borrowed from soviet communism, these theories came to be professed in the most unexpected quarters. Heads of institutions of higher capitalistic studies [10] vied with unsophisticated Marxian socialists in the ambitious endeavor to bring order out of chaos by the deliberate political organization of economic life. The task, stupendous even when undertaken only on a national scale in countries accustomed to a certain measure of individual freedom, is of course utterly inconceivable on the international plane. Thus planning also made for a recrudescence of economic nationalism. The following extract from Dean Donham's *Business Looks at the Unforeseen* clearly shows this causal relation:

The truth is that the effective organization of the world on the basis of constantly expanding interdependence is beyond human intelligence. Too many cultures clash at too many points. Too many facts, hopelessly beyond intellectual and practical mastery, prevent mutual understanding. Too many local economic and social problems require solutions not consonant with any general plan directed at the best average solution for the total population of the globe. Too great differences in standards of living exist in different parts of the world. The road to peace by the accentuation of mutual interdependence is hopeless. The only hope lies in the lessening of points of conflict so that in our remaining points of contact we may attain mutual understanding.[11]

Similar views held in the labor world have led one European socialist party after another recently to insert protectionist planks in its political program. Thus the freedom of international trade has come to be abandoned as a policy, even by the natural champions of the masses, most immediately interested in the maintenance of a low cost of living.

Finally, one may note that economic nationalism is today receiving support also from some international reformers. Peace, they argue, demands that political and economic institutions be developed in harmony one with another. Having been obliged, however reluctantly, to recognize that the states of today are still too passionately attached to their political sovereignty to allow for the creation of the true world federation which present economic international relations would seem to demand, they are led to favor a restriction of these relations. Having been disappointed in their hopes that a new political mold could be devised to fit the enlarged dimensions of the body economic, they urge as a makeshift the compression of this body into the existing molds of political sovereignty. And these suggestions of course again make for economic nationalism.

Thus, in an article entitled "The Limits of Economic Nationalism," Professor Quincy Wright, of Chicago, wrote some time ago:

If the amount of international contact can be reduced without arousing dangerous resentment, that is all to the good. International contact is probably a cause of war if not regulated by adequate international machinery. We might as well recognize that all nations cannot be economically independent without a degree of depopulation or a reduction of the standard of living which is unthinkable, that there is consequently a minimum below which international contact cannot be pushed, and that we must develop sufficient international organization so that that degree of contact can be regulated.[12]

This quotation shows that even such a leader of internationalist thought as Professor Quincy Wright has been driven to consider international trade and economic interdependence more as a curse than as a blessing. He tends to consider them not as allies, but as foes, of peace, to be disciplined and regulated in so far as it is found impracticable to abolish them.

The devastating torrents of economic nationalism which are flooding mankind in its national abodes and depriving it of most of the benefits to which the progress in the arts of production would seem to have entitled it thus spring from three main fountains: war, past and future, the spirit of nationalism, which is the main cause of war today, and state socialism, which is one of its most significant consequences.

III. *Whither Economic Nationalism?*

If such is the nature and such the origin of economic nationalism, may we ask ourselves in conclusion whither its tempestuous waters are carrying the frail raft of human destiny?

History, even when guided by economic and political science, can do no more than hazard explanations concerning the past. Even in its own domain, that of yesterday, its evidence is rarely such as to justify more than tentative conclusions. As for speculations concerning tomorrow, they are out of bounds for the historian, unless it be the historian of the imagination, as one might define the poet.

And was it not a poet himself who declared: "L'avenir n'est à personne"?

Are we thus, as men of science, inhibited from looking beyond today, from peering out of the windows of the past on the mysteries of the future? Most assuredly. If we students of the social sciences could only deny ourselves the forbidden fruits of prediction and of admonition, we should be far more respected, even if much less quoted, by our fellow creatures. Without betraying our scientific trust and without unduly indulging either in prophecy or in advice, we may legitimately, however, call attention to the striking dual parallelism of peace and free trade, on the one hand, and of war and economic nationalism, on the other, which past centuries reveal. This parallelism is both so undeniable and so readily explicable that to prolong its lines from the explored past into the unknown and unknowable future is, even if *ultra vires* for the historian, at least a forgivable, because a not unreasonable, assumption for the citizen of the world.

Ever since the dawn of economic thought in Western Europe, trade restrictions have been on the one hand urged and justified as weapons for the enhancement of the power of the national state, and on the other combated and condemned as obstacles on the road to peace and prosperity.

All historians of mercantilism, from Schmoller and Cunningham to their successors of today, however different their interpretations of the economic nationalism of the sixteenth to eighteenth centuries, have seen in it a doctrine and a policy of international belligerency. As Hekscher, the most recent of these historians, has well said:

While the medieval conception of the object of human effort was the salvation of human souls and while economic liberalism or *laisser faire* aimed at the temporal welfare of individuals, mercantilist statesmen and writers saw in the subjects of the state means to an end, and the end was the power of the state itself.[13]

To protect and to increase the power of the state, the Venetians, the Spaniards, the English, the Dutch, and the French all alike resorted to commercial policies which, however contrary to their immediate material welfare, were calculated to promote their warlike designs and to satisfy their lust for power. This is so true that the history of economic nationalism during the three centuries prior to the French Revolution is as much a history of international strife as of national consolidation. It is assuredly unnecessary to stress the point in this country, which owes its very independence to an armed revolt against the pressure of British economic nationalism.

As the practice of mercantilism inevitably led to war, so the reactions against it were inspired by the love of peace no less than by the desire to improve the lot of the individual.

As early as the beginning of the seventeenth century, the French publicist Emeric Crucé wrote his *Nouveau Cynée*. This curious work, of which one of the three original copies still extant is in the Harvard University Library, was, in 1909, re-edited by an American scholar. In bold opposition to the prevailing mercantilist prejudices, Cru005, as the subtitle of his book announced, advocated therein both "general peace" and "free trade for all." [14]

A century later, Boisguillebert attempted to show that nature herself, by distributing the fruits of the soil unevenly among the nations, had invited them peacefully to exchange their respective products rather than to wage war upon each other. [15]

Among the various reasons which incited the Physiocrats to revolt against the teachings of the mercantilists, the uselessly destructive wars to which their economic nationalism condemned the peoples of the earth was not the least potent. Quesnay, it is true, did not conceive of the nations otherwise than as "particular and distinct powers, which counterbalance each other and cannot be subjected to a general order." Although he consequently regarded international conflicts as inevitable, he held that "wars should be very rare between good governments, since a good government deprecates all wars undertaken under the absurd pretext of commerce and of all other misleading and captious claims to which one resorts for the violation of the law of nations, thereby ruining both oneself and others." [16]

As for Adam Smith, his denunciations of the "impertinent jealousy of merchants and manufacturers" whose mischievous policies have made of "commerce, which ought naturally to be a bond of union and friendship . . . the most fertile source of discord and animosity," are so well known that one hesitates to quote them. [17]

As is equally well known, Adam Smith's most faithful disciples, such as Say and Bastiat in France, Mill and Cobden in England, were apostles of peace no less than of free trade. Peace both as a necessary condition and as a beneficial and fruitful consequence of international commerce, war and military establishments as enemies both of liberty and prosperity, these have always been among the principal themes of economic liberalism. Two brief quotations may suffice to show how closely allied the ideals of peace and free trade have ever been in the inspiration and in the doctrines of this school.

The conclusions of John Stuart Mill's famous chapter on international trade read as follows:

. . . Commerce first taught nations to see with good will the wealth and prosperity of one another. Before, the patriot, unless sufficiently advanced in culture to feel the world his country, wished all countries weak, poor, and ill-governed, but his own: he now sees in their wealth and progress a direct source of wealth and progress to his own country. It is commerce which is rapidly rendering war obsolete, by strengthening and multiplying the personal interests which are in natural opposition to it. And it may be said without exaggeration that the great extent and rapid increase of international trade, in being the principal guarantee of the peace of the world, is the great permanent security for the uninterrupted progress of the ideas, the institutions, and the character of the human race.[18]

As for Cobden, not only did the pursuit of peace occupy a place hardly second to that of free trade in his public efforts, but we have it on his own authority that, in his advocacy of commercial liberalism, he was prompted by political no less than by economic motives. Thus, addressing a meeting on peace under the auspices of the Peace Society at Wrexham, in Wales, on November 14th, 1850, he declared:

When I advocated free trade, do you suppose that I did not see its relation to the present question, or that I advocated free trade merely because it would give us a little more occupation in this or that pursuit? No; I believed free trade would have the tendency to unite mankind in the bonds of peace, and it was that, more than any pecuniary consideration, which sustained and actuated me, as my friends know, in that struggle.[19]

Throughout the nineteenth century, also, and up to the present day, we may note as close a connection in the history of political thought between economic nationalism and war as that existing between the ideals of free trade and of peace.

No author ever extolled national self-sufficiency with greater fervor than Johann Gottlieb Fichte. The title of his famous book, *The Self-Contained Economic State*,[20] suffices to indicate to what lengths patriotic passion, when coupled with logical frenzy, can carry a German philosopher. Having established to his own satisfaction that humanity was predestined by nature to be divided into large empires, and having justified the extension of these empires at the expense of their smaller neighbors, if need be by conquest, so as to render them absolutely self-contained, Fichte continued:

It has always been the privilege of philosophers to sigh over wars. The present author does not love them more than anyone else. But he believes in their inevitability in the present circumstances and deems it uncalled for to complain of the inevitable. In order to abolish war it is necessary to abolish its cause. Every state must receive what it intends to obtain through war and what it alone can reasonably determine, that is its natural frontiers. When that is accomplished it will have no further claims on any other state since it will possess what it had sought.[21]

Then, but then only, when states will have become absolutely independent of each other within their natural frontiers and will have refrained from all foreign trade, can peace be envisaged. For Fichte, therefore, complete economic nationalism was the necessary condition of peace. But, as peace could be maintained only as between self-contained states and as these in turn could be constituted only by the processes of war, war thus became the inevitable price of economic nationalism.

Less crude in its conception, but no less ruthless in its exigencies, was the political philosophy of Fichte's compatriot of the following generation, Friedrich List. List's patriotic protectionism is the more provocative as no writer more clearly perceived and more convincingly analyzed the causal relations between peace and international trade than this great champion of German unity and power. Yet no one has done more to promote economic nationalism, not only in his own day and country, but in all industrially backward states ever since. How is this paradox to be explained?

That List considered universal peace and prosperity

promoted by international interdependence and free trade, not only as an Utopian ideal, but as the probable outcome of the evolution of civilized mankind, is unmistakably shown by the following quotation from his principal work, *The National System of Political Economy*, first published in 1840:

Reason as well as religion unquestionably call[s] for the ideas of universal confederacy and of eternal peace. If a duel between two individuals is clearly contrary to reason, how much more must a duel between nations be so? The proofs of the rationality of the union of all men under the same laws are perhaps of all proofs which sociology can draw from the history of the human race those which most appeal to common sense. History teaches that whenever individuals live in a state of war, the well-being of mankind is reduced to its lowest level and that it rises *pari passu* with their union. In the evolution of the race we witness alliances between families, then between cities, then city confederacies, then the union of whole territories and finally of many states under a common law. If nature has been powerful enough to extend to hundreds of millions this union which began among a few families, it would seem probable that it should bring about the union of all the nations. Since the human mind has been able to perceive the advantages of this great union, it should be permitted to deem it able also to understand the advantages of a universal union of the whole human race. Many signs point to this tendency of the world mind. Let us recall only the progress of the sciences, of the arts and of the inventions, of industry and of the social order. It is already possible to predict with certainty that after a few decades the most civilized nations of the world will, thanks to the improvement in the means of communication, be with respect to their material and intellectual relations united as closely or even more closely than were a century ago the counties of England. Already the governments of the continental states possess in the telegraph almost as convenient an instrument of conversation as if they were located in one and the same place. Already new and powerful sources of energy have raised industry to a point of perfection undreamed-of in former times and such sources still more powerful have already announced their apparition. Now the higher the development of industry, the more uniform its spread over all the countries of the world, the less the possibility of war. Two equally advanced industrial nations would be able, within one week, to inflict upon each other greater damage than they could repair in a generation. To this must be added that the same new forces which have heretofore primarily served productive purposes would not refuse their service to causes of destruction and that they would in the first instance benefit the continental states of Europe, depriving England of those advantages which it has so far derived from its insular position. In the congresses of the great powers, Europe already possesses the embryo of a future assembly of the nations. Clearly the tendency to reconcile national differences through negotiation already takes precedence over the endeavors to settle them by force of arms. A deeper insight into the nature of wealth and of industry has already convinced the best minds in all the advanced nations that the civilization of barbarian or semi-barbarian peoples and of such that are backward in their evolution and the establishment of colonies offer them a field for the exercise of their productive powers infinitely more promising and less precarious than mutual warlike or commercial antagonisms.[22]

The fundamental irrationality and the destructiveness of war, the beneficial effects of free trade, the pacifying possibilities of scientific and industrial progress and, if ill-directed, its deadly menace for the security of all states and particularly of Great Britain, indeed the coming of a league of nations, all this is clearly recognized in this truly prophetic page of Friedrich List.

How is it then that this lover of peace through technical and commercial progress, this friend of international trade, and this professed enemy of armaments, both military and economic, should be known as perhaps the leading advocate of European protectionism in the nineteenth century? The explanation is to be found not in any logical inconsistency, nor in any psychological evolution on List's part. It resides, purely and simply, in his deliberate subordination of the interests of the individual and of the human race to those of the national state, obviously prompted by an envious admiration of the industrial and commercial supremacy of liberal England. In the very same chapter from which the above quotation is drawn, List declares:

The system of the (liberal) school is based on a true idea, an idea which science, if it is to fulfill its purpose of guiding practical policy, should recognize and elaborate, an idea which this policy cannot ignore without going astray. But this school has neglected the consideration of the nature of nationalities, of their special interests and conditions, and of their relations to a universal union and to lasting peace.

The school has assumed as already existing a state of affairs which has still to be realized. It assumes the existence of a universal union and of lasting peace and therefrom draws its conclusions concerning the great advantages of commercial freedom. Thus it confuses effects and causes. Permanent peace prevailing between united provinces and countries has given rise to commercial unions which, thanks to this peace, have proved so advantageous. All historical precedents go to show that political unions go before and that commercial unions follow in their wake. There is no example of the opposite order. There are very strong and in our opinion decisive grounds for believing that under the present world conditions general free trade would result, not in an universal republic, but in the universal subordination of the less advanced nations to those possessing supreme manufacturing, commercial, and sea power.[23]

In spite of the economic and political advantages accruing to all individuals and to mankind as a whole from universal free trade, List therefore recommends policies of industrial protection for all but the most advanced states, and particularly for Germany. It is the task of economics, he declares — or rather of national economy, as he and all his fellow Germans significantly prefer to call the science of which Adam Smith is the father — "to promote the economic education of the nation in order to prepare it for its admission to the universal society of the future." [24]

When is a state fit to become a member of this society and how is it to be educated therefor? The main requisites for full statehood are, according to List, "a well rounded-out territory," a large population speaking the same language, and a well-balanced economic structure, in which agriculture, manufacture, trade, and sea power are all harmoniously developed. In order to enjoy such statehood, a nation must possess "sufficient military power by land and by sea to protect its autonomy, its independence, and its foreign trade," and it should normally be endowed with colonies to serve as an outlet for its surplus population. Thus Germany should be united and enlarged so as to possess "all the sea-coast from the mouth of the Rhine to the limits of Poland including Holland and Denmark."[25]

Moreover, in order to hasten its growth towards complete statehood, a nation should resort to industrial protection. Such protection, List observes, "is not the artificial product of political speculation, as the school erroneously teaches. History shows," he adds, "that trade restrictions are born either of the natural efforts of the nation to attain well-being, independence, and power, or of wars and hostile commercial measures on the part of the dominating manufacturing nations." [26]

As well-developed manufactures are, for a predominantly agricultural country, the condition of complete statehood, as such manufactures are best promoted by reasonable tariffs, and as wars are the most fertile source of protectionist measures, List, in spite of all his previously professed pacifism and economic liberalism, does not hesitate to conclude that "a war which promotes the transition from the purely agricultural to the mixed agricultural-manufacturing state is therefore a blessing for a nation. . . . Whereas a peace, which throws back into a purely agricultural condition a state destined to become industrialized, is a curse incomparably more harmful than a war." [27]

List's final championship of both economic and military armaments, as complementary means of promoting the independence and power of the nation, is nowhere more concisely and more clearly asserted than in the following statement:

> We ask: would not a government be mad in the estimation of every reasonable citizen if, invoking the advantages and the rationality of assured peace, it should disband its armies, destroy its men-at-war, and raze its fortifications? But such a government would be doing no more than what the school demands of governments, namely to renounce the advantages of protection, by reason of the advantages of free trade. [28]

Thus, with less brutality, with far greater political and economic intelligence, and with more moderation and subtlety, List arrives at conclusions not essentially different from those of Fichte. From the point of view of the world community, whose political organization he foresees, he condemns war as inhuman and trade restrictions as irrational. But from that of the national state, which, in his scale of values, is entitled to precedence over both the individual and mankind as a whole, he admits and even welcomes armaments, military as well as economic, as factors of progress.

This hasty sketch of the development of economic nationalism and of its political implications may suffice to show that, in their consistent advocacy of economic as well as of military armaments, the present-day dictators of Europe, did they not prefer the illusion of their own originality, might claim an ancestry as ancient as the oldest states of Europe. This ancestry, in fact, is more ancient than the states over which they rule.

It is assuredly not an accident that the two great powers

which today practice economic nationalism in its most aggressive and defiant forms are those whose national unity
was most recently achieved. What mercantilism was to
Spain, England, and France in their formative stages, at
the beginning of modern times, dictatorial economic nationalism seems to be to Italy and Germany today.

Are we to conclude therefrom that economic nationalism must, in Italy, Germany, and the other younger states
of Europe, run its course in the twentieth century as mercantilism exhausted itself in Western Europe before the
nineteenth? And may we hope that, having run its course,
it will make place for a more humane doctrine? Such a
conclusion might seem plausible and even hopeful, were it
not for a circumstance of absolutely decisive importance.

The qualitative and quantitative progress in the arts of
destruction has been such in the course of the last century, and more particularly since the World War, that the
civilization which has developed since the Middle Ages
could probably not survive the shock to which it would be
exposed tomorrow if economic nationalism were to engender the same political consequences to which it has ever
given rise in the past. Our imagination shrinks before the
vision of universal devastation, suffering, and death which
the thorough application of modern physics and chemistry
to the task of mutual annihilation must evoke.

But that, of course, is no sure protection. Men and nations have gone mad in the past, and previous civilizations,
no less ambitious than our own, have been engulfed in dark
ages in centuries and millenaries gone by.

Such a tragedy may be in store for our generation. It is,
however, not inevitable. Men may yet recoil before the
fatal consequences of their criminal folly. They may yet
allow reason to triumph over the promptings of inflamed
and misguided nationalism. They may yet realize that,

under the conditions of modern civilization, humanity is essentially one crew manning one and the same craft and that all may be lost if mutual animosity is allowed to wreck the common ship.

Economic nationalism, as it is universally practiced today, cannot but lead to the exasperation of such mutual animosity. To denounce the terrifying dangers of a doctrine so universally prevalent, although so manifestly incompatible with the welfare of the human race, may seem futile or presumptuous. Not in the name of science, which knows neither dangers nor welfare, but for the sake of science, as well as for the sake of all that is precious in this world, I am impelled however to conclude this brief study on economic nationalism on a note of extreme alarm. Alarm is indeed the only alternative to despair, because an alarmed, eleventh-hour conversion to more reason, to more liberalism, and to more humanity in international relations is, as I see it, the only alternative to impending catastrophe.

Lest an American audience attribute the pessimism of these views to the panic of the European scene in which they were conceived, my last words will be borrowed from Professor James T. Shotwell, of Columbia University. In the preface of his recent book, *On the Rim of the Abyss*, I read the following statement, which so clearly sums up the opinions above expounded that I may quote it here as my own conclusion:

The forces of destruction which mobilized industry can unloose today from the arsenals of science are greater than those of many Tamerlanes. Single factories now exist which could, by swift readjustment to war purposes already planned, turn out in a single day five times the destructive chemicals that were rained on England in the whole war. The armaments of 1918 compared with those of today were almost medieval. It does not necessarily follow that they would be used to the uttermost, and that the result of another major war would be a return to the Dark

Ages. But to attempt to escape such a fate by taking to the woods, erecting barriers to trade in order to make each country self-sufficing, like a feudal domain, is to anticipate disaster by bringing it upon us in peace time. [29]

Such, then, are my general conclusions.

It must not be said, however, that a citizen of the city of John Calvin has addressed an audience in the state of John Winthrop on such a solemn occasion as this without a closing appeal to our common puritanical instincts of self-accusation and self-improvement. May I therefore suggest that it may well be that the economic nationalism of the United States in the past, however pacific its own inspiration, has not been entirely foreign to the rise of aggressive economic nationalism in the European dictatorships of today? Who can assess the ultimate repercussions on the labor markets of the Old World, and thereby on the temper of its teeming millions, of the restrictions by America of imports and of immigration into the New?

However that may be, if by the example of the Good Neighbor the American people could bring about a New Deal in international relations, they would be adding still another and yet infinitely more significant obligation to the long list of debts which Europe already owes them. These debts of gratitude, of which none can feel the weight more keenly than the present European guests of Harvard University, are not the less real nor the less appreciated for not having always, as I am told, been fully and faithfully repaid in the past!

NOTES

1 *Oeuvres de Turgot* (Daire ed., 2 vols., Paris, 1844), II, 800. "... Quiconque n'oublie pas qu'il y a des États politiques séparés les uns des autres et constitués diversement, ne traitera jamais bien aucune question d'économie politique...."

2 *An Inquiry into the Nature and Causes of the Wealth of Nations* (1776; Cannan ed., London, 1925), I, 351.

3 *Ibid.*, p. 457.

4 Alfred Rosenberg, *Der Mythus des 20. Jahrhunderts* (53rd, 54th ed., Munich, 1935), p. 532. — "Die grosse Katastrophe unseres geistigen Lebens bestand darin, dass eine sündhafte, durch Blutvergiftung mitbedingte Verschiebung in der Freiheitsauffassung im deutschen Leben immer mehr zu herrschen begann: als sei *Freiheit* gleichbedeutend mit *Wirtschaftsindividualismus.* ... So hat eine scheinbar geringe erkenntniskritische Verschiebung ungeheures materielles Unheil über die Welt gebracht, denn Tag für Tag rächt sich die unerbittliche Natur bis zur kommenden Katastrophe, bei der die *sogenannte Weltwirtschaft* mitsamt ihrem künstlichen, naturwidrigen Unterbau, einem Weltuntergang vergleichbar, zusammenstürzen wird."

5 *Ibid.*, p. 638. — "Heute hilft kein Versteckspiel mehr, kein schwächlicher Hinweis auf 'innere Siedlung' als alleinige Rettung, da dadurch wenig am Gesamtschicksal der Nation geändert wird, heute hilft nur der in zielbewusste Tat umzusetzende Wille, Raum zu schaffen für Millionen kommender Deutschen."

6 Quoted from *Corriere della Sera*, March 24, 1936. — "La questione delle materie prime va dunque, una volta per tutte, posta non nei termini nei quali la poneva il liberalismo rinunciatario e rassegnato a una eterna inferiorità dell'Italia, riassumentesi nella frase ormai divenuta abusato luogo commune che l'Italia è povera di materie prime.

"Deve dirsi invece: l'Italia non possiede talune materie prime, ed è questa una fondamentale ragione delle sue esigenze coloniali; l'Italia possiede in quantità sufficiente alcune materie prime; l'Italia è ricca di molte altre materie prime.

"Questa è l'esatta rappresentazione della realtà delle cose e questo spiega la nostra convinzione che l'Italia può e deve raggiungere il massimo livello utile di autonomia economica per il tempo di pace e sopratutto per il tempo di guerra. Tutta l'economia italiana deve essere orientata verso questa suprema necessità; da essa dipende l'avvenire del popolo italiano."

7 Luck would have it that just as I was drafting these lines in my study at Geneva, on Tuesday evening, March 7th, 1936, the Radio-Paris brought me an unexpected confirmation of this statement. M. Franklin-Bouillon, president of the French so-called Republican Front, was addressing his constituents on the air with a view to the coming legislative elections. He declared: "France is above all a great agricultural nation. Fifty per cent at least of her population draw their subsistence from agriculture. In order to assure them of normal living conditions, the products of the soil must be revalorized." Having thus preached true economic nationalism — the revalorization of agricultural products can mean but more effective agricultural protection — the French deputy proceeded: "Our manufacturers and traders are suffering

cruelly . . . from the closing up of our traditional foreign markets, as a consequence of the ever increasing economic nationalism."

8 *Wealth of Nations*, I, 431.

9 W. E. Rappard, *L'individu et l'État dans l'Évolution constitutionelle de la Suisse* (Zurich, 1936).

10 Cf. for instance W. B. Donham, *Business Adrift* (New York, 1931) and *Business Looks at the Unforeseen* (New York, 1932).

11 *Business Looks at the Unforeseen*, p. 103.

12 Quincy Wright, "The Limits of Economic Nationalism," in *The Christian Register*, vol. cxii, no. 40 (1933).

13 Eli F. Hekscher, "Mercantilism," in the *Encyclopedia of the Social Sciences*, X (New York, 1933), 335.

14 *Le Nouveau Cynée, ou Discours d'Estat représentant les occasions et moyens d'establir une paix générale et la liberté du commerce par tout le monde* (1623; Balch ed., Philadelphia, 1909).

15 "Dissertation sur la nature des richesses," in Eugène Daire, *Economistes financiers du XVIIIe siècle* (2nd ed., Paris, 1858), p. 391 *et seq.*

16 "Despotisme de la Chine," in *Oeuvres économiques et philosophiques de F. Quesnay* (Oncken ed., Frankfurt, 1888), pp. 657–658.

17 *Wealth of Nations*, I, 457.

18 John Stuart Mill, *Principles of Political Economy* (1848; Ashley ed., London, 1909), p. 582.

19 Richard Cobden, *Speeches on Questions of Public Policy*, edited by John Bright and Thorold Rogers (London, 1870), II, 421.

20 *Der geschlossene Handelsstaat* (Tübingen, 1800).

21 *Ibid.*, p. 218.

22 *Friedrich Lists gesammelte Schriften*, herausgegeben von L. Häusser III (Stuttgart and Tübingen, 1815), 133 et seq.

23 *Ibid.*, p. 136.

24 *Ibid.*, p. 182.

25 *Ibid.*, p. 183.

26 *Ibid.*, p. 187.

27 *Ibid.*, p. 189.

28 *Ibid.*, p. 188.

29 James T. Shotwell, *On the Rim of the Abyss* (New York, 1936), pp. vii–viii.

II
STABILITY AND SOCIAL CHANGE

CONSERVATIVE FACTORS IN RECENT BRITISH HISTORY

JOHN HAROLD CLAPHAM, LITT.D.

Professor of Economic History, University of Cambridge

THE title of this paper is a frank imitation of that of Professor Charles M. Andrews which we are to hear shortly. Having learnt his title before I had decided on my own, it seemed to me fitting that, as he was to discuss conservative factors in that early colonial history of which he is a master, I should say what I could of the conservative factors in the recent history of Britain; for the economic history of most modern Britain is the part of history which I know best. By "recent" I mean very recent — approximately the last third of the nineteenth century and the first third of the twentieth: in British political terms, the history since the Reform Bill of 1867: in economic terms, since the effective opening of the age of electricity and steel, of American transcontinental railways, and of the Suez Canal.

Conservative factors of some kind have been very necessary to British well-being because of Britain's apparently unstable social and economic balance. Never before in the world's history has there been a great nation so thoroughly urbanized; never one so dependent on the outside world for essential foodstuffs and raw materials. Already in the forties of the nineteenth century this urbanization, with its associated industrial and social evils, had convinced one close foreign observer — Friedrich Engels — that a violent revolution was inevitable within three years. In the mid-

'eighties, when trade was slack all the world over but especially in Britain, he was sure that there would never be a revival and that the revolutionary Day of Judgment was again near. Engels, of course, was biased. He had imbibed, had helped to formulate, Marx's doctrine of the predestined catastrophe of so-called capitalism. He longed for that catastrophe and saw it coming when in fact it was not coming. Since his day — and until our own — the doctrine that industrial capitalism must stagger from depression to worse depression until it utterly falls has been an integral part of one body of socialist doctrine. Only the other day one of our ablest parliamentary socialists remarked that the recent economic recovery in Britain had shown him that there was more life in capitalism than he had supposed. With Engels, he was surprised that, like King Charles II, it was such an unconscionable time in dying. I do not hold this doctrine of socialist determinism; I mention it to emphasize the fact, admitted by observers of all schools, that there are grave elements of risk in the abnormal urbanization and industrialization of Britain. It was a revolution springing from industrial conditions that Engels anticipated, not a revolution predominantly agrarian like that of France in 1789.

These risks were underrated by the average British mind, and by many picked minds far above the average, in the peace of late Victorian and Edwardian times. They were underrated because to those minds peace seemed the natural state of nations, and the growing dependence of nations upon one another its best guarantee. The great free-traders of the nineteenth century had never tired of glorifying the peace-making nature of commerce. And they were half right; more nearly right, as I hold, than those of our contemporaries who would have us believe that struggle for markets is not merely a cause of particular wars — that it obviously is — but the dominant cause of war itself.

But many Continental thinkers, not dogmatic socialists nor single-minded free-traders, with the possibility of war always before them, rated British economic insecurity and instability exceedingly high at the opening of the present century. I have in mind such men as the late Professor Adolf Wagner of Berlin. They were debating how far it was desirable that Germany should follow Britain on the road of industrialism, urbanization, and lack of self-sufficiency. Britain, they said — with much truth — has sacrificed her agriculture to her industry. She first taught and then equipped other nations to be her industrial competitors. She has lost her leadership, or is losing it. With a little ill luck in war she might easily lose her life. Once beaten, her day is over, as the day of Carthage was. It may be recalled that in 1914–18 William II of Germany used to talk of the first and second Punic Wars against England.

The parallel is very far from exact, but there is this much in it. No great nation stood — and stands — to lose so much by defeat in a war as Britain. Your peasant country can recover from the most devastating war with extraordinary speed. Cheap homesteads are soon rebuilt; corn grows in much less than a year; pigs breed fast. Serbia after the war of 1914–18 is a case in point. Your country in which agriculture and industry, town and country, are approximately balanced, as they were in the France or — with a less even balance — in the Germany of 1914, has some of these advantages. Half or more of the defeated and discharged soldiers can go back to the land, as the peasant hero of Zola's *Downfall* did in 1871. But what the chaos might be, and how long it might continue, in a thoroughly defeated and thoroughly industrialized modern state we can only imagine — for the thing has never been experienced anywhere — with the aid of what we saw in Germany in 1918–25, a country more industrialized than France but much less than Britain.

So the first and most obvious conservative factor in the Britain of 1867–1914 was peace; for the Britain of 1918, victory. For Britain since 1918 it is again peace, or at least security. That needs no elaboration.

But those who in the nineteenth century prophesied revolution, believing that conservative factors were too weak to avert it, were not thinking of a revolution of defeat like the Paris Commune of 1871 or the German revolution of 1918. They were thinking of some social breakdown resulting from defects in the body economic which the governing powers were too weak, too foolish, or too selfish to remedy. Watching the growth of democracy in Britain, noting especially the Reform Bill of 1867 which, broadly speaking, gave votes to the urban wage-earners, Marx had allowed that England was the only country (I fancy he meant in Europe) "where the inevitable social revolution might be effected entirely by peaceful and legal means." He hardly expected that it would: he fancied that the English ruling classes would organize what he called "a pro-slavery rebellion" (what we today should probably call a Fascist movement) against the appropriate revolutionary laws; but he thought it just possible that there might be a peaceful transition from England as he knew it to England as he thought it was going to be. The change was to him quite inevitable. His economic determinism and his amazing self-assurance told him that. But there was just this doubt as to the *modus operandi*.

Obsessed by Marxian or semi-Marxian thought, many historians have scanned the nineteenth century to explain why there was not a British revolution in the tens or the forties or the eighties or somewhere. French scholars have been particularly impressed by the conservative force of popular religion in Britain, especially of Methodism. Bred among Methodists, I should be the last to deny the importance of that force. It is still at work. The late Arthur Henderson, our Foreign Secretary, had been a wage-earner and remained a Methodist lay preacher. Self-styled revolutionaries from our literary cliques mocked his conservatism; and undoubtedly men of his stamp have been conservative factors in British public life. But speaking for the moment as a *political* economist and historian — I underline the word political — I have never been able to find any moment in the nineteenth century at which, so far as I could judge, the risks of violent revolution, or of anything like it, were so great as to make it necessary for historians to explain why no violent revolution took place. Of course the existence of the definitely religious type, and its sustained prominence among the leaders of wage-earners' movements and of the modern Labour Party, was itself a minimizer of risks; but putting that aside in imagination, so far as one can, I should still be prepared to argue that the risk was never high. This is a mere *obiter dictum*: a volume would be not too much to sustain my point. But short papers on great subjects read at Conferences must contain many *obiter dicta*.

I hardly know whether I should class as a conservative or as a — what is the right antithesis in American usage to conservative? — shall I say radical? — as a radical factor the extreme flexibility of the British Constitution. If conservative implies conservation from physical violence, from revolutionary *journées*, from what Tennyson used to call "the blind fool-fury of the Seine," then it is without a doubt most conservative. That was what Marx saw to be true, once the franchise had been extended to urban wage-earners. Anything could and can be done quickly in their, or anyone else's, interests by Act of Parliament; nor is there any appeal. Why even consider violence when the law lies so ready to the hand of a majority? Revolutionary minorities of the right hand or the left may, and do, chafe at the slowness of our law-making machine; but ours, I think I may say without national vanity, is a politically educated people most unlikely to accept the lead of any small minority, excepting conceivably in some crisis of abominable distress, such as that which defeat in. a great war might have brought or might bring.

The Chartists of the forties did not even aim at the violent revolution which Engels, watching them, anticipated. They aimed at control of Parliament by universal manhood suffrage, realizing that this should suffice; for the Whigs had taught them in 1832 how to deal with the House of Lords; and twenty-five years ago, at the time of the Parliament Act of 1911, that method was illustrated. It was at a time when the flexibility of the Constitution as what I have called a radical factor was also being illustrated; when the way was being prepared for fundamental, if quiet, social transformations by the legislation of the last great British Liberal Government (there may yet be another, Liberal in our Party sense; but this I can hardly believe)—Campbell Bannerman's and Asquith's Government of 1905–15.

In the troubled years 1910–14, to which some young non-historical minds now look back rather ridiculously as times of rest and quiet, there was a real danger of civil war in the British Isles, but over the Irish Question, not over the radical — in the literal sense, going to the root of things — the radical legislative work of Asquith's Government. There was strong feeling enough about some of the social legislation as it affected Great Britain; but here the almost incredibly deep-rooted habit of automatic obedience to an

Act of Parliament, administered by a very powerful Civil Service whose integrity almost no one questions, prevailed. This habit viewed from one side is the most conservative, viewed from the other the most radical, factor in recent British history. True, when Lloyd George and Winston Churchill introduced the beginnings of our modern system of social insurance against sickness and unemployment in 1911, leagues were formed of people pledged not to lick stamps, as the phrase was. (The fixing of stamps to the insurance cards of insured persons was a novelty.) But these leagues were joined mainly by ladies in the West End of London and in spite of them the parlor-maids' cards, with all other cards, were very soon stamped — whoever did the licking. The system now works almost as smoothly as the penny post; though those who know our countryside best think that there may be some difficulty in getting farmers to lick the necessary stamps now that unemployment insurance has been extended, as from the present year, to the agricultural laborers.

Here, I believe, urbanization and the growing uniformity of urban habits help that semi-automatic obedience to a social Act of Parliament of which I have spoken. How that may be in America, with your more racially mixed urban population, I do not know; but I am strongly disposed to hold that it is so with us, though strict proof would not be easy. It is, I imagine, well known that the high British urbanization, combined with the high measure of dependence on imported foodstuffs, made the very difficult war time social experiment of food rationing easier, and, I believe, more successful, in Britain than in any other European country. Food rationing in a nation of food-producing farmers or peasants is infinitely difficult. It was never quite successful in the British countryside. But the countryside is, from many points of view most unhappily, so subordinated with us to the streets that relative failure there did not obscure the predominant success in our urban and suburban society.

In that society a food card, an insurance card, or any other instrument of experimental social legislation, readily takes its place alongside tram-tickets, pawn-tickets, rent and rates demand notes, savings certificates, and all the other printed records of social obligations and claims. Difficulties are most likely to arise among our small minorities of still imperfectly assimilated immigrants — such as Jews of the London East End — but I have no reason to think that these difficulties have been serious.

In this connection it may be worth while to point out the way in which, as it seems to me, the harsh experience of 1914–18 strengthened the habit of strict obedience to the law, even when obedience is greatly to the subject's disadvantage. The Great War came after nearly twenty years of what our propertied classes often described as confiscatory taxation — from Harcourt's death duties of 1895 to Lloyd George's budgets of 1910–11. The proceeds of that taxation went partly to pay for the South African war of a generation ago and the preparations for war on land and sea which, as we hold, were forced on us in the decade before 1914. But in part, though actually in subordinate part, they went to pay for the Liberal social legislation — the old age pensions of 1908, the social insurance experiments of 1911, and so on. Grumbling a little under their burdens already, our propertied classes found the country engaged in a war to win which they were prepared — wisely as well as honorably prepared — to shoulder almost any burden. They emerged in 1919–20 with a settled high-tax-paying habit which fifteen years earlier would have been quite unthinkable; a habit which today makes really rich men, with only a moderate amount of evasion and an occasional rather pathetic protest in their last wills and testaments, pay away a half or more of their incomes in taxes during life with the expectation that their heirs will hand over to the state a third or more of their capital at death.

The matter, it is said, was recently under discussion between an Englishman and a Frenchman. The Frenchman, having quoted a French parallel to every burdensome English tax, said, with disarming candor — "faut avouer que nous ne payons pas." It is not vaingloriously but, I believe, as a record of fact that I say of the English — "nous payons."

This financial docility may, like the flexibility of the British Constitution, be regarded either as a conservative or as what I have called a radical factor in recent British history. Conservative, in that it has allowed our immense — and not always well-regulated — social and other expenditure of the last fifteen years to be made with singularly little friction. (The central budget today is approximately one fifth of the statisticians' estimate of the aggregate national income: and there are the county and municipal budgets to be added.) Radical, in that almost any kind of experimental expenditure may be incurred with this guaranteed minimum of friction. The old age pension has been increased; pensions for widows have been introduced; unemployment insurance — applicable to only selected industries before 1914 — has, with the recent inclusion of agriculture, been made all but universal. Various industries have been experimentally subsidized. And so on. I make no attempt to assess the values of the different policies. Those vary. I am emphasizing merely the ease of their introduction. In 1913 the British public, and British Chancellors of the Exchequer bred in the Gladstonian tradition, thought a budget of £200,000,000 a terrible

thing and the total national debt was £650,000,000. Now
an expenditure of some scores of millions on widows' pensions or a proposed expenditure of £130,000,000 on national roads is taken as a matter of course. And yet the
taxable national income, in terms of pounds sterling, was
probably not more than twice as great in 1934 as in 1914.

That the free expenditure on social services has been a
conservative force is obvious. A century ago George Can-
ning used to say that the old English Poor Law, harsh as it
seems to the modern mind, had saved England from revolution during the great French Wars. I agree that it was
at least a very important conservative factor. So with our
health and unemployment insurances and their rather
lavish extensions — aided by the remains of our old Poor
Law — in the depressions of 1921–23 and 1929–33. Attention has been so much fixed, both at home and abroad,
on the black spots of concentrated unemployment that the
undoubted rise in average well-being among British wage-
earners is apt to be overlooked. This rise is the combined
result of anonymous economic forces and of these deliberate government policies. Anonymous forces have given
the greatest increase in real wages to the man who needed
it most — the unskilled. In London the percentage of
those living in tragic poverty, below the statisticians' revised "poverty line," has certainly decreased since the War;
and, thanks to social insurance, "the most dreaded features
of that life," as the 1930 Survey of London put it, "have
been largely removed."

London has been relatively fortunate in the incidence of
trade depression, but it is the same elsewhere — barring a
few specially hard-hit areas. In the depths of the post-1929
slump I spoke to a Liverpool business man. "There is no
trade in Liverpool," said he, in the sweeping way business
men do. "And the people?" said I. "Never so comfort-

able," said he. "In the old days you constantly saw bare feet: now they are unknown." That, of course, is no proof — only a picturesque illustration of what is in fact capable of proof. Anyone who can compare in memory the dress of British skilled or unskilled workers, especially the unskilled, over the two decades 1913–33 knows for certain that there has been improvement. Emphatically there are no *sans-culottes* in the Britain of today.

A conservative factor of a different kind, but connected indirectly with the disproportionate rise in the real wages of unskilled labor, is that decline in the British birth rate which has become so pronounced that, even if the rate continues at the present level and falls no further, an actual decline in population will shortly set in. With the sudden — if perhaps temporary — fall since 1928 in the power of younger countries to attract British emigrants, and with the actual reflux from those and other countries into the United Kingdom of more than 250,000 people during the six years 1930–35 — a thing unheard of during the last two centuries of British history — the social strain would have been most severe, although probably not insupportable, had our home population been growing at the old rate. Now, since the last sharp downward plunge in the birth-rate began in 1923–24, we are just nearing the years in which industry must adjust itself to a shortened annual supply of juvenile labor, and society to an abnormal proportion of elderly people, until those of us who, like myself, were born when the birth rate was more than twice what it now is are gathered to our fathers. Already our school population has declined, and we are beginning to think in terms of a stationary, or even a falling, population.

In this stabilizing society we have a powerful conservative factor — the last to which I shall refer — in our Parliamentary tradition which guarantees, as I believe, that the further social and economic changes which are certainly coming will come conservatively, that is gradually and with a minimum of friction. The British Labour Party has hitherto governed twice but not ruled. If it comes to rule, to have a clear majority of its own, as it well may in the near future, I do not anticipate Marx's "pro-slavery rebellion" of the former governing classes. If violence were tried by any group from the left, then there would be counter-violence from the other side; and I believe it would succeed. But rebellion against an Act of Parliament is infinitely improbable; and the Acts which might emanate from a victorious Labour Party, though they might be slightly revolutionary, are likely to be discreet. Our Labour Party, like our House of Commons, is a fascinating amalgam of social types; and the cross-connections of House of Commons life facilitate the traditional British compromise. Few Parliaments or parties of the left contain more men with personal experience of working for wages than the contemporary British House of Commons and its Labour Party. With them — in Parliament and party—are men from all Marx's "governing classes." The present leader of the Labour Party was educated at a public school — in the English sense — and at Oxford. His rival for the leadership started life as an errand boy. The two chief experts of the party on foreign affairs both came from my own College at Cambridge: one of them went to it from Eton. Arthur Henderson in his early days was an iron molder. Our present Foreign Secretary is the son of a seventh baronet. I am inclined to think — here I speak as an outsider, though with some inside information — that three of the most personally popular men in the House are the Prime Minister, educated at Harrow and Trinity College, Cambridge, Mr. Lansbury, educated at primary schools, and Mr. Maxton — well to Mr. Lansbury's left as a socialist — who is a graduate of Glasgow. Our solitary Communist, not University trained, is also well liked.

The strong development of late years of Parliamentary groups of Members drawn from all the parties who have some common interest — the latest is an Austrian group — is a great help to mutual understanding; and as all parties have now abandoned the doctrine that social and economic affairs should not, in the terminology of the nineteenth century, be "interfered with" by the state, the chief differences of opinion between them are those of time, pace, extent, and method of interference which lend themselves perfectly to compromise and adjustment.

These are some of the chief historical factors which seem to me to favor a conservative economic and social evolution in Britain, given — an important and fateful proviso — international security.

THE HISTORICAL PATTERN OF SOCIAL CHANGE

ROBERT MORRISON MACIVER, PH.D., LITT.D.

*Professor of Political Philosophy and Sociology,
Columbia University*

THE search for principles of order in history is beset
by peculiar difficulties. When the historian traces the
concatenation of events he generally treats them as falling
into parallel or marginally connected sequences and tends
to view these as together establishing an epoch or historical
stage or as revealing the life-course of a nation or a civilization. But two assumptions are therein implicit: first that
the epoch or the nation or the civilization is itself a distinctive unity, not merely a convenient name or label
under which to range the myriad activities that are taken
as its manifestations, and second that the unity is continuous through change, not merely from event to event
but throughout the whole sequence. These assumptions
are rarely examined and still more rarely justified. Yet
they supply the two dimensions, the space dimension and
the time dimension, of the historian's universe. Without
them history-writing on any scale becomes no more than
an assemblage of accidentally associated tales. On the
other hand, those writers who, not content with the more
academic mode, essay the task of discovering large-scale
patterns or recurrences in the web of history generally
postulate as the substratum of change an organic totality
that reveals afresh, age upon age, the persistent character
of its fundamental being. As recent instances of this more
ambitious style one may cite the interpretations of

Spengler, Pareto, and Arnold Toynbee.[1] The eclectic use
which such synoptic writers make of the historical data
and the persuasive manner in which they richly illustrate
and plausibly reinforce their very divergent conclusions
suggest the need for a re-examination and clarification of
the initial postulate. What is the nature of the unity that
at any given moment characterizes an area of human
society? What is the nature of the continuity that any
such area maintains throughout its changes? Is it an
integral unity of the organic sort that responds as a whole
and changes as a whole? Or is it a unity more loosely
woven of diverse strands that have different motions and
principles of change? If the latter, then we may be led to
approach history by another road and to find in the time-
sequence some other order than that of recurrent rhythms,
of like responses to like situations, or of the successive wax-
ing and waning of like organic forms.

It is an inveterate human tendency to conceive of unities
too simply and too absolutely, whether the unity be nation
or state or culture or religion or race or generation or anything else which we include within the bracket of a social
name. The practical consequences of this simplification
are rife in the world to-day. The theoretical consequences
alone concern us here. Falsely conceived entities cloud the
thoughts of the common man and invade the speculations
of the philosopher. The one philosophically-minded statesman of the Great War, General J. C. Smuts, said at its
close:

There is no doubt that Mankind is once more on the move.
The very foundations have been shaken and loosened, and

[1] Oswald Spengler, *Der Untergang des Abendlandes*, translated by C. F. Atkinson
as *The Decline of the West* (New York, 1926–28); Vilfredo Pareto, *Trattato di
Sociologia Generale*, edited by Arthur Livingston as *The Mind and Society*, see
especially vol. IV (New York, 1935); A. J. Toynbee, *A Study of History*
(London, 1934).

things are again fluid. The tents have been struck, and the great caravan of Mankind is once more on the march.

Some tents have been struck and some stand pegged. Some parts of the "great caravan" move in one direction and some in another, forward or backward. What is the whole that marches whither?

Let us admit with the synoptic historian that there is history only of that which in each of its moments is a unity and in all its sequences persists through change. Where this condition is lacking we have no history, but manifold histories. If the condition does not hold for human aggregates, then we still may have histories of industry and agriculture, of housing and of standards of living, histories of mathematics and magic and medicine and engineering and warfare and government, of all the conditions and arts and contrivances of man — but not of his peoples and tribes, countries and nations. Without this concept of unity historical research is only cutting separate trails through the jungle of events. If a hundred million agriculturists over the face of the earth suffered simultaneously from drought or famine, this would no more constitute a single historical event than if they enjoyed simultaneously the most diverse fortunes. Even were every one of the hundred million linked at some point with his neighbors so that a nexus of relationship threaded them all together, we should still be far from the necessary condition of a common history. All we could attain would be a multitude of cross-referenced biographies, lacking historical focus or significance. And even were the whole multitude subject to some single human organization, such as a tax-gathering and soldier-recruiting empire, that touched their lives sporadically from afar, we should still have to exclude from the content of a common history the vast extent of all they did and suffered. The incidents of their lives might have much human interest and in that sense they might attract the attention of the historian, who is — sometimes to the confusion of his art — a human being no less than an historian.

For there is history only of that which in itself, as a unity, undergoes processes of change. This proposition, being self-evident, everyone admits in principle. No one, for example, would set out to write a history of Patagonia-plus-Ethiopia. In the demarcation of an historical subject, whether it be the village of Blind Man's Gap or mankind itself, there is always, as we have stated, the assumption that here is a distinctive entity which grew and achieved and suffered as a whole. But the proposition may be accepted in principle and evaded in application. We may assume unities into whose reality and into whose nature we do not enquire. We may take a geographical area, a territory, as the equivalent of a social unity. We may regard a mere power-system, an empire, as the incorporation of a culture-system. Or we may use the term "culture" as an anthropological blanket to cover all the characteristics of human life within an area territorially defined. Or we may use the term "state" as if it connoted a common way of life, although frequently a system of government extends over many schemes of life and many creeds, and frequently a scheme of life or a creed extends over many systems of government.

Unless we define our unity, what criterion have we to distinguish the relevant from the irrelevant? In the multitude of affairs and changes, what matters for the record, in what degree and why? These are the embarrassing questions that the historian of commonwealths and peoples must answer — or fail to answer. These questions have little sting for the specialist of military history or political history or economic history or the history of science. But the general historian evades them at his peril. How much weight should he give to "the drums and tramplings of a thousand conquests" and how much to the changing tides of opinion that are revealed in the songs and gossipings of common men? Should Alexander, who wept that he had no more worlds to conquer, have more space in the record than his tutor Aristotle, who took all knowledge to be his province? What prominence shall Savonarola have beside Galileo, or Cesare Borgia beside Machiavelli? What significance shall the historian attach to the squabbles of politicians for spoils as compared with the quiet toil of scientists and inventors, to the money-makers as compared with the wealth-creators, to the leaders of men as compared with the dreamers of dreams? For what, *to what*, are they severally significant?

The historian cannot evade these questions, unless he is content to make the historical record an arbitrary reflection of his own selective interest in events or unless, in a vain objectivity, he is ready to assess events by the amount of clamor or commotion which they aroused. But no scientific observer could accept the latter criterion. A flaming meteorite is vastly less significant to the astronomer than a faint nebula. And so may the spectacular figures and events of history mean far less to the scheme of things entire than the dim processes of change that are unheralded by the fame of men.

The essential difficulty is that the historical data nowhere fall within a single closed system with determinate frontiers of space or of time. Systems, of course, abound; political systems, economic systems, class systems, community systems, technological systems, religious systems, language systems, thought systems, mode-of-living systems. These systems are interwoven and interdependent, but their interdeterminate and changing frontiers are bewilderingly non-coincident except perhaps in some rare fastnesses where small tribes still live remote from contacts — and from history. There alone, if anywhere, is the dream of totalitarianism realized in our present world. Elsewhere the various systems refuse the measure of any Procrustean bed devised by race fanatics or culture purists, who would make the world conform to the simplicity of their own thoughts. It has been so ever since what we name civilization began. In this fact, which could be amply demonstrated did space permit but which may be sufficiently obvious without demonstration, we find one main reason for rejecting the notion that societies or civilizations, on any scale whatever, are organic wholes, all of whose elements and systems are bound together in indissoluble unity, grow together, flourish together, and at length die together.

From this negative fact we start on the quest for another conception of social unity. But, if we do not accept the organismic hypothesis, are we not abandoning altogether the unity that historians desiderate? If we think of society as an array of diversely ordered systems overlapping and merging into one another, how can we find any coherence, any focus, any pattern even, in this flux? We can, of course, take any one system, say the economic, as our main interest, and seek to show its dynamic relation to all the others, but unless we assume, as in the Marxist position, that this particular system is primary and in effect determinant of all the rest, we come no nearer to a synthetic principle. For that we must look beyond the systems to the mentality that creates and sustains them. An economic system, a political system, a religious system, all systems of human relationship, exist only in and through the conscious experience of them. Take away that experience and they leave not a wrack behind. Likewise a technological system, apart from the contriving consciousness, is neither technology nor system. The engines and the guns become merely curious shapes of metal and the houses and gardens are houses and gardens no more. Territory is no longer country and the frontiers of men's allegiance fall into oblivion. These very obvious facts lead us through to a less obvious conclusion. In the realms that the historian of society explores the sole purely objective reality is the experiencing subject, the sole inclusive unity is the coherence of a scheme of life, over the range within which it determines the activities and the thoughts of men, and the sole available synthesis is that which interprets the character, the derivation, the conditions, the trends and the transformations of these socially established modes of being. All the systems we have referred to, economic, military, religious, and so forth, are but the articulations or instruments of some embodied vision wherein or whereby man lives. Egyptian priestly dynasties, familially-minded China, caste-bound India, Minoan and Mycenean societies, the Greek city states, the Roman imperium, the intestate civilization of Maya, Christian feudalism, Japanese feudalism, nineteenth-century capitalism, and the newborn orders of a shaken world are all to be understood, in the last resort, as nuclei of such relatively coherent schemes of life.

Whatever may be the relation of race or geography or economic nexus or control-institutions to such a scheme of life, the unity itself is clearly none of these things. It manifests itself dynamically as a system of incorporated values, and the scale of the unity is the range over which these distinctive human valuations are incorporated. We have thus three main elements in every historical situation and in every historical process. First and focal are the incorporated values themselves, which, using the term in the older, non-anthropological sense, we shall call the culture; in the second place come the utilitarian or instrumental systems that sustain the culture, though, of course, they serve to mold it as well — the economic, political, and technological systems with all their organizations, contrivances, authorities, controls, and educational devices. Finally, there is the third element, the material factors which, as such, exist apart from the scheme of life and its sustaining systems but which are essential determinants of them — the eternally interactive biological and environmental factors. When we bring these factors, the population as a biological entity and the geographical conditions, into relation to the scheme of life and the utilitarian systems, we discover various types and degrees of interdependence between them all. Thus we conceive of the totalities that we name peoples and nations and societies and civilizations.

The incessant change of these variously named totalities is the theme of history, and what I wish here to suggest is that in an analysis of the contingent and unstable adjustment of these three elements we shall find the main key to the interpretation of historical change. Further, I hope to show that, in the larger historical perspective, the changes in the mode of adjustment between these elements follow a particular pattern. This is what I mean by the historical pattern of social change. It is not a changing pattern with which I propose to deal, but a pattern of change itself. But before I proceed to elucidate it I shall endeavor to justify the selection of our three primary categories. Why mark off into these three groupings the myriad diverse phenomena of social life? Why assume that they are more adequate and more relevant than any other categories? Why assume a certain order of relationship between them that gives logical priority to subjective group values, regards the nexus of institutions mainly as their instruments, and lumps together the concrete realities of human stock and physical environment as though they were merely the oil and the lamp for the flickering flame of these insubstantial values?

If we are to answer these questions, a fuller definition of our first two categories is necessary. We are distinguishing here between the activities, personal relationships, products, and finally states of being, which are in normal human experience immediate values, and those which are by contrast conditional or indirect values. We are distinguishing between the things men pursue because they want them and those they pursue because they are the conditions of their attaining what they want. Taken from a psychological standpoint this distinction does not help us. One man reads because it helps him to sleep and another because he enjoys reading. One man plays golf because it is good for his health and another because he likes golf. One man preaches because he finds it a comfortable profession and another because he believes in his message and calling. From the psychological standpoint values-as-ends and values-as-means are inextricably and hopelessly intermingled. But from the sociological standpoint, as I have elsewhere shown, the distinction is tenable and serviceable.[2] For values-as-means cohere into characteristic systems which differ in important respects from the systems that express values-as-ends. The economic, the technological, and the political systems are *typically* embodiments of values-as-means; while the family, the church, the club, the discussion group, the gossip party, the sports organization, the associations of the fine arts and of the sciences, the alumni association, and certain

---

[2] In my book, *Society: Its Structure and Changes* (New York, 1931), ch. XII.

forms of educational institution, are *typically* embodiments of values-as-ends.

The importance of the distinction lies in the fact that we can envisage the utilitarian systems, the economic, the technological, and the political, as constituting one great nexus of means, and find in the relation of this nexus to the cultural life, to the colorful confusion of the realm of ends, the clue to a major problem of human history. It is a commonplace observation of our times that the nations of the world, in spite of their manifold cultural apartnesses, are meshed in the same expansive machine-technology, and it is scarcely less obvious that their economic systems are interdependent in spite of strong attempts on the part of many to assert independence, and that their political systems laggardly follow, in uneasy compromises with their sense of sovereign isolation, the inevitable demands of economic-technological expansion. This current situation is a phase of the larger pattern with which I wish to deal. I refer to it here since it may serve to illustrate one of a number of reasons why for the discovery of this pattern of change we draw a line between the utilitarian order and the cultural life.

For this nexus of means has a mode and tempo of expansion other than those of the creeds and the philosophies, the *Weltanschauungen* and the mores, which dominate cultural expression. Technology and scientific application move always forward. They march to ever new conquests. The economic system is caught up in the advance, being the area which first and always receives the impact of technology. The political system follows in the rear, slowest to respond to that impact, but follows, nevertheless, with strange twistings and tergiversations, as it is forced to abandon the trenches of ancient authority. The economic and the political cannot for long go separate ways, still less so the economic and the technological. For together these constitute an interwrought scheme of means and powers, and there is chaos where they are not conjoined. Every economy is, and always has been, even in the extreme moments of laissez-faire, essentially a political economy. And since means can be added to means and powers added to powers, the utilitarian nexus is inevitably expansive and tends to embrace within one homogeneous organization ever larger areas of society. Here it stands in contrast to the characteristic organizations of the cultural life. The latter, with their deeper bite into human personality, with their appeal to final values and goals of living, as variable as the minds that respond to them, have more limited, precarious, and temporary conditions of expansion. Culture tends to be a subjective possession, enjoyed and cultivated in congenial person-to-person relationships, and even the one culture-aspect which makes universalist claims, religion in certain of its forms, arouses in the minds of those who accept its claims a thousand competing interpretations of that universality. But traders will deal with one another across any culture barrier and machines will work as well for pagans as for Christians, for Soviet collectives as for American capitalists. Hence a phenomenon that emerges in various degrees from the dawn of history to the present. The South Sea Islander embarks on a bartering expedition to alien tribes; the ancient empire incorporates in its political system the outer barbarian; and modern nations gladly enter into alliance with others whose ways of life and thought they abhor.

But the utilitarian order has an inner as well as an outer principle of expansion that differentiates it from the cultural order. The steady, seemingly irresistible advance of technology has no counterpart in the realm of cultural values. In technology the highest attainments of yesterday are surpassed to-day, and those of to-day will be surpassed to-morrow. These attainments are not merely outmoded, like the popular songs and plays of yesteryear. They are replaced by more effective devices, by finer instruments, by more powerful engines, by more ingenious mechanisms. For in this sphere, once it grows distinct, the appeal is no longer to authority or to phantasy or to tradition. Here only the pragmatic appeal, the demonstrable test of competitive efficiency, is determinant, and here alone, in spite of the yearnings of certain philosophers, is that test available. If one machine will, at less cost, do more work than another, that machine will send the other to the scrap heap, and no odor of sanctity or cherished sentiment will save it. Cultural variations can be subjected to no analogous test. There is no clear or accepted criterion whereby to compare them. The values by which men live also conform to processes of change but, as we shall see, the processes are very different, though interrelated, and the results are far less predictable. Here there is ebb and flow, oscillation, recurrence, and neither triumphant march nor yet any clear sign posts to point the way of indubitable advance.

It is scarcely possible that an older technology should overpower its later developments, but it is nothing remarkable in the history of values that an older culture type should reassert itself over a newer one, either in its original home or in some other cultural focus. The vitality of culture is of an entirely different order from that of technology. Frequently, in designs of living and in the fine arts, there is a return to earlier styles, but the technological arts reject the cyclical mode. On the grander scale of world-history, as Rome and Byzantium and Islam and Renaissance Europe can testify, there is offered again and again the spectacle of an older culture successfully invading the newer. "Conquered Greece has taken us captive" admitted a Roman poet. But the language of victory and defeat is not fully applicable to the relation of culture to culture. Cultures do not normally replace one another. They blend and permeate and fuse, forming new coherences of elements, new and old. And the elements that reassert themselves from out the past are not only those that represent what we may regard as the higher values. The more primitive aspects lie quiescent in the dominant higher culture, and may at any time, and particularly as war or crisis or disaster or panic beats on the spirit of a people, emerge triumphant, to defeat our fond notions of progress. We may have less reason than past civilizations had to fear the invasion of primitivism from without, but we have still good reasons to fear its eruption from within. The study of the recurrence of cultural primitivism is full of interest, and it is perhaps not without present significance than an historical investigation of this theme has recently been inaugurated.[3] But in technology primitivism is a rare and evanescent dream. When modern states seek to return to the good old ways they still develop modern diplomacies, modern police methods, and the most modern instruments of war.

Many other contrasts could be drawn between the utilitarian process and the cultural process, but what has been said may suffice to validate our distinction and to permit us to proceed to the last of our preliminary questions. We have tentatively taken the position that what enables us to conceive of a people as a unity in space and time is something other than the biological stock and the geographical environment, and something other than the

---

[3] H. O. Lovejoy and associates, *Primitivism and Related Ideas in Antiquity* (Baltimore, 1935).

economico-political organization. We are not denying that these things are essential conditions, even determinants, of that unity, but we are suggesting that the unity itself, however begotten and however conditioned, must be understood in other terms. We are suggesting that in the configuration of cultural values is to be found the inner bond, the factor of cohesion that alone entitles us to claim that what we call a people, a nation, or a civilization has any unity through space and time, that alone entitles us to speak of Egypt and Greece and Palestine and China and England and the United States of America as historical entities. Think away the sense of common values, and what cohesion remains? Remove the participation in common values, and what gaunt framework of power can hold a people together? In so far as there are common or inclusive cultural attachments — not merely *like* attitudes, but *common* ends — there is social unity as well.

It is not the culture in its entirety that sustains this collective being, but the cementing efficacy in it which we may roughly identify with the sense of *common* values. There may be great divergences in culture, and yet the sense of common values may be triumphant, a situation that tends to be characteristic of modern nations. On the other hand, there may be great uniformity of culture, and yet no transcendent sense of community. Nor is mere distinctiveness of culture enough. Ancient Greece possessed this to an unusually high degree, but ancient Greece was never a coherent unity. And modern China possesses it to a high degree, but is at present socially disrupted. Repeatedly in the course of socio-cultural change the awakened sense of a larger community has been lost or dissipated, sometimes to be restored, sometimes to disappear altogether. Thus, for example, the vision of community that grew clear at certain times in medieval Europe broke into a multi-colored series of separate visions, and the mechanism of international organization that in recent days has attempted to create a new unity has been powerless against the ideals of national separatism. The sense of grave common peril is too negative to overcome the aggressive sense of cultural difference.

The unity, then, that we find in human societies is in the last resort a quite subjective bond, the operative sense of community, institutionally incorporated, sustained by and responsive to a utilitarian order, and ultimately dependent on the biological adjustments of man to his total environment. Being itself subjective, it has been generally identified, though at the risk of serious misconceptions of its nature, either with the systems of our second order, such as dynasty, state, and empire, or with the biological or the environmental factors of our third order, such as kin, tribe, race, and country. It was an historical advance over these conceptions when culturally united groups began to think of themselves as nations, for the term "nation" does not connote a biological or a territorial or even a political datum, but only that degree of cultural cohesion in a people which makes them desire to have or to maintain a politically unified life. It does not imply uniformity of culture, such as established religion, but only the cementing quality of a culture that permits differences to live together in relative peace and freedom. Unfortunately the drive of separatism, seeking for its own ends to dissever the larger unities of culture, attempts to recapture the concept of the nation and to give it the meaning of the older terms which it was replacing.

But that issue belongs to another theme. What we are here maintaining is the logical priority, in the quest for historical unities, of collective valuations, collectively sustained quests and designs of living, with their attendant thought-forms, myths, creeds, and dreams. This conclusion will seem very unsatisfactory to those who regard such things as mere ideologies, mere epiphenomena, compared with the economic facts, the possession of material resources, the strength, size, and vigor of populations, and so forth. But again we are not disputing the dependence of cultural values on the concrete realities. We cannot conceive the former apart from the latter, any more than we can conceive a painting apart from its pigment and canvas; but we are unable to resolve either the unity of a picture or the unity of a people into material elements that in themselves present no such unity. The unity in both instances belongs to the realm of idea-values. Therein lies their essence, meaning, reality. And it is no difficult task to show that those who reject such interpretations, in the name, it may be, of blood or of iron or of property or of economic necessity, and are therefore scornful of ideologies as ineffective phantasms, are themselves actuated to this scorn by other ideologies, other value-impregnated thought-forms, which can come to terms with the former only in the eternal arena of ideas. Our age, like every other, is in the grip of its own changing and conflicting thought-forms, and in our age, as in every other, the historian, the philosopher, and the sociologist essay the understanding alike of the present and of the past in the light of their own cultural loyalties. Thus history is never written but always re-written. The energy with which we attack ideologies is ideologically derived, and even the armies of objective scholarship, when they advance to battle, have idea-symbols inscribed on their banners. Frequently their leaders do not read the symbols, and then they are like generals who plan a war in great detail and with much calculation but without asking what they are fighting for.

The scholar who deals with the value-facts of society

cannot achieve objectivity by denuding these facts of
value, for if he treats them as non-values he does not treat
them at all. The best he can aspire to is the catholic comprehension and the tolerance that find nothing alien in anything human. Even so, he cannot escape from the rela-
tivity of values. For every culture-system persistently
attempts, as scholars like Dilthey have shown, to interpret
in its own terms the total given reality, persistently
evaluates it all, means and ends in one, together with the
sustaining earth and the indifferent cosmos itself. The
culture-system turns fact not only into value-fact but also
into symbol. That is its necessity, its life, as well as its
peril. And that is why, in our search for historical unities, we give logical priority to what we have, for lack of
another term, called the culture-element.

In the typical sequences of the modes of interaction of
these three orders we shall look for our pattern of social
change. In passing we may remark that the history of
cultural values has received much less attention than the
history of the sustaining economic, political, and technological systems. In particular, the history of the ideas that
permeate a people in their everyday behavior, in their
love-making, in their family life, in their relations to
authority and power, in their strivings and their fears, is
rarely traced with the devotion that is bestowed on the
history of scientific or philosophic ideas. Consequently,
we know far more of the rise and fall of monarchies than of
the changing conceptions of authority that sustained or
undermined them, of the establishment and dis-establish-
ment of churches than of the breathing faith and doubt
that made these institutional changes possible, of the heyday and decline of patriarchal systems than of the sentiments that clustered about them and gave them or bereft
them of strength.

Within the limits of this paper, all we can hope to do is to suggest in briefest outline the manner in which the changing inter-relation of the three orders follows a distinctive pattern. We shall first consider it in the broadest evolutionary sense. As society evolves from primitive types to developed civilizations, the three orders undergo a process of demarcation from one another, a process which also marks the expansion of each particular civilization. We cannot deal with the curious context of tensions, liberations, fusions, and again separations that complicate the process; we can but point out the main result. In primitive life the utilitarian system is utterly undetachable from the cultural life. No device, no lore, no art, is solely utilitarian. The cultural is deeply interfused with the utilitarian, and *vice versa*. Ritual is as important as craftsmanship in the making of a canoe or in the cultivation of the soil. Prayers are as important as arms in the conduct of war. Religion is compounded with magic and cannot be divorced from the business of living. The dance is as much a means of warding off evil spirits or of inducing fertility as it is a mode of social recreation. The success of a fishing expedition is as much endangered by a woman's touching the fishing tackle as by unfavorable weather. Sickness comes from spells and the breaking of taboos. The people are bound in spirit to the soil, the home of their ancestors and their gods. Everything in nature is instinct with social meaning and enshrined in social ceremony. Culture, technique, authority, people, and land are subjectively unified.

It is obvious that in this primitive scheme of things ends and means are fused. Everything has simultaneously a cultural and a utilitarian aspect. In this fusion, primitive society lies poles apart from our present civilization, which has carried further than any previous one the demarcation of utility from cultural significance. In the process that brought our modern civilization into being, the land, the focus of feudal values, gradually lost most of its cultural associations and has become a marketable commodity, overpowered by the impersonal category of capital. Capital itself has grown so detached from specific ends, so purely utilitarian that it embodies itself in ageless and anonymous corporations, served by transient myriads of workers bound to them by the ephemeral nexus of cash. Finance, the most intangible and the most protean form of capital, inherently neutral and free to enlist on the side of any cultural alternatives, to serve war or peace, tyranny or freedom, has in turn detached itself from industry, thus becoming impersonal control raised to the second power. Technology, inspired by experimental science, has loosed itself from tradition and become a closed system of means, closed in the sense that it need no longer placate an established culture but develops almost entirely in response to its own particular incentive, utilitarian efficiency. And in doing so it devises modes of relationship between man and man that stand as remote as its own instruments and engines from any other considerations than those of sheer utility. No ceremonies salute the time clock and the steam whistle, no hierophants unveil the mysteries of the counting house, no myths attend the tractor and the reaper-binder, no dragons breathe in the open-hearth furnace. For multitudes the art of living is detached from the business of living and must find what refuge it can in the now lengthened interval between today's work and tomorrow's.

In making this contrast we are not at all implying the reversionary attitude that accents the cultural loss as against the cultural gain of the process of detachment. The terms of the comparison cannot be drawn in so naïve a way. The enormously more complex potentialities of cultural development that emerge in the process are beset by problems unknown to the primitive world, unknown precisely because they are concerned with the controllable relationship of the now detached systems, economic, technological, and political, to the primary desires and the final wants of men. But here we are interested in the fact of social evolution, not in the hypothesis of progress. And within that fact we are minded particularly to show how the all-inclusive unity of primitive society breaks up into a number of partial semi-independent systems of diverse social range — economic systems such as capitalism in its various forms and with its necessary but insecure relation to political systems such as democracy; technological systems representing various stages of the one all-conquering system of industrial mechanization; cultural systems infinitely variable in many respects though cohering around certain foci of devotion and certain symbols of loyalty; with ancillary systems, such as the educational, which perplexedly move in response to the divergent currents of change. In such a world the corporate unity of the primitive is unattainable, and the subjective absorption of the individual life into one all-inclusive solidarity is attained only by those who in their atavistic need blind themselves to large areas of the presented reality. In this multifarious world other concepts of integral unity are discovered that were unrealized before, the concept of the organism as a whole, of nature as a whole, of the cosmos as a whole. But the primitive concept of a society as a corporate whole is obsolete, though there may be many who set out along strange paths in quest of its restoration.

The process of demarcation which our own civilization so markedly exhibits has occurred in various modes and degrees in the civilization of the past. One or two glimpses must here suffice, even though they can suggest but little of the rich variety of historical experience in which the pattern of change unfolds itself. Of all the examples that history offers none surpassed in its cultural adventurousness that which ran through the Greek world from the Homeric age to the fourth century B.C., with its amazing intensification in the Athenian sector between the Persian invasion and the Peloponnesian War. Pareto somewhere remarks that to the Greek sailor prayers to Poseidon were just as much a part of the art of navigation as rowing with oars. But from this fusion of culture and utility the Greek went further in emancipating himself than probably any human being on the earth before. There is a Greek epigram which, reflecting on the votive tablets to Poseidon of sailors who had escaped shipwreck, quietly asks: Where are the votive tablets of those who have been drowned? Even before the city-state was attained, while the Greeks were still a congeries of tribal bands under chieftains, they had attained a degree of cultural liberation that was fatal to the primitive fusion. Their receptive culture was not straitened in the bonds of tradition, of caste, and of religious taboo. In a manner beyond precedent they made technique the servant of their art. They exhibited more than any other people the attitude that Lucretius ascribes to one of their great thinkers, the attitude that dares to lift the eyes to heaven and without dreading the thunderbolt of Zeus seeks boldly for the causes of things. The heroes of Homer, in their less sophisticated way, revealed this same attitude in their free encounters with the gods, even on the battlefield. Thus was set the stage for the extraordinary development that culminated in the fifth century B.C., during which Prometheus, the daring inventor, removes one by one the shackles in which Zeus, the Father-God of the static order, would have held bound the race of men. The gradual untrammelling of Greek culture is witnessed in the history of its philosophy, of its drama, of its art, of its festivals and sports; and the unique fact is that in all these directions the Greek élite was as freely responsive to creative need as it was to the utilitarian urge of economic enterprise and political adventure. More so, in truth, for after achieving a characteristic form of political union, the city-state, the Greek genius was unable to advance beyond it when the combined perils of inter-Hellenic warfare and external invasion threatened its very existence. In the culminating period the analytic spirit that detaches the cultural from the utilitarian at length attacked the social bond. "Custom is the king of men," Herodotus had said, viewing with dispassionate curiosity the opposing mores of different peoples, and the sophists were quick to draw the conclusion that the union of men in society has no warrant but convention. But the sorely needed constructive principle that transcends the differences of culture in a larger loyalty was never available. At this point alone, and fatally at this point, the Greek adhered to the primitive concept of unity. Nor was this due solely to the prejudice of the masses, for when the need was most instant the intellectual leaders too found no remedy but in a return to primitivism. Euripides in the *Bacchae* recants his flouting of the old traditions, Plato dreams of a rigid totalitarian Utopia, and both he and Aristotle advocate a caste-system on the Spartan model within the confines of a narrowed city-state; and this at the time when the Spartan system was collapsing with the Athenian into common ruin for lack of a larger concept of political unity.

The case of Greece illustrates one aspect of an eternal problem that presents itself wherever the pattern of change, from the fusion to the demarcation of the three

orders, witnesses to the growth of a civilization. We have
suggested that the tempo, pulse, and style of change are
inherently different for the three orders; that, for example,
technological change, once the primitive fusion is broken,
is not subject to the same authoritarian controls or to the
same reversals of direction as religious change, and that, to
take another example, the expansion of population is not
subject to the same principle as the growth of economic
wealth. Moreover, within each order, the mode of change
varies for the different factors in accordance with their
closer or remoter attachment to factors of the other orders.
Thus the fundamental institutions of the political system,
being more deeply embedded in the older culture-com-
plexes, adapt themselves with more difficulty to changing
conditions than do the institutions of the technological
system. Hellenic civilization, in the face of obvious perils,
proved incapable of devising a political order more inclusive than the city-state, a situation not dissimilar to that
which, on a greater scale, is menacing our own civilization.
This problem of the re-adaptation of the political system to
the needs of a changing world is but one aspect of the more
inclusive problem that attends the growth of every civilization, the problem of the rediscovery and reinterpretation of the social unity that man, the pre-eminently social
animal, is bound to seek when the former narrow home of
his spirit transforms itself into a seeming maze of many
changeful mansions.

The endlessly variant situations in which the general
pattern of social change is for ever presenting itself anew
are well revealed in the growth of our own civilization.
Its matrix was a social system that, concreted out of
heterogeneous elements in an age-long turmoil and min-
gling of populations within the broken frame of an older
civilization, at length took definite shape in Western

Europe. This medieval system was formally dominated by a universalist religious culture, hierarchically organized and rigidly doctrinal, in such wise that it did not so much respond to the cultural impulses of the populations it embraced as impose itself upon them in the name of a higher and unequivocally supra-social rule of life. Both its strength and its weakness lay in this authoritarian superimposition. Beneath it lay indigenous cultures that spoke with indigenous tongues instead of the universal Latin and that through persistent strife with one another pursued their respective ambitions and cherished their respective myths. But the formidable authoritarianism of religion cloaked with its mystic orthodoxy the contradictions and tensions inherent in the situation. While the ecclesiastical authority could achieve only an uneasy compromise with the political powers of feudalism it impressed itself more effectively on the underlying social system and in particular it determined the thought-form of the patriarchal family. Thus the everyday life of man revolved again within a circle as closed as that of Ptolemaic astronomy. The scheme of things was subjectively unified, the cultural and the utilitarian were fused, and whatever failed to conform to the established principle of relationship was conveniently dismissed as heresy in thought and sin in deed. A caste system prescribed for men their lot on earth, and the Most Holy Inquisition safeguarded their souls.

The manner in which this closed system broke up and the ever-new energies of ever-new generations resumed the quest for socio-cultural unities, amid endless confusion and trampling back and forth, reveals with peculiar significance the different roles of our three great orders in the processes of historical change. But we must limit ourselves to a very few observations. Medieval civilization, unlike the Hellenic, made authority the palladium of unity. This

authority underwent assaults initiating in each in turn of
the three changing orders.

First, within the culture itself, there came the challenge
of new valuations, the inevitable diversities of school and
sect that arise from the variety of human nature and
human experience no matter what indoctrinations they are
subject to or what sanctions they must confront. Next
there came the new formations of land and people, turning
the universalist culture into a patchwork under the formula
of *cuius regio eius religio* and at length splitting with the
keen wedge of nationalism the inclusive loyalties that remained. But a third mode of assault was also maturing,
unheralded, impalpable, cumulative, and irresistible, the indirect assault that came from the changing utilitarian order.

Technology, once set on the road of change, follows the
principle of efficiency, a principle that has no clear application in the realm of culture. It has thus a continuity of
direction that cultural movements do not exhibit. While
faiths veer and fashions oscillate, techniques advance.
Advancing, they not only transform the economic system
and the social relationships entangled in it, they subtly and
profoundly change the scheme of values. Authority may
resist the frontal attack of heresy or repair the schisms
that it causes, but neither the secular nor the spiritual
sword is potent against the habituations and attitudes that
respond to new ways of earning a livelihood, to the manipulation of new mechanical powers, to the new resources,
new luxury, new leisure, new freedom, and new servitude
that their exploitation brings with it, and to the new relations between men and groups of men that they engender.
We need not pursue this theme, since it has been effectively
presented by Veblen and his followers. It is not unreasonable to hold that in the course of Western civilization the
line of technological innovators, from Roger Bacon to —

shall we say? — Henry Ford, have done more, unwittingly more, than any other men to dissolve the sanctity of tradition and to transform the nature of authority.

New schools and sects usually attack the established order from premises that belong within it. But new technology, by changing the basis of life, prepares for a change in the very basis of thought. It is thus of particular potency in undermining the established notions of authority held by the masses of men. For these masses, subjected to continuous discipline and immersed in the struggle for livelihood, do not freely conceive new loyalties or new goals. If they have advanced from primitivism it is not because they have thought their way, or fought their way, out of it, but only because they have responded to ideas congenial to the new conditions of life that technological change has gradually substituted for the old.

The epochal example of Soviet Russia might at first sight seem an exception to this rule. In reality, it illustrates remarkably well both the fact that new technology prepares the way for revolutionary cultural change and the fact that cultural and not merely utilitarian ideas determine the unity and character of a society. The Marxist idea, bred in the transition from a feudal to an industrial economy, seized the minds of powerful leaders brought up in a similar stage of transition and through them was conveyed to a people shattered and disillusioned, thus breaking the resistance of their bankrupt traditions and becoming for them a gospel of liberation from chaos and despair, the vision of a new scheme of life.

Though technology, unlike culture, marches continually in the same direction, it does not advance at an even pace. When it conquers certain strategic points, its march is vastly accelerated. Such conquests occurred especially in the later history of our own civilization and have given it its most distinctive character. In consequence of this acceleration the utilitarian, as we have already pointed out, has become more completely detached from the cultural life than ever before. This fact has had very important repercussions on the nature of authority and on the problem of social unity. With a brief reference to each of these closely related aspects we must bring our argument to a close.

The detachment of utility, involving among other things the vast growth of organizations specifically and exclusively economic, has been a powerful solvent of class distinctions, of political dynasties, and of all vested powers that claim an intrinsic right to rule the lives of men. This new condition does not spell the greater liberty of the individual, but it does mean that authority must, as never before, specify its objectives and justify them in the eyes of the masses, a corollary being that the arts of propaganda have been enormously developed. Authority must constantly readapt itself to technological change, a principle of which Bismarck provided a remarkable illustration. But Bismarck applied the principle to maintain a traditional class dominance that was nevertheless fundamentally out of accord with the process of technological change. The groups that control the levers of power may represent, according to the conditions, any cultural level of the population. In England, for example, the control of municipal politics is in the hands of a very different type of leadership from that which is generally dominant in the cities of the United States. Recent transformations of authority in various European countries witness on the national scale to the new contingency of power.

Power and cultural leadership are thus apt to be divorced — a situation that stands in marked contrast to the union of the two in medieval civilization. It is this change that most of all spurs the modern quest for socio-cultural unity. If we seek for unity of the old type we can find it only by a resort to a totalitarianism that suppresses the varieties of culture and does violence to the principle of cultural growth. The alternative is to accept alike the contingency of power and the diversity of culture, and to be content with partial unities of different range, with a series of loyalties none of which is absolute or all-inclusive, so that the focus of unity must in the last resort be the integrating personality itself. The direction in which the pattern of change moves is towards a greater variety of divergent and interpenetrating cultural coherences within an ever more inclusive and uniform utilitarian order. This solution makes greater demands on human nature and is possible only in a society that is not subject to severe exploitations from within or oppressions from without. But, given these conditions, it becomes a hopeful alternative. For there are two great types of common interest that have always aroused the loyalties of men. One is the social group, the kin, the tribe, the community, the nation. The other is the cultural value in itself, the things conceived of as good and beautiful and true, as desirable in any degree or on any level. These things, no less than their social groups, unite men in social bonds, because they must be pursued in co-operation, even in communion. The unity they create is the unity of the like-minded seeking common goals, and it cannot be identified with the unity of the social group. But from their dwelling-place in the social group men may pursue it through a thousand vistas of challenge and adventure. This is the alternative we set up against the organic theory of society, which requires that the cultural system and the social system be one and indivisible and which, on mystical grounds, assumes that the differentiation of the primitive totality, as the pattern of change unfolds, is also the dissolution of society.

CONSERVATIVE FACTORS IN EARLY COLONIAL HISTORY

CHARLES MCLEAN ANDREWS, LITT.D., LL.D.

Professor of American History, Emeritus, Yale University

IT IS an interesting fact, Mr. Chairman, that among the many fields of inquiry provided for this conference the only one which bears a close and intimate relationship to the early history of Harvard herself is the one that I have chosen to speak upon this afternoon. The three hundred years of Harvard's Tercentenary trace back to the seventeenth century. For nearly sixty years of that century Harvard was the only institution of the higher learning, a beacon light in the midst of an undeveloped educational world. Some of my ancestors went to Harvard; all of my ancestors lived in the New England that Harvard illumined; and one of my greatest enjoyments of life has been to spend many years in the study of the century during which Harvard was beginning her great career. You will not be surprised, therefore, if to me the address that I am to deliver is more than an academic treatise; it is an effort to describe certain conditions of the larger colonial world within which Harvard men, as well as other colonists, lived and moved and had their being — the world of the seventeenth century. It is of this world that I would say something here today.

Several years ago, while on a walk with the late Lord Bryce through the woods of Mount Desert, that eminent statesman and historian plied me, as was his wont, with questions regarding our American colonial history. One of them I remember particularly, for I have been pondering it ever since. When, he asked, did the English colonists first begin to be American-minded; when did they cease to think English and begin to think American; in other words, when did our colonial history take on an unmistakable American form? This very comprehensive question strikes at the root of our subject today and assumes one thing, that there was a period when our colonists, though on American soil, still thought of themselves as Englishmen. As evolution of any sort is by its nature slow, it is difficult to say at any given moment just how far it has progressed; but where human beings have been uprooted from one soil and planted in another quite different and new, it is not impossible, I think, to discover their state of mind, at least during the earlier years of their settlement.

Under the spreading branches of the subject selected for this paper I am to discuss the relationship of constituted authority and the individual as it existed in the seventeenth century of our colonial history, laying particular stress on the degree of conservatism and liberalism present in the colonial governments of the period. Along the way I want to find, if I can, an answer to Lord Bryce's question, for in that answer lies the key to the enigma of the seventeenth century of our history. Too often the layman, and sometimes also the older historians, having assumed that the colonies from the very beginning were inhabited by independent and restless individuals, who were not only liberal but revolutionary in spirit, have concluded for that reason that the conservative factors of the period were so inconspicuous as to call for little more than a passing glance, and that American-mindedness began then and there. This view of the case I believe to be erroneous.

The subject has been a good deal obscured by the fact that the dynamic and progressive phenomena of history have always made a stronger appeal to mankind than have the conservative and reactionary factors which belong mainly to institutions and ideas that have been vanquished and have disappeared. Furthermore, writers on English and American history, in their enthusiasm for the growth of popular representation and the control of government by the people, often have ignored or belittled executive authority as a subject for serious investigation, and not infrequently have condemned its exercise as sinister and evil and inherently wrong. They have dubbed "liberty" a virtue and "conservatism" a vice, and have dismissed many an institution as "iniquitous" and many a person by calling him a "malcontent" or a "henchman." They have carried the beginnings of democracy much too far back and have made its progress far too simple and rapid, interpreting frequent references to the word "people" as something connoting democracy. What they do not understand is that the word "people" is among the most easily misunderstood words in history, and as used in the seventeenth century has quite a different meaning from that which Lincoln had in mind in his Gettysburg address. We have been led astray, too, by the writings of the Hallam, Green, Freeman school of historians, who exaggerated enormously the antiquity of democracy in England; and by the writings of Macaulay and his followers, who set up the Whig tradition of progressive liberalism, execrated the Stuarts, and, by implication, intensified the hostility already existing in this country toward Great Britain and all her works.

But of recent years a change has been coming over the face of the historical waters owing to the growth of new ideas regarding the purpose and object of historical research, which demands that we approach our subject in the spirit of the scholar and, freeing ourselves of prejudice, follow the truth wherever it leads.

If we are to discuss seriously the subject of the conservative factors of our seventeenth-century colonial history, and to discover when American-mindedness began first to appear, we shall have to forget for the moment that there is a United States of America, and remember, not only that our great republic had not yet come into being, but that England, the land from which the colonists came and to which they owed their allegiance, was the only country that was a living, visible reality to them. We shall have to put out of mind such disturbing thoughts as those which concern manifest destiny, triumphant democracy, rugged individualism, and the inherent rights of men — a heritage to us of a later century than that under discussion. We shall have to forget that the descendants of our colonists a century later were to engage in revolution and to demand separation from Great Britain, because their ancestors of the seventeenth century had not, either in thought or by any act, begun to feel the slightest desire for political or economic independence. It is imperative that we keep in mind one thing, and that the most important of all, namely, that the colonies were colonies and not sovereign communities, and that they were subject to the authority of a sovereign across the seas and in law bound to obey such rules and orders as were framed for their guidance. In that connection we must hold strictly to the contemporary point of view of the seventeenth century, grasping, if we can, the seventeenth-century ideas regarding the status of a colony and its place in the schemes of expansion that were in process of formulation by the leading maritime states of the time, of which England was one of the greatest; and we must take into consideration the fact that England's attempt to organize her colonies according to a uniform plan, as worked out later by her statesmen in greater detail, was not in itself, nor was it meant to be, a blow at colonial "liberty." In other words, it is necessary that we approach the seventeenth century of our history in complete freedom from all prejudgments born of events that were yet to come.

The English individual, accustomed to the life and laws of his own country and inclined under normal conditions to reproduce them wherever he went, would have found himself, on coming to America, at any time during the seventeenth century, confronted with three types of constituted authority. Of the three only one paralleled in any way the English system with which he was familiar. That type was the colony of Virginia, the only royal colony during the greater part of the seventeenth century and the only one that followed the English pattern down to minute details of procedure. Virginia even modeled the room in which her burgesses sat after that of the House of Commons in St. Stephen's Chapel at Westminster, and, as was the case with some of the other colonies, particularly Maryland, demanded the privilege and adopted the procedure of the English parliamentary body. Like the mother country, she made the Church of England the established church of the colony and, in demanding conformity, drove out Roman Catholics and Puritans as undesirable members of her population. During the greater part of the seventeenth century, Virginia's method of government ran true to form on a fairly even keel, and even the expulsion of Governor Harvey in the thirties, the subjection to the authority of the Commonwealth of England in the fifties, and the rebellion of Nathaniel Bacon in the seventies did not alter the main structure of her constitution. Even Bacon's rebellion, which has often been construed as a revolt against England and her policy, was in no sense an uprising against the higher constituted authority of the mother country. It was rather a protest against the hardships of frontier life and the evils of local administration. Similar protests, though not always taking the form of a resort to arms, were not uncommon during the years of settlement, when the whole business of colonization was an experiment, privately conducted, and when England (before 1660), in the throes of civil war and the Puritan revolution, was incapable of fashioning any adequate kind of organized oversight, such as came into existence at the end of the century. It is a witness to the normality of the Virginia system that the people of the colony, unlike those in nearly all the colonies to the northward, remained largely unaffected by the English revolution of 1688 and 1689, which had notable repercussions elsewhere in America.

But whereas Virginia was a normal colony, in which the status of the individual toward constituted authority as exercised within its boundaries remained pretty much the same as the status of his fellow subject in England toward constituted authority there, the two remaining types of continental colony followed a different course. In those colonies we find factors that are more than conservative — factors that are ultra-conservative and even reactionary. For instance, Massachusetts, Connecticut, and New Haven cannot be considered normal colonies in the English interpretation of the word. They were Puritan religious commonwealths, each of which placed limitations upon the co-operation of the people in government that were not only unlike anything prevailing in England or elsewhere, but were of such a kind as would not have been tolerated for a moment at home. Massachusetts and New Haven made church membership a requisite for voter and office-holder alike, and Connecticut was scarcely more politically generous in that she built her government on a Trinitarian foundation and made a selected few of her people the arbiters of her policy as a colony. The Puritan colonies were unique in centering authority in a small number of regenerate men. They paid very little attention to the political rights of the individual; they exalted the state and community as divine or semi-divine institutions; and they abhorred democracy as something unwarranted by the Scriptures and disapproved of by God and his faithful elect. That the Puritan leaders governed honorably and well no one can deny, and that they had high ideals for the advancement of learning and the promotion of good works these Tercentenary exercises at Harvard University amply demonstrate; but in Puritan eyes the rights of God were more important than the rights of man, and the individual was always made subordinate to the authority of God and the religious integrity of the state. Even the Pilgrims in actual practice formed something of a petty autocracy ruled by William Bradford, thirty times governor and autocrat in chief. I know of no instance when the Plymouth people ever gave voice against their leaders to a will of their own. These conservative religious systems were really a curious combination of trading company, primitive church, and city of God.

But as far as constituted authority was concerned, the colonies forming the third type were even more conservative than were those in New England. Whereas Massachusetts and Connecticut were the property of private chartered corporations, Maryland, New York, the Jerseys, the Carolinas, and Pennsylvania were the property of private individuals, each one, two, or more of whom, by royal charter, held the government of the colony in the hollow of one hand and the ownership of the soil in the hollow of the other. This proprietary system was a reversion to a method of guarding England's frontier in vogue in the fourteenth century, and was adopted for America because that land was deemed a frontier constantly menaced by Spanish,

French, and Indians. The system was a throwback to an earlier period, in that it made the proprietor largely independent of the royal authority in England; granted him more power than the king himself exercised in the realm; placed the inhabitants in the position of tenants to an absolute lord instead of giving them full recognition as subjects of the king; and required that these same inhabitants take an oath of fidelity to the proprietor, from whom alone, by patent, they could obtain a legal title to their lands. The extent and effectiveness of these proprietary prerogatives varied with the different proprietary provinces. Maryland, chartered in 1632, was the most regal of them all, for there the individual was almost entirely subordinate to the proprietary authority. Pennsylvania, chartered fifty years later, at the end of a period of tremendous happenings in English history and at a time when England was shaping her own colonial policy, was the least so, though Penn still preserved many of the privileges of the proprietor. These proprietary prerogatives are not negligible factors in our history. They presented a formidable obstacle to the colonists in the latter's struggle to obtain the normal rights of Englishmen, because they stood between a subject and his allegiance to the throne and placed him in a feudal relation to a true and absolute lord. By virtue of these prerogatives the inhabitants of the proprietary provinces were subjected to a private authority that imposed many limitations upon their freedom of action and made upon them many demands that were burdensome and sometimes oppressive. Thus it is evident that if the Puritan colonies were reactionary in admitting a religious test into the operation of their government, the proprietary provinces were reactionary in that they were built on a plan which for a long time had been out of date in England.

If this was the character of the constituted authority

exercised in nearly all the American colonies in the seventeenth century, we may ask ourselves whether the individuals there, thus debarred from political privileges, did not
express their dissatisfaction in such form as to support the
belief that something akin to democratic discontent was
abroad in the land. The answer comes quickly. There were
manifestations of discontent and many protests and statements of grievance, it is true, but they cannot be construed
as agitations for democracy. From 1634 in Massachusetts,
when the freemen of that colony revolted against Winthrop's administration, down to 1701 in Pennsylvania,
when Penn was forced to grant the charter of liberties of
that year, we have a succession of efforts both in the Puritan and in the proprietary colonies to coerce those in authority and to obtain for the individual greater rights and
privileges. But among the many utterances to which these
efforts gave rise, there never appears any demand for a
widening of the franchise on a democratic basis, any evidence of interest in the theory of the inherent rights of men,
or any mention of the individual's sacred state of political
freedom, such as are associated, at least in principle, with
the democratic ideas of today. One never reads in these
utterances that men are born free and equal and entitled
to life, liberty, and the pursuit of happiness. Such speculative ideas had not entered the mind of the colonist in the
seventeenth century. Colonial unrest, which may often be
described as unruliness, was frequently directed against
abuses in local government, but more frequently it was a
protest against those in the Puritan and in the proprietary
colonies who refused to allow the individual what he considered to be the ordinary rights of Englishmen, or as the
phrase went — and we find it repeated over and over
again — "that which every liege and freeborn subject of
the crown of England may and of right ought to have."

This form of protest was voiced very early by Samuel Gorton in Rhode Island, and that was one reason why the Puritans hated him so, because he was demanding the enforcement of English authority, English law, and English court procedure and denying the competency of the Puritan jurisdictions. One cause of the fall of the New Haven colony was the revolt of those who claimed as their due the protection which only an English title could provide, and in Massachusetts, particularly after 1660, the Puritans resisted the king's order, based on complaints from the colony, that the non-freemen there should be allowed in church and state the same rights that they would have been entitled to had they remained at home. In so doing, Massachusetts added one more to the charges that brought about the annulment of her charter. In all the proprietary provinces, from New York to South Carolina, this demand for the rights of Englishmen was continuously and vociferously expressed. Even the inhabitants of New York and the Puritan towns of Long Island, under the proprietary rule of the Duke of York, demanded no more than equal rights with their "fellow Brethren and subjects of the Realme of England in our neighboring Plantations." This demand must be interpreted, not as something unusual or ahead of its time, but as an outcry against the reactionary forms of government under which these protestants were obliged to live.

The longer I study the subject the more I am driven to believe that the colonists were, if anything, more English-minded after 1660 than they were before. They were more English-minded because Englishmen were becoming more colonially-minded and because the influence of religion in politics was passing away. The romanticism and religiosity of the first period of English colonization had gone forever. Jamaica had been conquered in 1655. New possessions in five different parts of the world — Dunkirk, Mardyck, Jamaica, Bombay, Tangier, and New Netherland — had been brought, though some of them not permanently, under England's control. In the City of London was an influential body of merchant capitalists, with their hard, self-satisfied commercial spirit, whose slogan was "Trade follows the flag." At Whitehall was coming into prominence a similarly-minded group of courtier promoters, whose leader was the Duke of York and who were interested in New Netherland, the Jerseys, the Carolinas, the Bahamas, the Royal African Company, and the Hudson's Bay Company. New colonies were erected, and Englishmen, who were neither Puritans nor Pilgrims, were coming over in large numbers, men who were just as much colonists as those who came to Massachusetts in 1630, and much more English in their political outlook. Let me cite one illustration. In 1692, almost at the end of the seventeenth century, when an American-mindedness ought to have appeared if it ever was to appear in the seventeenth century, the commons house of assembly in South Carolina objected to the presence of Huguenots as members because they were alien and should be governed by alien law. The house took the ground that only Englishmen, able to speak the English language and possessed of the privileges and rights of Englishmen, should be allowed to make the laws. It was not until 1696 that an act was finally passed making aliens not Americans but naturalized Englishmen, and admitting them to the full enjoyment of the franchises and immunities possessed by the Englishmen at home.

Just what were the rights, immunities, and franchises of Englishmen at this time it would be difficult to state exactly. One thing, however, is quite clear: they were neither theoretical nor metaphysical but specific and concrete — rights that men were actually enjoying in England at the time. They were not the "liberty" but the "liberties" — quite a different matter — that Englishmen had won in the long years of their history and that concerned their position before the law, the titles to their lands, their freedom from arbitrary exactions, and the right of their representatives in parliament to certain privileges, particularly in matters of taxation. These immunities and franchises cannot be briefly described because they rested on the common law, of which they were integrally a part, and therefore were based on nothing more certain than custom, judicial decisions, and statute law. But whatever these rights were, they had nothing to do with democracy and represented nothing that was in advance of the age in which the colonists lived. In our search for the conservative factors in our early colonial history we shall find nowhere any manifestations of democracy or even the suspicions of democracy in any form, any aspirations that anticipated future political ideals, any beginnings anywhere of an American mind. What else should we expect to find? The American wilderness, it is true, was a vast frontier, but in that century it was filled with Englishmen, men who had been born in England and brought up in English surroundings and habits of life, men whose minds had been shaped by English experiences and English institutions. They did not come all at once, but arrived in a continuing stream throughout the century; and though their children born in America might feel the influences of a new country, even they would continue to think the thoughts of their fellow Englishmen at home, because they knew no other. Those in America who were bold enough to express their discontent merely wanted to be treated as were the king's subjects elsewhere. They wanted to be the king's subjects and not the disfranchised members of a

Puritan oligarchy or tenants owing fidelity and obedience
to a medieval lord.

These colonists never at any time drafted a statement of
political principles containing ideas that were in the least
original or out of accord with the ideas prevailing at the
time. Why should they? Their highest aim was to get from
the legal authorities over them such concessions as would
put them on a par with their fellow subjects in England, an
aim that called for no originality. We have made too much
of certain dicta emanating from such men as Roger Williams, Thomas Hooker, Lord Baltimore, and William
Penn, dicta which should be studied not so much in their
written form as in their actual application. I cannot see
that any one of the schemes presented by these men accomplished any important results that were destined to be
permanent. The utopia of Roger Williams ended in turmoil and confusion; that of Thomas Hooker, of which we
know very little, probably never found actual enforcement
in the form that modern writers have given to it; the noble
attempt of Lord Baltimore to persuade Roman Catholic
and Protestant to live together in harmony came to an
untimely end in eleven years; while the holy experiment of
William Penn, which took too little account of human frail-
ties, proved in operation to be anything but holy.

The only systematized programs of the century, designed for use in the colonies, originated not in America,
but in England. They were drafted by the proprietors of
the Jerseys, the Carolinas, and Pennsylvania, who living
in England were influenced by the spirit of their age and,
in the case of William Penn, by the prickings of Quaker
idealism. The period of the Commonwealth and the Pro-
tectorate had been a time of experimentation, when hosts
of new ideas, both social and political, had been let loose
and had found lodgment in many minds in the colonies as

well as in England. The sufferings of twenty years had brought men greater tolerance and sympathy and had broken down uncompromising attitudes on all sides. Men were softening their asperities and, despite the persecuting policy of the government under the Clarendon Code and the recusancy laws directed against the nonconformists, they were feeling more and more the necessity of avoiding extremes. So generally was this conviction held after the Restoration that men interested in colonization knew that to secure settlers they would have to offer the most favorable possible terms. Some of these men, borrowing ideas from the *Utopia* of Sir Thomas More and the *Oceana* of James Harrington, embodied them in their own Concessions, Agreements, and Fundamental Constitutions, frames of government and codes of moral conduct and judicial procedure that were liberal rather on the humanitarian than on the governmental and tenurial side. They promised liberty of conscience, but this they promised only to Christians or to those who believed in God. They included in these concessions certain other broad-minded provisions, particularly in those programs for which Penn was wholly or largely responsible, touching morals, social behavior, legal privileges, and kindness toward one's fellow men. But in general, in all that concerned property and civil rights, these concessions were conservative, in that they made land the sole basis of the governmental and social structure. In some respects, quite apart from the features which reproduced the terms of the medieval charters, they were reactionary, as when the Carolina proprietors introduced into their colony a complicated system of hereditary nobility and Penn refused to allow the popular assembly in Pennsylvania any real share in the administration of the province. In none of their schemes are there any concessions to democracy, for even Penn's frames of gov-

ernment disclose a latent want of faith in the competency
of the people to rule.

It was in the eighteenth century, not the seventeenth,
that England's colonial policy was for the first time put
into operation as far as it was ever successfully enforced.
It was in the eighteenth, not the seventeenth, century that
were born the men who made the American Revolution,
and not until the eighteenth century was well under way
did the spirit of opposition in the colonies to the royal prerogative and England's policy reach a point at which appear the first glimmerings of a revolt against a constituted
authority represented by the English king and his parliament. Then it was, and then only, that ideas which we can
begin to call American took shape in the colonial mind, and
even those were not the ideas that foreshadowed the
Americanism of Jefferson.

In this very brief treatment of a large subject I have
attempted to show that the spirit of government in the
colonies during the seventeenth century was conservative
and even reactionary; that there was nothing akin to
modern ideas in the minds either of those in authority or of
those under authority living at the time on the soil of
America; and that the grievances of the people at large
looked no farther than to the recovery of political and legal
rights which they had lost in coming to the New World. I
do not doubt that there were precedents formed, habits
and practices well rooted, and traditions established, particularly in the struggle against the proprietary prerogatives,
that in one way or another contributed to the strengthening of those who carried the struggle to completion in the
eighteenth century. There was a measure of liberalism in
the colonies in the seventeenth century, but it was limited
entirely to the men who had property to defend. It was not
a liberalism that had at heart the political well-being of the

entire community. Unless we decide that any form of resistance to any constituted authority is to be interpreted as an indication of American-mindedness — and we know that such form of resistance is as old as the beginnings of civilization — and unless we are to call an American any one who happened to make his home in America, without regard to his origin, his habits of mind, or the direction of his aspirations, then we can reach but one conclusion: the colonies in the seventeenth century were the abode not of Americans but of Englishmen, who were not essentially different from their fellow Englishmen at home, who were English-minded and not American-minded, and who looked on themselves as English, with England still the home of their affection, and the rights and privileges there established the height of their political ambitions. If this be the case — and I am unable to see how it can be argued otherwise — then these men of the seventeenth century contributed little or nothing to the cause of progressive liberalism or to the advancement of those democratic ideals that are a characteristic of the United States of America at the present time.

AUTHORITY AND SOCIAL CHANGE

JOHN DEWEY, PH.D., LL.D.

Professor of Philosophy, Emeritus, Columbia University

THE last four centuries have displayed an ever-increasing revolt against authority, first in the forms in which it was manifested and then against the principle itself. None of its important forms has been immune from assault. The assault was first directed against dominant institutions of Church and State. But the control exercised by Church and State in combination had entered into all phases and aspects of life, in belief and conduct alike. Hence attack upon ecclesiastic and political institutions spread to science and art, to standards and ideals of economic and domestic life. For the practical movement of assault, like every other such movement, had to defend itself on intellectual grounds. The best intellectual defense was attack, and so defense grew into systematic justification, and a social philosophy developed that was critical of the very idea of any authoritative control.

The theoretical system spawned watchwords, rallying-cries, slogans, for popular consumption. One of the latter, by constant iteration, has assumed the status of a comprehensive social and political idea. To many persons it seems to be itself the summary of a profound social philosophy. According to the formula, the one great intellectual problem is the demarcation of two separate spheres, one of authority and one of freedom; the other half of the formula is to maintain this theoretical demarcation as a sharp division in practice. The formula has a corollary. The inherent tendency of the "sphere" of authority is to extend itself unduly, to encroach on the "sphere" of freedom, thus enstating oppression, tyranny, and, in the language of today, regimentation. Hence the right of way must belong to the idea and actuality of individual freedom; authority is its enemy, and every manifestation of social authority and control is therefore to be zealously watched, and almost always to be vigorously opposed. However, since the sphere of liberty has its boundaries, when "liberty" begins to degenerate into "license" the operation of authority is properly to be called upon to restore the balance.

The formula, like most slogans that attain popularity, owes its vogue and influence to the fact that it seems to afford a solution of an outstanding problem while in fact it evades the problem; and, by postponing effort at genuine solution, gives temporary support, sometimes to one of the contending forces, sometimes to the other, and always at the expense of both. For even when it is accepted in its own terms at face value, it leaves the fundamental issue of the rightful extent of the two alleged spheres undecided, their rightful metes and bounds a matter of constant dispute.

The genuine problem is the *relation* between authority and freedom. And this problem is masked, and its solution begged, when the idea is introduced that the fields in which they respectively operate are separate. In effect, authority stands for stability of social organization by means of which direction and support are given to individuals; while individual freedom stands for the forces by which change is intentionally brought about. The issue that requires constant attention is the intimate and organic union of the two things: of authority and freedom, of stability and change. The idea of attaining a solution by separation instead of by union misleads and thwarts

endeavor whenever it is acted upon. The widespread
adoption of this false and misleading idea is a strong
contributing factor to the present state of world confusion.

The genuine import of the formula which divides and
apportions the total field of human life and action between freedom and authority is to be found, not in its
theoretical statement, but in its relation to the historic
events of the last few centuries. As a purely theoretical
formula, it claims an inherent validity and universal
application which I, for one, find absurd. But when the
formula is taken to be the record of a historic period, the
case is otherwise. The formula then achieves the significance of a symbol of the distinctive crises of western civilization in recent centuries; it becomes representative of a
great historic struggle. In its dual character, the formula
celebrates, with one hand, the decay of the institutions
which had exercised sway over men's minds and conduct;
and, with the other hand, it signalizes the rise of the new
social and intellectual forces. The old traditions and established social organizations resisted the new forces in
human life and society on their emergence, as being
dangerous, even mortal, rivals who came to dispute for the
power and privileges they had hitherto exclusively enjoyed. The formula, instead of supplying a means of cop-
ing with and solving this historic struggle, offers as a solution what is none other than a theoretical transcript of
the nature of the conflict itself. As a guide to understanding and action, the formula is, as I said, absurd. But as a
symbol of historic events it is deeply revealing.

Unfortunately, when the struggle first got under way,
the newer forces tended to accept the established institutions at their own evaluation, namely, as necessary expressions of the very principle of authority. Finding the existing institutions oppressive, the new movement reacted

against authority as such and began to conceive of authority as inherently external to individuality, and inherently hostile to freedom and the social changes that the overt expression and use of freedom would bring to pass. In consequence, while the new movement should have the credit for breaking down a system that had grown rigid and unresponsive, and for releasing capacities of individuals that had been dormant, its virtual denial of the organic importance of *any* embodiment of authority and social control has intellectually fostered the confusion that as a matter of practical fact in any case attends a time of transition. More particularly, as I shall show later, the new movement failed to acknowledge as authoritative the very power to which it owed its own vitality, namely, that of organized intelligence. Such are the propositions I desire to advance.

For, in the first place, I think a survey of history shows that while the individualistic philosophy was wrong in setting authority and freedom, stability and change, in opposition to one another, it was justified in finding the organized institutional embodiments of authority so external to the new wants and purposes that were stirring as to be in fact oppressive. The persons and classes who exercised the power that comes from the possession of authority *were* hostile to the variable and fresh qualities, the qualities of initiative, invention, and enterprise, in which change roots. The power exercised was the more oppressive and obstructive because it was not just physical but had that hold upon imagination, emotions, and purpose which properly belongs to the principle of authority. Underneath, it was not a conflict between social organization and individuals, between authority and freedom, but between conservative factors in the very make-up of individuals — factors that had the strength that is derived from the inertia of customs and traditions engrained by long endurance — and the liberating, the variable and innovating factors in the constitution of individuals. It was a struggle for authoritative power between the old and the new; between forces concerned with conservation of values that the past had produced and forces that made for new beliefs and new modes of human association. It was also a struggle between groups and classes of individuals — between those who were enjoying the advantages that spring from possession of power to which authoritative right accrues, and individuals who found themselves excluded from the powers and enjoyments to which they felt themselves entitled. The necessity of adjusting the old and the new, of harmonizing the stability that comes from conserving the established with the variability that springs from the emergence of new needs and efforts of individuals — this necessity is inherent in, or a part of, the very texture of life. In the last few centuries the necessity of effecting this adjustment has manifested itself on an unparalleled scale in the arena of human culture. The philosophy which transforms this historic and relative struggle into an inherent and fixed conflict between the principle of authority and the principle of freedom tends, when accepted and acted upon, to present authority as purely restrictive power and to leave the exercise of freedom without direction. To a considerable extent these untoward conditions depict our contemporary estate.

Let me explain briefly what is meant by calling the struggle one between forces that belong to individuals and that, in the interest of individuals as such, need to be adjusted to one another. It is folly psychologically and historically to identify the structure of the individual simply with the elements of human nature that make for variation and that mark one person off from another. The force of habit that leads individuals to cling to that which has been established is a genuine part of the constitution of individuals. In the main, it is a stronger and deeper part of human nature than is desire for change. When tradition and social custom are incorporated in the working constitution of an individual, they have authority as a matter of course over his beliefs and his activities. The forces that exert and exercise this authority are so much and so deep a part of individuals that there is no thought or feeling of their being external and oppressive. They cannot be regarded as hostile to individuals as long as they are built into the habitual beliefs and purposes of the individual. They support him and give him direction. They naturally compel his allegiance and arouse his devotion. Attack upon the authoritative institutions in which custom and tradition are embodied is, therefore, as naturally resented by the individual; it is deeply resented as an attack upon what is deepest and truest in himself.

For by far the greater number of millennia man has lived on the earth, man has been, for the most part, content with things as they, from time to time, are. This is true even of social organizations that seem to us arbitrary exhibitions of despotic force. For ages untold, the human disposition has been to attribute divine origin and sanction to whatever claimed for itself the authority of long tradition and custom. Individuals, instead of seeking change, are more generally afraid of it. If we were justified in putting authority and freedom, stability and change, in opposition to one another, we should be compelled to conclude that for the greater period of human history individuals have preferred authority and stability.

This state of affairs has been reflected in theory. Until a very recent time, the accepted doctrine was that authority existed by nature; or else, by that which was beyond nature — the supernatural. In either case, it was held to exist in virtue of the inherent constitution of the universe and of individual man as part of the universe. In philosophy the conception that social authority exists by nature was formulated by Aristotle. In subsequent periods, the underlying idea was restated by the Stoics, in that quasi-idealistic, quasi-materialistic form that has always been — and still is — the means by which ideas obtain their strongest hold on the popular mind. The Christian philosophers of the Middle Ages re-enstated the doctrine of Aristotle — but with a significant revision. Ultimate authority, they said, must be sought in the supernatural Author of Nature and in the Redeemer of man, for in them alone does it reside. This authority had its earthly representative, interpreter, and agent in the divinely instituted and constituted Church.

Even when the rise of secular dynastic states challenged the supremacy of the Church, the basic idea was not even questioned, let alone challenged. The secular state only claimed that it also existed by divine right or authority, and that its authority was therefore supreme in all the affairs of this life, as distinct from those of the soul in the life to come. Even when popular governments began to flourish, they continued the old idea in a weakened form: the voice of God was now the voice of the People.

The new science endeavored to smooth its thorny path by asserting that it was engaged in thinking the thoughts of God after Him. The rise of new economic forces in turn threatened the supreme authority of existing political institutions. But the new economic forces also claimed the right to supreme authority on the ground that they were pure and literal expressions of natural law — in contradistinction to political laws and institutions which, in so far as they did not conform to the play of economic forces, were artificial and man-made. Economic forces, through their representatives, interpreters, and agents— the official economists and industrialists— claimed the divine prerogative to reign supreme over all human terrestrial affairs. The economist and industrialist and financier were the new pretenders to the old divine right of kings.

The conclusion that emerges from this brief historical survey — a conclusion that would be confirmed by any intensive study of the field — is that the identification of the individual with the forces that make freely for variation and change, to the exclusion of those forces in his structure that are habitual and conservative, is something new and recent. Speaking in general terms, the identification is an expression of special and specific historic events. These events may be condensed and summarized. New methods and conclusions in natural science, with their technological application in new modes of industrial production and commercial exchange of goods and services, found themselves checked and limited by the institutional agencies of Church and State which were the possessors of actual social power and the claimants for exclusive and rightful authority in all the variegated fields of human endeavor. In this conflict, the new forces defended and justified themselves by restricting the very idea of authority to the ecclesiastical and political powers that were hostile to their own free expression, and by asserting that they and they alone represented and furthered the interests of the individual and his freedom. The formula mentioned at the outset of this address, the formula of two separate and independent spheres of authority and freedom, in which primacy in case of doubt belongs to the individual and to freedom — this formula is the net product of the historic conflict.

The final result was a social and political philosophy

which questioned the validity of authority in *any* form
that was not the product of, and that was not sanctioned
by, the conscious wants, efforts, and satisfactions of individuals in their private capacity — a philosophy which
took the form of *laissez faire* in economics, and individualism in all other social and political affairs. This philosophy
claimed for itself the comprehensive title of liberalism.

Two general conclusions, it seems to me, clearly emerge.
First, the older forms of organized power that had exercised authority were revealed as external and oppressive
with respect to the new forces that operated through the
medium of individuals, and as hostile, in consequence, to
all important social change. Second, the new philosophy so
tended to decry the very principle of authority as to deprive individuals of the direction and support that are
universally indispensable both for the organic freedom of
individuals and for social stability.

The result is the present scene of confusion, conflict,
and uncertainty. While decrying the principle of authority, and asserting the necessity of limiting the exercise
of authority to the minimum needed for maintenance of
police order, the new philosophy in fact erected the wants
and endeavors of private individuals seeking personal gain
to the place of supreme authority in social life. In consequence, the new philosophy, in the very act of asserting
that it stood completely and loyally for the principle of
individual freedom, was really engaged in justifying the
activities of a new form of concentrated power — the
economic, which new form, to state the matter moder-
ately, has consistently and persistently denied effective
freedom to the economically underpowered and under-
privileged. While originating as a social force that effected
widespread social change in opposition to, indeed in despite of, the powers that had authority when it began to

emerge, economic power has now become, in its turn, an organized social institution that resists all further social change that is not in accord with itself, that does not further and support its own interests as at present existing.

It is for such reasons as these that I affirm that the real issue is not that of demarcating separate "spheres" for authority and for freedom, for stability and for change, but that of effecting an interpenetration of the two. We need an authority that, unlike the older forms in which it operated, is capable of directing and utilizing change, and we need a kind of individual freedom unlike that which the unconstrained economic liberty of individuals has produced and justified — we need, that is, a kind of individual freedom that is general and shared and that has the backing and guidance of socially organized authoritative control.

If the history of man in the past be taken to provide conclusive evidence, it would show that the problem of union of freedom and authority is insoluble as well as unsolved. We have had organized social authority that limited the expression of the variable factors in individuals from which orderly and intentional change proceeds. We have had a time of relatively unconstrained and unchecked individualism, and of resultant change going on rapidly on a wide scale. The suppressive and stagnating effect of institutional authority of a political type has been weakened. But security, and co-operative, ordered, and orderly change, are conspicuous by their absence.

It is completely possible, in my opinion, to recognize the need and important social consequences of the individualistic movement and yet also see that in its past mode of operation it has already run its socially justified and justifiable course. It is possible to acknowledge not merely the valuable historic services it has rendered, but also that its assertion, practical and theoretic, of the value of the variable tendencies of human beings — those that mark off one person from another and that are expressed in initiative, invention, and energetic enterprise — is something that should be permanently embodied in any future social order: — it is possible, I say, to acknowledge all the admirable traits and products of the individualistic movement and yet hold that the movement as it has operated up to the present has suffered from a great defect, owing to its absolutistic opposition to the principle of organized authority.

It requires little if any argument to prove that the institutional forms in which authority has been embodied in the past are hostile to change. It suffices, perhaps, to recall that those who have labored to change the forms authoritative power had taken were denounced as heretics, as elements subversive of social order. And, I need hardly add, those who are engaged in similar labor today are similarly denounced. The point that does require emphatic attention is that in spite of possession of power, and in spite of persecution of heretics and radicals, no institution has in fact had the power to succeed in preventing great changes from taking place. All that institutions have ever succeeded in doing by their resistance to change has been to dam up social forces until they finally and inevitably manifested themselves in eruptions of great, usually violent and catastrophic, change.

Nor is argument necessary to prove that the individualistic movement has been allied with a period of immense and rapid changes, many of which, taken one by one, have brought positive benefit to society. The facts speak so loudly for themselves, argument is unnecessary. The intimate connection between the new individualism and social change is seen in the watchwords of the movement:

Initiative, Invention, Enterprise. For all of these words stand for the variable elements in the constitution of individuals; they point to the loci of departure from what has been; they are the signs which denote the sources of innovation. It is just because they are these signs that they can be so effectively used as watchwords, as signals that arouse the individual to effort and action. Indeed, the connection with change is so intimate that the movement produced that glorification of change as sure and necessary progress which marked the heyday of its influence. But I venture the statement that just as the past manifestation of the principle of authority has failed precisely where its claim was most vehement, namely, in the prevention, or at least in the guidance, of change, so the individualistic movement, taken historically and in the large, has failed to secure freedom for individuals on any commensurate scale — and in any assured way — even for its temporary possessors. The individualistic movement has tended to identify the exercise of freedom with absence of any organized control, and in this way it has in fact identified freedom with mere *de facto* possession of economic power. Instead of bringing freedom to those who lacked material possessions, it has imposed upon them further subjection to the owners of the agencies of material production and distribution.

The scene which the world exhibits to the observer at the present time is so obviously one of general instability, insecurity, and increasing conflict — both between nations and within them — that I cannot conceive that any one will deny the *desirability* of effecting and enstating some organic union of freedom and authority. Enormous doubt will well exist, however, as to the possibility of establishing any social system in which the union is practically embodied. This question, it will be justly urged, is *the* issue that emerges even if the substantial validity of the points so far made is admitted. In fact, it may even be justly urged that this question confronts us as the controlling and decisive question just because, or to the degree that, the validity of my argument thus far is granted.

The weight of the evidence of the past is assuredly strongly against the realization of any such possibility. As far as the idea of organized authority is concerned, the pathos of the collective life of mankind on this planet is its exhibition of the dire human need for some authority; while its ever-mounting tragedy is due to the fact that the need has been repeatedly betrayed by the very institutions that claimed to satisfy it. That all is not well, on the other hand, with the principle of individualistic freedom in the form in which it has been influential up to now, is shown by more than one fact in the present scene of discord and insecurity. Above all is this manifested by the recrudescence of the principle of authority in its most extreme and primitive form — the rise of dictatorships.

As if in substantiation of the old idea that nature abhors a vacuum, it might be contended that economic competitive individualism, free from social control, had created a moral and social vacuum which recourse to dictatorships is filling. In many countries, the demand for collective and organized guidance and support has become so urgent that the very idea of individual freedom has gone into the discard and become an ideal, not to be praised, but to be despised. The regime of economic individualistic liberty is attacked by dictatorships from both the right and the left. In countries in which there are no open and acknowledged dictatorships, the conceptions of liberty and individualism seem to be losing their magic force; and security, discipline, order, and solidarity are, by social transfer, acquiring magic power in their stead. The actual concrete conditions that produce resort to dictatorships vary from country to country. But the phenomenon is so widespread it demands a generalized explanation. The most obvious one is the virtual bankruptcy and moribund state of a regime of individual initiative and enterprise conducted for private gain and subject to no control by recognized, collective authority.

Neither the past nor the present afford, then, any ground for expecting that the adjustment of authority and freedom, stability and change, will be achieved by following old paths. The idea that any solution at all can ever be attained may seem to some romantic and utopian. But the most fantastically unrealistic of all notions is the widely prevalent belief that we can attain enduring stable authority by employing or re-exhuming the institutional means tried in the past; equally fantastic is the belief that the assured freedom of individuals can be secured by pitting individuals against one another in a pitiless struggle for material possessions and economic power. The issue, in my judgment, can be narrowed down to this question: Are there resources that have not as yet been tried out in the large field of human relations, resources that are available and that carry with them the potential promise of successful application?

In raising this question I am aware that it is almost inevitable that what I have said about the human necessity for some kind of collective authority to give individuals direction in their relations with one another, and to give them the support that comes from a sense of solidarity, will appear to be a plea for a return to some kind of social control brought about through, and perpetuated by, external institutional means. If my question is so taken, then the criticism I have made of the alliance that has taken place between the principle of individual freedom and private initiative and enterprise in economic matters will necessarily also seem to be merely an argument for social control by means of a collective planned economy — put forward, of course, with some change in vocabulary. However, the argument in fact cuts in both directions. It indicates that while movements in the direction of collective, planned economy may cure evils from which we are now suffering, it will in the end go the way of all past attempts at organization of authoritative power unless some hitherto untried means are utilized on a large and systematic scale for bringing into life the desired and desirable organic co-ordination. Otherwise we shall finally find ourselves repeating on a different plane the old struggle between social organization and individual freedom, with the oscillation from one principle to the other that has so characteristically marked the past.

The resource that has not yet been tried on any large scale, in the broad field of human, social relationships is the utilization of organized intelligence, the manifold benefits and values of which we have substantial and reliable evidence of in the narrower field of science.

Within a limited area, the collective intelligence which is exemplified in the growth and application of scientific method has already become authoritative. It is authoritative in the field of beliefs regarding the structure of nature and relevant to our understanding of physical events. To a considerable extent, the same statement holds true of beliefs about historical personages and historical events — especially with those that are sufficiently remote from the present time. When we turn to the practical side, we see that the same method is supreme in controlling and guiding our active dealings with material things and physical energies. To a large and significant extent, the Baconian prophecy that knowledge is power of control has been

realized in this particular, somewhat narrowly circum-
scribed area. To be sure, it cannot be said that intelligence, operating by the methods that constitute science,
has as yet completely won *undisputed* right and authority
to control beliefs even in the restricted physical field. But
organized intelligence has made an advance that is truly
surprising when we consider the short time in which it has
functioned and the powerful foes against which it had to
make its way: the foes of inertia, of old, long-established
traditions and habits—inertia, traditions, and habits all of
them entrenched in forms of institutional life that are
effulgent with the prestige of time, that are enveloped in
the glamor of imaginative appeal, and that are crowned,
severally and collectively, with an emotional halo made of
the values that men most prize.

The record of the struggle that goes by the name of
"conflict between science and religion," or, if you please,
"conflict between theology and science," was essentially a
conflict of claims to exercise social authority. It was not
just a conflict between two sets of theoretical beliefs, but
between two alignments of social forces — one which was
old and had institutional power that it did not hesitate to
use, and one which was new and striving and craving for
recognition against gigantic odds.

What is pertinent, what is deeply significant to the
theme of the *relation* between collective authority and freedom, is that the progress of intelligence — as exemplified
in this summary story of scientific advance — exhibits their
organic, effective union. Science has made its way by releasing, not by suppressing, the elements of variation, of
invention and innovation, of novel creation in individuals.
It is as true of the history of modern science as it is of the
history of painting or music that its advances have been
initiated by individuals who freed themselves from the

bonds of tradition and custom whenever they found the latter hampering their own powers of reflection, observation, and construction.

In spite of science's dependence for its development upon the free initiative, invention, and enterprise of individual inquirers, the authority of science issues from and is based upon collective activity, co-operatively organized. Even when, temporarily, the ideas put forth in science by individuals sharply diverge from received beliefs, the method used is a public and open method which succeeds only as it tends to produce agreement, unity of belief among all who labored in the same field. Every scientific inquirer, even when he deviates most widely from current ideas, depends upon methods and conclusions that are a common possession and not of private ownership, even though all of the methods and conclusions may at some time have been initially the product of private invention. The contribution the scientific inquirer makes is collectively tested and developed and, in the measure that it is co-operatively confirmed, becomes a part of the common fund of the intellectual commonwealth.

One can most easily recognize the difference between the aim and operation of the free individual in the sphere of science and in that of current individualistic economic enterprise by stretching the fancy to the point of imagining a scientific inquirer adopting the standards of the business entrepreneur. Imagine the scientific man who should say that his conclusion was scientific and in so saying maintain that it was also the product of his private wants and efforts goading him on to seek his private advantage. The mere suggestion of such an absurdity vividly discloses the gap that divides the manifestations of individual freedom in these two areas of human activity. The suggestion brings into bold relief and in typical form the

kind of individual freedom that is both supported by collective, organic authority and that in turn changes and is
encouraged to change and develop, by its own operations,
the authority upon which it depends.

The thesis that the operation of co-operative intelligence
as displayed in science is a working model of the union of
freedom and authority does not slight the fact that the
method has operated up to the present in a limited and
relatively technical area. On the contrary, it emphasizes
that fact. If the method of intelligence had been employed
in any large field in the comprehensive and basic area of
the relations of human beings to one another in social life
and institutions, there would be no present need for our
argument. The contrast between the restricted scope of its
use and the possible range of its application to human relations — political, economic, and moral — is outstanding
and depressing. It is this very contrast that defines the
great problem that still has to be solved.

No consideration of the problem is adequate that does
not take into account one fact about the development of
the modern individualistic movement in industry and
business. There is a suppressed premise in all the claims
and reasonings of the individualistic school. All the beneficial changes that have been produced are attributed to
the free play of individuals seeking primarily their own
profit as isolated individuals. But in fact, the entire
modern industrial development is the fruit of the technological applications of science. By and large, the economic changes of recent centuries have been parasitic upon
the advances made in natural science. There is not a
single process involved in the production and distribution
of goods that is not dependent upon the utilization of results which are consequences of the method of collective,
organic intelligence working in mathematics, physics, and

chemistry. To speak baldly, it is a plain falsehood that the advances which the defenders of the existing regime point to as justification for its continuance are due to mere individualistic initiative and enterprise. Individualistic initiative and enterprise have sequestered and appropriated the fruits of collective co-operative intelligence. This they have done alone. But without the aid and support of organized intelligence they would have been impotent — perhaps even in those activities in which they have shown themselves to be socially most powerful.

In sum, the great weakness of the historic movement that has laid claim to the title of liberalism and that has proclaimed its operating purpose to be that of securing and protecting the freedom of individuals — the great weakness of this movement has been its failure to recognize that the true and final source of change has been, and now is, the corporate intelligence embodied in science. The principle, as I have already said, cuts in two directions. In so far as the attempts that are now being made in the direction of organized social control and planned economy ignore the role of scientific intelligence, in so far as these attempts depend upon and turn for support to external institutional changes effected for the most part by force, just so far are they re-enstating reliance upon the method of external authority that has always broken down in the past. For a time, while in need of security and a sense and feeling of solidarity, men will submit to authority of this kind. But if history shows anything, it shows that the variable factors in individuals cannot be permanently suppressed or completely eradicated. The principle of individual freedom expressed in the modern individualistic movement is deeply rooted in the constitution of human beings. The truth embodied in it cannot die no matter how much force is brought down upon it. The tragedy of the movement is that it misconceived and misplaced the source and seat of this principle of freedom. But the attempt to uproot and eliminate this principle on behalf of the assurance of security and attainment of solidarity by means of external authority is doomed to ultimate defeat no matter what its temporary victories.

There is no need to dwell upon the enormous obstacles that stand in the way of extending from its present limited field to the larger field of human relations the control of organized intelligence, operating through the release of individual powers and capabilities. There is the weight of past history on the side of those who are cynical or pessimistic about the possibility of achieving this humanly desirable and humanly necessary task. I do not predict that the extension will ever be effectively actualized. But I do claim that the problem of the relation of authority and freedom, of stability and change, if it can be solved, will be solved in this way. The failure of other methods and the desperateness of the present situation will be a spur to some to do their best to make the extension actual. They know that to hold in advance of trial that success is impossible is a way of condemning humanity to that futile and destructive oscillation between authoritative power and unregulated individual freedom to which we may justly attribute most of the sorrows and defeats of the past. They are aware of the slow processes of history and of the unmeasured stretch of time that lies ahead of mankind. They do not expect any speedy victory in the execution of the most difficult task human beings ever set their hearts and minds to attempt. They are, however, buoyed by the assurance that no matter how slight the immediate effect of their efforts, they are themselves, in their trials, exemplifying one of the first principles of the method of scientific intelligence. For they are projecting into events a large and comprehensive idea by experimental methods that correct and mature the method and the idea in the very process of trial. The very desperateness of the situation is, for such as these, but a spur to sustained, courageous effort.

III
THE PLACE AND FUNCTIONS
OF AUTHORITY

THE CONSTITUTION AS INSTRUMENT AND AS SYMBOL

EDWARD SAMUEL CORWIN, PH.D., LL.D., LITT.D.

Professor of Jurisprudence, Princeton University

ON AN early page of his celebrated *Constitutional Limitations*, Judge Cooley defines "constitution" in the following curt terms: "That body of rules and maxims in accordance with which the powers of sovereignty are habitually exercised." Returning later to the subject he quotes with approval a more elaborate conception, couched in these words:

What is a constitution, and what are its objects? It is easier to tell what it is not than what it is. *It is not the beginning of a community, nor the origin of private rights; it is not the fountain of law, nor the incipient state of government; it is not the cause, but consequence, of personal and political freedom; it grants no rights to the people,* but is the creature of their power, the instrument of their convenience. *Designed for their protection in the enjoyment of the rights and powers which they possessed before the constitution was made, it is* but the framework of the political government, and *necessarily based upon the pre-existing condition of laws, rights, habits, and modes of thought. There is nothing primitive in it, it is all derived from a known source. It presupposes an organized society, law, order, property, personal freedom,* a love of political liberty, and enough of cultivated intelligence to know how to guard it against the encroachments of tyranny. A written constitution is in every instance a limitation upon the powers of government in the hands of agents; for there never was a written republican constitution which delegated to functionaries all the latent powers which lie dormant in every nation, and are boundless in extent, and incapable of definition.[1]

The first of these definitions answers to what I mean in this paper by the term "constitutional instrument"; the second approximates, particularly in the passages I have stressed, what I have in mind when I speak of "constitutional symbol."

To the modern mind, confident in the outlook afforded by science and its achievements, the word "instrument" connotes the future and things needing to be done in the future. It assumes that man is the master of his fate, able to impart a desired shape to things and events. And regarded from this point of view a constitution is an *instrument of popular power* — "sovereignty," if you will — *for the achievement of progress.*

American constitutional symbolism looks, on the other hand, to the past and links hands with conceptions which long antedate the rise of science and its belief in a predictable, manageable causation. Its consecration of an *already established order of things* harks back to primitive man's terror of a chaotic universe, and his struggle toward security and significance behind a slowly erected barrier of custom, magic, fetish, and tabu. While, therefore, the Constitutional Instrument exists to energize and canalize *public power*, it is the function of the Constitutional Symbol to protect and tranquillize *private interest or advantage as against public power*, which is envisaged as inherently suspect, however necessary it may be. What has been the relation of these two conceptions in the case of the Constitution of the United States? To answer this question is the main purpose of this paper.

The aspect of the Constitution of the United States as an instrument of popular government for the achievement of the great ends of government is stamped on its opening words:

We, the people of the United States, in order to form a more perfect union, establish justice, insure domestic tranquillity, provide for the common defense, promote the general welfare, and secure the blessings of liberty to ourselves and our posterity, do ordain and establish this Constitution for the United States of America.

The aspect of the Constitution as symbol and bulwark of a previously achieved order of human rights appears most evidently in the ninth article of the Bill of Rights: "The enumeration in the Constitution of certain rights shall not be construed to deny or disparage others retained by the people." The same idea was expressed by Webster in the following words: "Written constitutions sanctify and confirm great principles, but the latter are prior in existence to the former." Or as Governor Landon put the same idea recently: "The Constitution was not framed to give us anything, but to protect inherent rights already possessed." [2]

That the attitude of the members of the Federal Convention toward their task was predominantly instrumentalist and practical is clear at a glance. They had not gone to Philadelphia merely to ratify the past, Governor Landon to the contrary notwithstanding, but with *reform* in mind, and specifically the creation of *a strong, effective national government*. Theirs, it must be remembered, was one of the great creative periods in the history of political institutions, and they were thoroughly imbued with the faith of their epoch in the ability of the human reason, working in the light of experience, to divert the unreflective course of events into beneficial channels; and in no respect did they deem man more evidently the master of his destiny than in that of statecraft. Furthermore, most of these men had been reared in the Mercantilist tradition, and accordingly regarded governmental intervention in the field of economic activity as one of the chief reasons for the existence of government; while the importance to government in turn of engaging the self-interest of groups and

individuals by its active policies was a thing constantly
present to their minds. The atmosphere of the Convention
was, in fact, almost scandalously secular. Despite the
social pre-eminence of the cloth in 1787, not a clergyman
was listed among its fifty-five members, and when Franklin
suggested that one be recruited to open the meetings with
prayer, the proposal was shelved by his obviously embarrassed associates with almost comical celerity. Nor did the
Constitution as it came from their hands contain a Bill of
Rights.

And naturally the party which brought the Constitution
into existence continued to regard their work pragmati-
cally while they elaborated a working government under it.
"You have made a good Constitution," a friend remarked
to Gouverneur Morris shortly following the Convention.
"That," Morris replied, "depends on how it is construed." And in his characterization of the Constitution as
"an experiment" Hamilton voiced the same pragmatic
point of view. The new Ship of State was quickly crowded
with all the canvas of powers "implied," "resultant,"
"inherent," that its slender, vibrant phrasing would carry;
and it is a significant fact that the constitutional validity
of not a single item of the Hamiltonian program was challenged judicially even in principle until a generation later.

The Constitutional Instrument was the work of a
limited class, comprising those whose "interests and outlook," as Woodrow Wilson put it, "transcended state
lines." The Constitutional Symbol, on the other hand, *being a symbol*, was the work of the many — a creation of the
mass mind. Indeed, prevision of the symbolic role of the
Constitution is older than the Constitution itself. In that
number of *Common Sense* in which he urged independence,
in February, 1776, Thomas Paine urged also "a Continental Conference. He said:

The conferring members being met, let their business be to frame a Continental Charter or Charter of the United Colonies (answering to what is called the Magna Charta of England) fixing the number and manner of choosing members of Congress and members of Assembly . . . and drawing the line of business and jurisdiction between them (always remembering that our strength is continental, not provincial), securing freedom and property to all men . . . with such other matters as it is necessary for a charter to contain. But where, say some, is the King of America? That we may not appear to be defective even in earthly honors, let a day be solemnly set apart for proclaiming the charter; let it be brought forth placed on the divine law, the word of God; let a crown be placed thereon, by which the world may know that so far we approve monarchy that in America the law is King.[3]

That so able a propagandist as Paine proved himself to be should have sensed the popular need for a symbol, as well as the fact, of authority is perhaps not to be wondered at. At any rate, the Constitution had not long been in operation when his prediction was fulfilled most amazingly. The outbreak of the wars of the French Revolution, by increasing British and Continental demand for American products, brought a hazardous prosperity which minds unaccustomed to looking so far afield for causes attributed to the Constitution. Speaking on the floor of the Congress in 1794, Richard Bland Lee declared:

I will only mention the stimulus which agriculture has received. In travelling through various parts of the United States, I find fields a few years ago waste and uncultivated filled with inhabitants and covered with harvests, new habitations reared, contentment in every face, plenty on every board; confidence is restored and every man is safe under his own vine and fig tree, and there is none to make him afraid. To produce this effect was the intent of the Constitution, and it has succeeded.[4]

To be sure, there were skeptics. "It has been usual with declamatory gentlemen," complained sour old Maclay, "in their praises of the present government, to paint the state of the country under the old Congress as if neither wood grew nor water ran in America before the happy adoption of the Constitution."

Such disparagement, discreetly confided to the pages of a private journal, did not stem the course of opinion. Hardly has Holy Writ itself been more eulogized than the Constitutional Symbol presently came to be. "In the Constitution of the United States," wrote Justice William Johnson in 1823, "— the most wonderful instrument ever drawn by the hand of man — there is a comprehension and precision that is unparalleled; and I can truly say that after spending my life in studying it, I still daily find in it some new excellence."[5] And inevitably the virtues of the Framers were imputed to their handiwork, as were its virtues to them. Jefferson, ordinarily no reverent spirit, at first described the Convention as an assemblage of "demi-gods," though he later reconsidered this appraisal. On the other hand, while Hamilton's cold evaluation of the Constitution as "an experiment" was repeated by Washington in his Farewell Address eight years later, Jackson in his Farewell Address in 1837 demurred to this description as no longer suitable. Even in the midst of civil war, when the "experiment" seemed to have failed, it was apostrophized as embodying much more than "calm wisdom and lofty patriotism," as "providential," "God's saving gift," "His creative fiat over a weltering chaos: 'Let a nation be born in a day.'"[6]

But when one says that the Constitution had become "a symbol," one has not advanced very far, for the question remains, *symbol of what?* Initially the symbol was, it would seem, hardly more than decorative — the tribute which the American people rendered their own political sagacity for ordaining such a marvelous Constitution. Yet this

symbol of high political achievement became in time a
symbol of distrust of the political process — a symbol of
democracy's fear of democracy. How explain this seeming
paradox, and what have been the results?

It is no contradiction of what has been said in preceding
paragraphs to point out that the *original* attitude of the
American masses toward the document which came from
the Philadelphia Convention was far from being one of
worship. The said masses were small farmers with slight
social experience and vast social suspicions, suspicions
which had been given by the agitation leading to the Revolution a decided anti-government — and especially *an anti-
central-government* — set. Nor, in fact, was the Constitution which its former opponents presently vied with its
former champions in praising altogether the same Constitution as the one over whose merits they had originally
divided. Not only had it now a Bill of Rights, but what
was vastly more important, the authors of the Virginia and
Kentucky Resolutions, squaring the logical circle, had
succeeded in affixing to it, for those who chose to welcome
the improvement, a gloss of the extremest State-Rightism.
It is true, of course, that Marshall was still to propound
from the bench, for more than a third of a century, the
original conception of the Constitution as the ever adapt-
able instrument of national needs; yet only, as it were,
academically, and in behalf of statutes for which the Congresses of the period were enacting few counterparts. The
national sovereignty had become in truth, in great measure, a sovereignty *in vacuo*.

But certain environmental factors have been, perhaps,
even more potent than intellectual currents in finally affixing to the Constitutional Symbol its distinctively negative
quality. The presence to the eastward of the Atlantic
Ocean, with its fair assurance against hostile invasion, dis-

credited from the outset any plea in favor of strong government in the name of defense. The presence to the
westward of endless stretches of cheap lands opened to
even the humblest members of society an opportunity for
self-assertion on a scale never before approached in the
history of mankind. Lastly, the presence throughout this
richest of continents of vast mineral and other natural resources which public policy, or rather the lack of it, threw
open to private pre-emption with little restriction, vested
the acquisition of wealth with a moral and legal sanction
of its own. People were content with the answer that the
country was being developed.

It is a commonplace that Constitutionalism has worked
in this country to impress upon the discussion of public
measures a legalistic — not to say theological — mold. By
a terminology which treats *doctrines* as *facts*, the actuali-
ties which should control statesmanship have been too
often kept at arm's length; while for the question of the
beneficial *use* of the powers of government has been substituted the question of their *existence*. The tendency in
question manifested itself at an early date. Said W. H.
Crawford in a speech in the Senate in 1811:

Upon the most thorough examination I am induced to believe
that many of the various constructions given to the Constitution are the result of the belief that it is absolutely perfect. It has
become so extremely fashionable to eulogize the Constitution,
whether the object of the eulogy is the extension or contraction
of the powers of the government, that whenever its eulogium is
pronounced, I feel an involuntary apprehension of mischief.[7]

Crawford's words carry the significant suggestion that
there were those who looked upon the constitutionality of
a measure as a positive quality, a reason by itself for the
measure's enactment. Such an attitude is, in truth, a normal phase of the psychology of Constitutionalism. What

better reason can there be for doing a thing than the right
to do it when that was challenged in the first instance?
Generally speaking, nevertheless, constitutional debate
proceeds characteristically from the point of view of *negation* and treats the Constitutional Symbol as a source of
tabu; and the "great constitutional lawyer" is one who
knows how to make two constitutional restrictions grow
where one grew before. Indeed, it is astonishing the extent
to which the taint of constitutional obliquity has always
dogged the footsteps of the American people and their representatives. The Constitution itself was unconstitutional
by an argument to which Madison felt it necessary to reply
in the *Federalist*. Most of Hamilton's legislative program
was unconstitutional in the opinion of half of Washington's
Cabinet. The Louisiana Purchase was unconstitutional in
the opinion of the President who accomplished it. The
most important measure by which the slavery question
was kept in abeyance for years was unconstitutional in the
opinion of large numbers of people, and finally in the
opinion of the Supreme Court. The Civil War was brought
to a successful issue by resorting to measures which two
out of three Americans alive at that time would have voted
to be unconstitutional; and according to the *Democratic
Almanac* of 1866, the Thirteenth Amendment was unconstitutional. And the enumeration might easily be prolonged to include almost every measure of scope and of
somewhat novel character that the Congress of the United
States has enacted within the last half-century.

Despite all which, it may be remarked of constitutional
negativism, as Lord Acton remarked of liberty, that it
must have remained impermanent and inefficient had it
not found embodiment in an implementing institution. I
refer, of course, to judicial review, and especially to the
power of the Court to disallow acts of Congress on the

ground of their being in conflict with the Constitution. Recently there has been a renewal of the old debate as to the intentions of the Framers in this respect. Neither side, perhaps, has quite all the truth on its side. That the Framers anticipated some sort of judicial review of acts of Congress there can be little question. But it is equally without question that ideas generally current in 1787 were far from presaging the present vast role of the Court.

Thus, as we saw earlier, constitutional negativism exalts the Bill of Rights as the bulwark of achieved liberties. In the Virginia convention, on the other hand, which ratified the Constitution, Marshall declared of bills of rights that they were "merely recommendatory. Were it otherwise," he continued, ". . . many laws which are found convenient would be unconstitutional." The principle of the Separation of Powers, too, was originally thought of as "directory only," and hence as not affording a judicially applicable restriction upon legislative power. Again, the Constitution is today assumed to comprise *a closed, a completed system*. Indeed, this assumption is asserted by Cooley to be the underlying basis of judicial review. Yet in the debate on the location of the removal power in the first Congress to assemble under the Constitution the most strongly-held theory was that the Constitution did not declare itself on the point, as obviously it does not, and that accordingly Congress was confronted with a *casus omissus* which under the necessary and proper clause it was entitled to supply. And no less paradoxical by modern standards is Chief Justice Marshall's suggestion early in 1805, while the Chase impeachment was pending, that the power of impeachment ought to be surrendered by Congress in return for power to reverse such "opinions" of the Court as Congress found objectionable. In a recent discussion of this episode in the Senate, it was confidently asserted that what

Marshall had in mind was an amendment to the Constitution. But quite clearly this was not the case. The situation was an urgent one; Marshall was trembling not only for the safety of the Court but for the safety of his own position. What he evidently had in mind was an *ad hoc* understanding between the two branches, one that would ripen in time into a fixed custom of the Constitution.

The opinion of our Senatorial wise men confirms Professor Maitland's statement as to the tendency of the law (i.e., of the lawyers) to "antedate the emergence of modern ideas," and it may be added that they sometimes antedate other things too. How account otherwise for that door-panel of the new Supreme Court Building which — according to the earliest explanations of it — pictures Chief Justice Marshall as handing to Justice Story the former's opinion in *Marbury* v. *Madison*, although this opinion was rendered some nine years prior to Story's appointment to the bench; [8] or for that repeatedly encountered motif in court-house murals, the *signing* of Magna Carta by King John, although John probably could not write, and at any rate the great seal, affixed by the Chancellor, was thought to serve such occasions very adequately? Nor is this to mention Senator Borah's speech last February 22nd, in which Washington is represented as delivering the Farewell Address in the new capital named for him, some four years before said capital was open for business!

Judicial review of national legislation first disclosed its potentialities seventy years after the framing of the Constitution, in the Dred Scott Case, where it is placed squarely on a symbolic basis. The Constitution, Chief Justice Taney there declares, speaks always "not only with the same words, but with the same intent," as when it came from the Framers. Thus is the miracle which is the Constitution of 1787 to be maintained and preserved by the mystery which is judicial power — its clairvoyance into the intentions of men long dead as to things which did not exist when they lived!

And by the same token, if judicial review has conserved the Constitutional Symbol, the Constitutional Symbol has conserved judicial review, by screening its operations behind the impersonal mask of the unbiased past. Even today the notion of the judicial mouthpiece of a self-interpreting, self-enforcing law has its adherents. Listen, for instance, to this defense by a correspondent of the *New York Times* of the decision in the Rice Millers' Case, which awarded some two hundred millions of dollars to people most of whom were probably not entitled to it:

> For so long as the Constitution of the United States endures in its present form, it must operate with the infallibility of the laws of nature. Sound and fecund growths will be fortified by its influences. Its impact will always strip the fruit from any governmental tree which is too defective to maintain its own integrity. The office of the Supreme Court is simply to elucidate the process.[9]

Coming now to the heart of the problem here under discussion, I propose to point out briefly certain restrictions upon the national legislative power which the Court has from time to time ratified in favor, primarily, of certain minority interests, on the theory that such interests comprised an essential part of a prior order of things which it was a fundamental — *the* fundamental — purpose of the Constitution to put beyond the reach of popular majorities. Viewed from this angle the Constitutional Symbol is seen to part company with the Constitutional Instrument very radically. *The symbol of the many becomes the instrument of the few, and all the better instrument for being such symbol.*

The two minority interests which have left the deepest imprint on our constitutional law so far as national power is concerned are slavery and that fairly coherent group of interests which are commonly lumped together as "Big Business." Slavery was awakened to its situation by the Tariff of 1828. But as no appeal could be taken to the Court with any hope of success so long as Marshall dominated it, Calhoun, reversing his constitutional creed almost overnight, fashioned a fantastic substitute from the Virginia and Kentucky Resolutions of thirty years previously; and by the aid of Nullification the South was presently able to force a compromise with the adherents of the American System.

Twenty years later the question of slavery in the Territories was to the fore, and meantime the menacing possibility had presented itself that the rising forces of anti-slavery in Congress would attempt to put a stop to the interstate slave trade. Whether by dint of foresighted management or by accident, the slave-holding states had now a majority on the Court, and the drive which culminated nine years later in the Dred Scott decision, to get a judicial determination of the territorial question, was launched. But what line ought the Court to take in handling questions of national power affecting slavery? Should it treat slavery as constituting a special case, a sort of enclave, withdrawn by the intention of the Framers from the constitutional powers of the national government; or should it construe these powers in such a way as to render them harmless for slavery considered simply as any proprietarian interest? In his opinion in the Passenger Cases, Justice Wayne of Georgia, the strongest nationalist on the Taney bench, suggested the former expedient, but without success. The consequence is that the two doctrines which have proved most restrictive of the powers of Congress in recent years are directly traceable to the Taney Court. The first of these is the doctrine that the Tenth Amendment segregates to the states certain "subjects," "fields," or "interests," and hence forbids Congress to exercise any of its powers, but especially its interstate commerce and taxing powers, with the effect or intention of governing such "subjects," "fields," or "interests." The second is that the due-process clause of the Fifth Amendment authorizes the Court to invalidate any act of Congress which it finds to impair property rights "unreasonably." Furthermore, from the defenders of the Dred Scott decision came the doctrine of the "finality" of the Court's interpretations of the Constitution — a doctrine which Lincoln assailed in his first Inaugural as transferring to the Court the people's right of self-government.

And it is on these bases, shaky as they are in both logic and history, that the Court has chosen to rest the most outstanding of its recent decisions.[10] There is no need to review these holdings in any detail in order to show their bearing on our subject. The climax is reached, when they are considered for their impairment of the Constitutional Instrument, in the A. A. A. Case, which, when evaluated in the light of Justice Roberts' opinion, appears to assert that Congress may not legitimately employ its granted powers in order to further on a *national* scale anything which states may legitimately attempt on a *local* scale. Others of these decisions have suddenly thrust into prominence as a restrictive principle the heretofore innocuous and unused doctrine that a legislature may not delegate its power, but without giving that doctrine coherent or understandable form. Still another decision rejects the principle of emergency power on the basis of the equivocal or erroneous assertion that the powers of the national government have proved "adequate," "both in war and peace." Still another implies a theory of judicial autonomy in relation to legislative power which represents a *vast* departure from the views of the Framers. Lastly, the American Liberty League, whose mission it is to spread the gospel of the Constitution as symbol of "The American Way," informs us that the Constitution may be amended "in harmony with its fundamental principles" — that is, may *not* be amended in disharmony therewith. Perhaps it is to be regretted that the judicial history of the Prohibition Amendment contains small assurance of this doctrine ever receiving that acceptance which would round off most conclusively and artistically the triumph of the Constitutional Symbol over the Constitutional Instrument. [11]

Considered, in short, from the point of view of the national legislative power, especially in the important fields of taxation and of interstate-commerce regulation, the Constitution has passed through the following phases: from (1) an instrument of national government, a source of national power, to (2) an object of popular worship, finally valued chiefly for the obstacles it interposed to the national power, to (3) a protection of certain minority interests seeking escape from national power; or, in other words, from constitutional instrument to constitutional fetish, to constitutional tabu, to constitutional instrument again, albeit the *negative* instrument of certain special interests, not the *positive* instrument of a government of the people.

And with what final result for national legislative power? The question is answered admirably by Mr. Irving Brant, in his recent *Storm over the Constitution*: "During this later period the United States shifted from a Constitution of *implied powers* under the express powers [of Congress] to a Constitution of *implied limitations* on the express powers. It was virtually the same thing as writing a new, and infinitely narrower Constitution" [12]— the same thing, that is, as permitting the Court to do this.

It would be easy to ascribe this conversion, partial but immensely important, of the Constitutional Instrument of the many into the Constitutional Instrument of the few, to a conspiracy of the latter; or, to use Sir Thomas More's words, to a "conspiracy of rich men, procuring their own commodities under the title of commonwealth." And the truth of the matter is that the effluvia of conspiracy are never altogether absent when authority joins itself to a mystery, such as the Constitution of the United States has to many intents and purposes become today. On the other hand, the propensity of the professional exalter of the Constitutional Symbol for modern propaganda technique, even if it does not quite dispose of the charge, yet does little to confirm it, inasmuch as propaganda rarely builds *de novo*, but works upon existing beliefs. We may concede therefore that the propagandist against the expansion of national power *thinks* that there is something in the popular mind to which he can appeal successfully; and he may be right. For, as a colleague suggests, we are today in the presence of the reverse of the situation which elicited from Mr. Dooley his famous remark anent the Supreme Court's following the "election returns." The question at present is, will the election returns follow the Supreme Court?

Certain of the characteristics of popular thinking which go to explain the rise of constitutional negativism, and thereby the implementation of certain minority interests by the Constitution, were adverted to early in this paper. One, however, I have reserved for more special mention in these closing paragraphs, and it is the fundamental premise of economic individualism. I mean the assumption that economic power is *natural* and political power *artificial*, from which the conclusion is drawn that "*arbitrary*" power

is characteristically *governmental* power. The latter idea
clearly underlies the more significant of the Court's recent
decisions. Thus, in the A. A. A. Case the Court held that
in requiring agriculturists to sign contracts as a condition
of receiving payments from the Treasury, the government
"coerced" the agriculturists who "involuntarily" accepted
its terms. Yet had Mr. Henry Ford stood in the place of
the government in such a transaction, who would even
have thought of using such language about it? Moreover,
there are still cases in good standing which hold that a
laborer is not coerced when confronted by his employer
with the alternative of giving up his job or quitting his
union, although it *is* coercion for government to forbid the
employers to do this! Likewise in the Alton Case the Court
holds that for Congress to require a carrier to pension a
superannuated employee is to deprive the carrier of liberty
and property without due process of law, the "liberty" in
question being the carrier's right to dismiss a superannuated employee without pensioning him.

The unreality of such thinking is hardly travestied in the
following passage from Professor Arnold's witty little
volume, *The Symbols of Government*:

If the American people were actually free from countless petty
restrictions, it is not likely that they would build a mansion in
the judicial heavens dedicated to the principle, before which we
make such curious sacrifices, that there should be no such restrictions. If we were not so constantly subject to arbitrary and
uncontrolled power over our very means of existence, we would
not require the dramatization of the abstract ideal that no such
power could exist in America, provided that the case could be
properly presented to the Supreme Court of the United States.
The only absolute essential of a heaven is that it be different
from the everyday world.[13]

The American people are today moving rapidly toward
a constitutional crisis of unpredictable gravity, a crisis

due chiefly to the Court's endeavor to put Big Business and its methods — "The American Way" — out of reach of effective government. Thanks to the Court's excessive preoccupation with this problem, the question has even been raised whether the entire system of constitutional limitations, judicially implemented, is not incompatible with popular government. Personally I am not convinced that this is so; but I do think that if the dilemma suggested is to be avoided, short of formal constitutional change, the Court will have to enlarge some of its conceptions; and especially will it have to enlarge its conception of *public power to include economic power*. For when this is done certain other important truths will also emerge. It will be seen that most people have to take orders from some source or other, and that therefore the problem of human liberty is not to be completely solved by the purely negative device of setting acts of Congress aside as contrary to the Constitution. Also recognition will dawn that there is no reason underlying the nature of things why acts or procedures which are regarded as unjust when they are resorted to by government are necessarily more defensible when resorted to by business management. Lastly, it will appear that unless we are to resign ourselves to economic autocracy, governmental power must be as little embarrassed by boundary lines as is economic power.

All this, however, I am conscious, is somewhat negative; and I would conclude on an affirmative note. I find it to hand in a passage from Señor Ortega's *Revolt of the Masses*:

The State is always, whatever be its form — primitive, ancient, medieval, modern — an invitation issued by one group of men to other human groups to carry out some enterprise in common. That enterprise, be its intermediate processes what they may, consists in the long run in the organization of a certain type of common life. State and plan of existence, programme of human activity or conduct, these are inseparable terms.

And he elsewhere adds: "When there is a stoppage of that impulse towards something further on, the State automatically succumbs . . . breaks up, is dispersed."[14]

Revision of the Constitutional Symbol there must be, I submit, to bring it into conformity with the Constitutional Instrument, regarded as the instrument of a people's government and of a unified nation which has not yet lost faith in its political destiny.

NOTES

1 T. M. Cooley, *A Treatise on the Constitutional Limitations which Rest upon the Legislative Power of the States of the American Union* (2d ed.; Boston, 1871), pp. 2, 38–39. Italics mine.

2 Address at Topeka, January 29, 1936.

3 *The Political Writings of Thomas Paine* (Granville, Middletown, N. J., 1837), I, 45–46.

4 Frank I. Schechter, "Early History of the Tradition of the Constitution," *American Political Science Review*, IX, 707, 720 (November 1915). The quotation from Senator Maclay is taken from the same place.

5 Elkinson *v.* Deliesseline, 8 *Federal Cases*, 593.

6 Quoted by Fletcher M. Green, in *Bulletin of Emory University* (Atlanta, Ga.), vol. XXII, no. 5, p. 7 (May 1936).

7 T. H. Benton, *Abridgment of the Debates of Congress*, IV (New York, 1858), 226. See also page 308.

8 Mr. Benjamin Ginzburg sets out the facts in his communication to the Washington, D. C., *Evening Star* of September 15, 1936.

9 *New York Times*, May 5, 1936.

10 See in this connection my recently published *Commerce Power versus States Rights* (Princeton University Press, August 1936), *passim*.

11 Very likely it was with the American Liberty League in mind that Professor Radin wrote recently: "The search for a new capitalist religion in the United States is rapidly taking the form of consecrating patriotic symbols and multiplying rituals which will inevitably be associated with the existing type of economic organization" (13 *New York University Law Quarterly Review*, 1935–36, p. 505).

12 Indianapolis and New York, 1936, p. 129.

13 Thurman Wesley Arnold, *The Symbols of Government* (New Haven, 1935), p. 224.

14 José Ortega y Gasset, *The Revolt of the Masses* (London, 1932), pp. 183, 176.

CENTRALIZATION AND DECENTRALIZATION*

HANS KELSEN, DR.JUR., DR.(HON)., LL.D.

Professor of International Law and of Legal Philosophy, Institut Universitaire des Hautes Etudes Internationales, Geneva, and Deutsche Universität, Prague.

1. The Problem:
Centralization and Decentralization as Juridical Problems

FROM among the subjects proposed for scientific discussion on the occasion of the Tercentenary of Harvard University, I have chosen the subject of centralization and decentralization. I have done this not only because it concerns a central problem of society; it also offers me an opportunity to show the application to a concrete problem of the Pure Theory of Law, which I and my scientific friends have represented for a quarter of a century.[1]

This, however, implies a certain, if not essential, limitation of the subject matter in two directions. First, I shall consider a theoretical, not a political, problem. I shall not be concerned with the merit or demerit of centralization or decentralization and decide for one or the other on the basis of this valuation, but I shall try to understand the essence of both phenomena from the point of view of a structural analysis of society, to determine the different forms in which these two types of organization take concrete shape, and to show how many apparently heterogeneous facts can be systematically understood from the point of view of centralization and decentralization, and only thus be fully

* Translated from the German by Wolfgang Herbert Kraus, Dr.Jur., S.J.D., Instructor in Government, Harvard University.

seen in their relatedness. Such exact knowledge is at the same time by far the best foundation for practice, which as social technique synthesizes the elements of analytical social theory.

The theory which I am going to develop here is a juridical theory. Accordingly, centralization and decentralization shall be treated as forms of organization found in communities of law. It is true that these phenomena may also be encountered in other than communities of law, but are there most clearly developed. As far as centralization and decentralization are concerned, the difference between legal and other social norms is of no importance. Therefore, the results of a juridical theory concerning these phenomena are open to generalization. Apart from this consideration, this juridical theory also has a sociological character, inasmuch as sociology is also concerned with the typical forms of society, forms which are determined by the particular formation of the norms constituting the social groups.

2. *Validity and Sphere of Validity of the Legal Norm*

As this examination is to be made on the basis of the Pure Theory of Law, I shall have to dwell first on some of its fundamental conceptions which will subsequently be applied to our problem.

For the Pure Theory of Law, law is a norm prescribing a certain human behavior. The specific existence of the norm consists in its validity, i.e., in the conception that human beings shall behave in accordance with the norm. As the content of the norm is human behavior which takes place in time and space, several spheres of validity of the norm may be distinguished: (1) the spatial sphere of validity, that is to say, the space for which the norm is valid, the space within which human beings shall behave in the way prescribed by the norm; (2) the temporal sphere of validity, that is the time for which the norm is valid, the time within which human beings shall behave in the way prescribed by the norm; (3) the personal sphere of validity, i.e., the persons to whom validity extends, who shall behave as prescribed by the norm; (4) the material sphere of validity, i.e., the behavior prescribed by the norm — in short: the where, when, who, and how of the behavior prescribed by the norm. Instead of sphere of validity we usually speak of jurisdiction, the authority of organs to create or to administer norms of a certain sphere of validity. But as the jurisdiction (*Kompetenz*) of the organ is determined by the sphere of validity of the norm created or administered by the organ, the conception of the sphere of validity certainly is the primary one.

3. *The Legal Norm as a Coercive Norm*

The specific difference between the legal and other social norms, between the social technique known as "law" and other methods designed to bring about a certain behavior of men, is to be found in the material sphere of validity. Legal norms are coercive norms. In order to bring about the desired behavior, the norm threatens the person disobeying it with a coercive act which he deems an evil. Such coercion would lie in depriving an individual, against his will, of life, liberty, or property. Thus the specific structure of a legal norm is revealed as the typical rule of law (*Rechts-Gesetz*); it connects two facts, a certain fact, as the condition, with another fact — the coercive act — as the consequence. The simplest example is the norm of criminal law. If some one commits larceny, he shall be punished. It is one of the most important contentions of the Pure Theory of Law that the whole material of positive law can be rendered in rules of this fundamental form.

4. *Legal Order and Basic Norm*

A plurality of norms forming one system constitutes an order. The unity of an order is based on the fact that all the norms constituting this order have the same ground of validity, i.e., they can be traced back to one and the same basic norm. The basic norm of the legal order is the one which determines in what way the norms belonging to the order are to be created. All these norms are valid because, and insofar as, they have been created in the way prescribed by the basic norm. It is in this sense that they are positive legal norms. They belong to one and the same legal order because and insofar as their validity is established upon the same basic norm. The supreme basic norm cannot be "created" in the same sense as the norms of the legal order whose unity is founded upon it. This basic norm is not created by the organs of the legal order, but is presupposed by legal cognition; the basic norm is therefore not a positive but a hypothetical norm.

5. *The "Pyramid of Law"* (*Hierarchy of the Legal Order*)

If one views the law in its dynamic aspect of creation, rather than in its static aspect of validity, and observes that it is the law itself which regulates its own creation, he finds that the norms of a legal order are not all on the same level. They must be thought of as being divided into the several layers of a structure within which the relation of sub- and superordination prevails. It is not possible here to go into the details of the theory of the pyramid of law; one illustration will suffice: the constitutional norms regulate the creation of the statutes, i.e., of the general norms of the legal order; the statutes regulate the creation of the individual norms, i.e., of judicial and administrative acts.

The constitutional norms are, therefore, higher than statutory ones, and the latter are higher than the ones created by judicial decisions and administrative acts. The contrast between the creation and application of the law (*legislatio* and *legis executio*) is, therefore, only relative. In relation to the determining higher constitutional norm, the creation of a lower norm, e.g., of a statute, is not merely an application or execution of law, but it is law-making, as far as the created norm — the statute itself — is concerned. A judicial decision is application of the law with regard to the controlling statute, and lawmaking insofar as it creates an individual norm regulating the behavior of the parties to an action, their rights and duties. The legal order consists not only of general norms, i.e., of norms which regulate in an abstract way an unlimited number of cases, but also of individual norms, which, on the basis of general norms, authorize and oblige only a single individual in a single case, and whose validity is exhausted with the carrying out of the particular ruling. Thus, the norm of a judicial decision imposes the duty on a certain individual of paying a sum of money to another individual under threat of forced execution; or an administrative act requires a certain employer to install a protective device on a certain machine in his factory. Only by recognizing that the individual norms, also, are a part of the legal order, is it possible fully to understand their structure. The acts by which the individual norms of judicial or administrative decisions are executed no longer belong to the legal order as a system of legal *norms*. They are legal *acts*, but only acts of application, no longer creative of new norms. The distinction between legislation and execution, therefore, merely refers to two or more stages in the process of lawmaking.

6. *Law and the State*

It is a traditional conception that every legal order constitutes a community of law. This distinction, however, between an order as a system of norms and the community constituted by this order is a superfluous duplication which is the source of many misunderstandings. The "community," which is to be distinguished from the individuals who are said to "constitute" it, is nothing but the order regulating the behavior of these individuals. Juridical cognition cannot have any object but the legal order, i.e., the legal norms constituting this order. Juridical cognition can grasp the community of law only in the legal order; consequently, it can recognize the state only as a legal order. It is one of the most important, and hitherto unrefuted, doctrines of the Pure Theory of Law that the state, as an order of human behavior, is not a being different from the law, but the law itself; or, more precisely, the legal order or its personification. The legal order known as "the state" is distinguished from the other legal orders in the following way: its spatial sphere of validity is limited in a specific manner (the territory of the state); its personal sphere of validity is "the nation"; its general validity signifies the "sovereign power," just as the state's "powers" or functions — legislation, adjudication, and administration — are different phases in the process of law-making; and, lastly, this legal order is centralized to a specific degree. It is by this last fact that the state is distinguished from the pre-statal, primitive community of law and from the super-statal community of international law. It is only as a consequence of its decentralization that the international community does not constitute a super-state.

A legal co-ordination of the individual states' legal orders (or, what amounts to the same thing, of the individual states themselves), i.e., their legal delimitation in their several spheres of validity — spatial, temporal, personal, and material — is only conceivable if there be above them an all-embracing legal order which provides for a division of their respective spheres of validity. The Pure Theory of Law has shown that either this supreme legal order is positive international law or that the function of international law can be interpreted in this sense. Thus the unity of all positive law can be understood as the unity of a universal system of legal norms, of a legal order which embraces international law and the municipal laws of all the states. This unity, of course, is not to be understood in a political sense, but exclusively in the sense of a theory of cognition.

7. *Centralization and Decentralization as Forms of the Legal Order*

From the preceding discussion it appears that the state must be recognized as identical with the legal order, and the so-called elements of the state as merely the validity and spheres of validity of this order. Consequently it is evident that centralization and decentralization, generally considered as forms of organization of the state with reference to its territorial division, must be understood by a juridical theory as particular forms of this legal order (and only secondarily, of the community itself established by this order); they must therefore be understood as problems of the validity or of the creation of legal norms. In fact, all the relevant phenomena in this connection are comprehended in a juridical theory which is concerned with the sphere of validity of the norms constituting the legal order, and with the organs creating and administering them. It may even be said that an exact determination of the problem is possible only in this way.

8. *The Static Concept of*
Centralization and Decentralization

The conception of a centralized legal order implies that all its norms have the same spatial sphere of validity, i.e., that they are valid throughout the whole territory over which it extends. A decentralized legal order, on the other hand, consists of norms which have different spatial spheres of validity, so that all or certain norms are valid only for parts of a given territory. These are territorial subdivisions (part-territories) only because and insofar as other norms of the same legal order are valid for a sphere embracing these subdivisions, that is, for the total territory of that legal order. The norms valid for the subdivisions form partial legal orders and constitute partial communities of law which are the members, differentiated in space, of a total community of law. That the territory of such a community is subdivided means that certain norms of the legal order constituting that community are valid only for those territorial subdivisions, that the norms of this legal order have different spatial spheres of validity, and that this legal order is decentralized. If one considers in particular the community of law of the state, the so-called territorial division is nothing but the decentralization of the legal order of the state.

Two norms valid for different regions, but relating to the same subject matter, that is, norms which, while having a different spatial, have the same material, sphere of validity, may regulate their subject matter (e.g., trade) in different ways for the two different spatial spheres. Basically, this possibility of regulating the same subject matter in a different way for different partial territories is one of the principal reasons for the decentralization of the state. The considerations which render such differentiation of the legal order of the state for different partial territories advisable are manifold. Geographical, national, and religious differences within the material to be regulated by the law must be taken into consideration; the larger the territory and the greater the possibilities of differentiation in the social relations which are to be regulated the more necessary will be this territorial division of the community of law.

9. Principles of Organization
Based on Territory or on Personal Status

The community of law may be divided on a basis other than the territorial. The partial communities of which the total community consists need not be established on a territorial basis; it may be personal, i.e., the norms of the legal order, or certain of them, may have the same material and spatial, but a different personal, sphere of validity. The same subject matter is regulated for the whole territory, but in a different way for different groups, as these groups vary in religion, language, race, profession. In this fashion all the norms regulating religious life may be valid for the whole territory, but among them one set would apply only to Catholics, another to Protestants, and a third to Mohammedans; thus, of course, the religious affairs of the different faiths would be variously regulated in accordance with the differences in belief. Such organization based on personal status is necessary, if the members of the various communities of religion, language, race, profession, are not settled exclusively in a particular part of the territory; territorial organization alone would not in this case permit the desired differentiation of the legal order with regard to its content. The principle of personal status is, therefore, a principle of organization totally different from the territorial. Only if the organization is carried out according to the territorial principle do we

speak of decentralization; we may also speak in this case
of a system organized by provinces, inasmuch as the territorial subdivisions for which certain norms of the legal
order are valid, and according to which the whole territory
is organized, may be called "provinces" in the widest
sense of the term.

10. *Total and Partial Centralization and Decentralization*

The decentralization, or territorial division of the community of law, as also the corresponding centralization,
may be of quantitatively varying degree. This degree is
determined by the relative proportion of the number and
importance of the central and decentral (local) norms of
the legal order. The "central" norms are the norms valid
for the total territory; the "decentral" or "local" norms
are the norms which are valid only for the territorial subdivisions. We distinguish, therefore, total, and partial,
centralization and decentralization. Total centralization
prevails if all the norms of a legal order are valid without
exception for the total territory; total decentralization
prevails if all the norms without exception are valid only
for territorial subdivisions. If there is total centralization or
decentralization, the quantitative degree of decentralization or centralization, respectively, is zero. But total
centralization and total decentralization are only ideal
extremes (poles). Even in the case of an extreme decentralization, at least one norm, even if only the hypothetical
·basic one, must be valid for the total territory embracing
all partial territories; even in this case, therefore, a minimum of centralization is necessary; otherwise, we could not
speak of decentralization as the territorial division, or organization in space, of one and the same community of
law; we could not speak of decentral (local) norms of a

single legal order. Neither this highest quantitative degree
of decentralization nor total centralization is to be found
in the reality of positive law. Positive law knows only the
most varying types of partial decentralization, between the
two extremes of total centralization and total decentralization, which at the same time always constitute types of
partial centralization.

11. *Criteria of the Quantitative Degree of Decentralization*

Essentially there are two criteria which determine the
quantitative degree of partial decentralization and, in consequence, of the corresponding centralization: the number
of stages in the legal order to which decentralization and
centralization extend, and the number and importance of
subject matters regulated by decentral (local) or central
norms. Only one stage, or several stages, of the legal order
may be decentralized or centralized, and decentralization
or centralization may refer only to one, to several, or to all
the subject matters of legal regulation. The constitution
alone, for example, may be centralized, i.e., only the norms
controlling legislation may be valid for the whole territory,
while the other stages of the legal order (legislation and
execution, adjudication and administration) are decentralized in regard to all matters of legal regulation. In this
case all the norms of the two lower stages — the abstract
norms of the statutes created in conformity with the constitution, and the individual norms of a judicial and administrative type based on these statutes — regardless of their
subject matter, have a decentral or local character: they
are valid only for territorial subdivisions. It is further possible that legislation and administration be only partially decentralized, when only the general norms regulating specific
subject matters and the individual norms which are to put

them into execution have a local character; for example, decentralization may apply only to the administration of agriculture and industry, while the other subject matters of legal regulation are centralized, in which case the material sphere of validity, the material jurisdiction, is divided between the central order and the local orders. As an alternative, not only the stage of the constitution, but also that of legislation, may be centralized in regard to all subject matters of legal regulation, and only the executive stage (adjudication and administration) be decentralized. In other words, all general norms, not only constitutional but statutory ones as well, are central, whereas the individual norms (judicial and administrative) have a decentral or local character, their sphere of validity being restricted to certain parts of the total territory. In this case again the execution may be totally or only partially decentralized, depending on whether all individual norms or only those pertaining to particular subject matters have a local character, i.e., a restricted spatial sphere of validity.

12. The Method of Restricting the Spatial Sphere of Validity

In order fully to understand this restriction of the spatial sphere of validity and with it the nature of a decentral (local) as distinguished from a central norm, we must keep in mind the structure of the legal norm as it has been outlined above. The spatial sphere of validity of a legal norm may be restricted to a given part-territory by relating to it the two legal determinants (*Tatbestände*) which the norm connects as condition and consequence, i.e., the conditioning as well as the conditional part of the legal rule. In other words, the norm will attribute legal consequences only to (conditioning) facts occurring within the part-territory, and the legal consequence — the coercive act and its procedural preparation — must take place within the same part-territory. On the other hand, the restriction of the spatial sphere of validity may be limited to only one of the two parts of the legal rule. If the international legal order delimits the sphere of validity of the legal orders of the particular states, this delimitation is accomplished in principle by restricting to its own territory only the coercive acts provided for in the norms of that particular state's legal order. In other words, the legal order of each individual state, according to international law, must direct the coercive acts it prescribes to be carried out only within its own territory, which, therefore, is a partial territory of the universal international legal order. However, the legal order of the individual state may attach the coercive act as a consequence to conditioning facts which have occurred even outside of its territory. In the above-mentioned case of partial decentralization of the legal order of the state, decentralization refers only to the stage of individual norms; constitution and legislation remain centralized, and only adjudication and administration are decentralized for the most part; the spatial sphere of validity of the decentral (local) norms is restricted in this case by the provision that only the conditioning, not the conditioned, fact defined by the norm (the coercive act) must take place within the partial territory to which the validity of the individual norm is restricted. The decentralization of the administration of justice provides an example. The territory of the state is divided into several judicial districts. Each local court has jurisdiction only for its district, which means that individual norms created by the court, such as its criminal decisions, must refer to delinquencies committed within the district of the court; but the penalty provided need not necessarily be so ordered that it can be executed only within the same district.

13. The Dynamic Concept of
Centralization and Decentralization

The problem of centralization and decentralization has not only its static aspect, in which it is concerned with different spatial spheres of validity of the norms constituting a legal order, but also its dynamic aspect, in which it is concerned with the methods of norm-making, with the organs creating and executing the norms. Whether the central or local norms are created and executed by the same organ, or by several organs, and how these organs are created, become important questions. Centralization in the static sense is, therefore, possible, whether there are one or more organs which create the central norms. But the idea of centralization finds a more significant expression if all central norms are created and executed by a single and simple organ, i.e., an organ which is not composed of several individuals.

As we have said, a centralized as well as a decentralized legal community (in the static sense) is possible, regardless of whether there is unity or plurality of organs creating the norms. Nevertheless, the concept of centralization is commonly connected with the idea of norms valid for the whole territory and created by a single organ which, so to speak, forms the center of the community and is generally located in the geographical center. On the other hand, the concept of decentralization is generally connected with the idea of a plurality of organs, which are not located in the center but spread over the whole territory, and are competent to create norms valid only for partial territories. There is, therefore, a certain inclination to speak of decentralization, even if there is only a plurality of organs creating norms and regardless of the sphere of validity of the norms created. If, for instance, central norms of a differing material sphere of validity, i.e., norms regulating different subject matters, are not created by the same, but by different organs (and this is the case in the system of different ministries in a modern central government), there is by no means decentralization in the static sense. If also in this case we speak of decentralization and distinguish it from the case in which all central norms, regardless of the difference of their material sphere of validity, are created by the same organ, the term acquires a dynamic meaning, totally different from its static meaning. In theory it is possible for all local norms valid only for partial territories, and even the central and all local norms, to be created by the same organ, i.e., by one and the same individual, even if by different acts. This would amount to the coincidence of a partial static decentralization and a total dynamic centralization. If the same individual functions here as the organ creating the central and the local norms, a personal union must be held to exist between the organs of the different orders (or communities) which are constituted by the central and by the local norms. But it should be borne in mind that, in this case of a partial static decentralization, there are one centralized and several local orders with different spatial spheres of validity. It is true that decentralization may be resorted to because it permits the creation of different norms for different partial territories, relative to the same subject matter; in other words, the regulation of the same subject matter in a different way for different partial territories. In this case, it will generally be preferable, for psychological reasons, not to allow the same individual to create the norms of the central order as well as those of the different local orders. It will be preferable to have different individuals act as norm-making organs of the different partial orders, and thus to avoid a personal union of the organs of the different orders.

For the dynamic conception of centralization and decentralization not only the unity or plurality of the organ but also the manner of its creation is of importance. A hereditary monarch or a minister appointed by him (whose jurisdiction extends over the whole territory of the state) on the one hand, and a president elected by the whole nation on the other, clearly illustrate the contrast between a centralized and a decentralized creation of organs. This becomes more clearly evident if one contrasts a president elected by the whole nation with a legislative and executive organ composed of representatives of territorial partial communities, i.e., of individuals elected by one of the partial communities into which the nation is divided, such as the upper house of a federal state. As far as the creation of organs is concerned, the house has a much more decentralized character than the president, regardless of the respective spatial spheres of validity of the norms created by those two organs. There is both static and dynamic decentralization if the legal order valid for only a partial territory is established by organs created (by election especially) by that partial community which is itself a creature of the partial order. Statutes, for example, are valid only for a member-state if they have been passed by the popularly elected legislature of this member-state. There is both static decentralization and dynamic centralization if a hereditary monarch creates different religious statutes for different territorial parts of his realm because of their religious divergencies whereas his other statutes are valid for the whole territory.

14. *Form of the State and Form of Organization*

The manner in which norms are created yields, as we have pointed out, the criterion of the dynamic concept of centralization and decentralization. It also determines the difference between autocracy and democracy. It is the essence of democracy that the individuals themselves who are entitled by and bound by the norms create these norms, while under the system of autocracy they are excluded from the creation of legal norms. This constitutes the contrast between autonomy and heteronomy. In the ideal, so-called direct, democracy, the legal order is created by the assembly of the whole nation; the persons creating the norms and bound by these norms are the same. The question arises: Is there an internal connection between the contrast in the forms of state (autocracy and democracy) and that in the forms of organization (centralization and decentralization)?

No such connection exists, if we proceed from the static conception of centralization and decentralization. Autocracies and democracies may be centralized as well as decentralized, i.e., the organs creating the central and the organs creating the local norms may have an autocratic or democratic character. In other words, democracy and autocracy are possible with or without territorial subdivision. But given the dynamic concept of centralization and decentralization, democracy may be characterized as a decentralized method of creating norms. For here the norms are created by the plurality of the individuals whose rights and duties they regulate, while under an autocracy they issue from a single individual set apart from the plurality of individuals who are subject to them. As the creation of norms is concentrated in the person of the autocrat, we may speak of a centralization of lawmaking.

In the same sense, the difference between statutory law and customary law may be understood from the point of view of the contrast between centralization and decentralization. The creation of the norms of customary law by the uniform and continuous behavior of individuals who are to be subject to the norm in formation has a decentralized character for the same reason as the democratic process: it is in fact a form of democratic lawmaking, since it is based on a real, though unconscious, autonomy. The difference between customary and statutory law consists in the fact that the latter is created by a special organ authorized for the creation of law. It is the principle of the division of labor which characterizes the progress from the customary to the statutory creation of law. And the development of organs functioning according to the principle of the division of labor always signifies a certain centralization of the community in the dynamic sense. Once more it must be emphasized that the dynamic concept of centralization and decentralization is wholly different from the static one. Whether the term in question should be reserved for the static concept only, or applied to both, is a rather unimportant, merely terminological, question. It is essential, however, clearly to distinguish these two different phenomena, which the traditional theory has confused.

15. *Democracy and Decentralization*

Apart from the fact that the autocratic creation of norms has a centralistic, the democratic creation of norms a decentralistic, character (the term being used here in its dynamic sense), autocracy has a centralistic, democracy a decentralistic, tendency. A plurality of organs under an autocracy is possible only when the autocrat appoints different organs as his representatives, organs for the creation of norms of certain categories (belonging to different stages or to different material spheres of validity). The very existence of such a plurality of norm-making organs involves a weakening of autocracy, which essentially is a monocracy (and ought to be described as such). The autocrat is, therefore, always inclined to concentrate the greatest possible number of powers and jurisdictions in his person and to regulate the greatest possible number of subject matters by central norms, i.e., by norms valid for the whole territory. Democracy, on the other hand, tends towards decentralization in the dynamic and in the static sense. This tendency is nothing but the inevitable consequence of the principle of majority inherent in a real democracy. The idea of democracy is the principle of liberty in the shape of the principle of self-determination. The realization of democracy demands the utmost conformity between the general will — as it finds expression in the legal order — and the will of the individual members of the community; that is why the legal order is created by the very individuals who are bound by it. Since this creation is consummated by the vote of a majority, central norms valid for the whole territory may easily be in contradiction with the majority will of partial communities. For the fact that the majority of the entire community belongs to a certain political party, nationality, race, language, or religion, is wholly compatible with the fact that in certain partial communities the majority of their members belong to another party, nationality, race, language, or religion. The majority of the entire nation may be socialistic or Catholic, the majority of one or more provinces may be liberal or Protestant. In order, therefore, to diminish the possible contradiction between the content of the legal order and the will of the individual members of the community, in order to approximate as far as possible the real organization to the ideal of democracy, it is necessary that the legal norms constituting the order be valid only for partial territories and, therefore, be created only by the inhabitants of these partial territories so that they may correspond to the majority will of the population in these partial territories. A thoroughgoing spatial organization of the legal community to suit the cultural and political structure of the population, decentralization in other words, is therefore a definitely democratic postulate. Certain circumstances of settlement may render it impossible to adjust a territorial organization to the cultural and political structure of the population. In such a case territorial organization, i.e., decentralization in the static sense, would have to be replaced by organization according to personal status, although its technical possibilities are admittedly very limited.

16. *Perfect and Imperfect Decentralization*

Apart from the quantitative distinction between total and partial decentralization, a qualitative one between perfect and imperfect decentralization is necessary. We speak of perfect decentralization if the creation of norms valid only for a partial territory is final and independent. It is final when there is no possibility that the local norm be abolished or replaced by a central norm. The division of legislative power in the federal state between a central and several local organs furnishes an instance; a certain subject matter then is reserved to local legislation; but in some instances a local statute may be abolished or replaced by a contrary central statute on the principle that federal law overrides state law. The creation of norms valid only for a partial territory is independent when the content of the local norm is not determined by a central norm. Accordingly, there is imperfect decentralization if legislation is divided between a central and several local organs while the content of the local law is determined by the central law in the following way: the central law contains the general principles of regulation, while the local law is restricted to a more detailed application.

17. *Administrative Decentralization*

"Administrative decentralization" is a case of imperfect decentralization in the domain of the executive. Under this system it is typical to have the state divided into administrative and judicial provinces, the provinces into counties, the counties into districts. These are the spheres of validity for the individual norms (judicial or administrative decisions). Certain organs within the hierarchy are authorized to create such norms (ministers, administrators of a province, of a county, of a district; supreme courts, courts of a province, county courts, district courts). Application ("execution") of a statute consists here in the creation of an individual norm with the narrowest sphere of validity by the official of the district or the district court. But this decision is not final. His act may, as on the petition of a party, be reversed or altered by a norm issued from a higher organ. Consequently, the difference between judicial and administrative action is this: in the former, the contents of the norm created by the lower instance cannot be determined by a norm of the superior instance; courts are independent in principle, administrative authorities are dependent.

18. *Decentralization by Local Autonomy*

The so-called decentralization by local autonomy constitutes another type of state organization. As far as local autonomy is concerned, the principle of decentralization is directly and consciously connected with the idea of democracy, i.e., of self-determination. The organ which is authorized to create the individual, and to a certain extent also the general local norms, is elected by those who are bound by the norms it is to create. The resultant legal order constitutes the unit of local self-government of which the municipality is typical. The municipal council, elected by the members of the community, and the mayor, et cetera, elected by the municipal council, are decentralized, local organs. The decentralization refers only to certain subject matters; the scope of municipal authority is restricted to the stage of individual norms. But there is also a possibility of general norms, so-called autonomous statutes which have to stay within the framework of the central statutes. Such decentralization is theoretically perfect, at least with respect to the autocratically organized central organs of the state. These, however, generally have a right of supervision and are authorized to annul acts of the community which violate statute law: but they may not modify them by norms they create themselves. A local unit may be combined with others to form a more comprehensive (superior) unit of local autonomy, so that its administration is not only in the first but also in the higher stages democratic self-government. Then the degree of decentralization in the relation between the inferior and the superior self-governing body may be diminished. Nothing prevents in this case the establishment of a series of hierarchic instances proceeding from the smaller to the larger unit, in which the superior organs would have the authority to reverse and revise the acts of the inferior ones. The high degree of decentralization of the autonomous bodies within the modern state can in the main be traced back to the fact that the modern state was, particularly as far as its central organs are concerned, in principle autocratically organized, whereas the local organs, particularly the municipalities, always had a democratic constitution. Decentralization of these democratic organs of the state meant the elimination of the influence of autocratic central organs. The struggle for local autonomy is — or was originally — a struggle for democracy. Within an essentially democratic state the grant of local autonomy to any territorially defined group means only decentralization. The "autonomous" right of local self-governing bodies against the state, a right so often asserted in theory, is nothing but the natural law construction of a political postulate. If the whole state is democratic, there is no longer any reason to affirm a theoretical contrast between state administration and local autonomy ("self-government"). Local autonomy is only a specific form of the administration of the state.

19. *Decentralization by "Countries"*

The degree of decentralization realized by local autonomous bodies may be increased so that the decentralization extends not only to the individual but on principle also to the general norms. This is normally connected with a relatively greater spatial sphere of validity of the local norms. It represents the type of decentralization by "countries" (*Länder*) which existed in the Austrian monarchy before the dismemberment of that state. In this case, legislation and execution are distributed between central and local organs. "Countries" (*Länder*) is a term applied to the partial communities which are represented by local legislative and executive organs and constituted by decentralized partial orders consisting of general and individual norms. It is difficult to distinguish them from larger autonomous bodies, particularly from so-called autonomous provinces; especially if the latter possess to a limited degree the power to create general norms (autonomous "provincial statutes"), and if the legislative and perhaps even the executive organs of the so-called *Länder* are of a democratic character (like elective functionaries). In this case the difference lies solely in the greater extent of legislative power.

20. *Decentralization in the Federal State*

Only a relatively small step separates this latter type from what is known as the "member-state" of a federal union. And even this step consists only in an increase of the degree of decentralization. It is attained if the decentralization does not refer solely to the individual and general norms, so that not only are legislation and execution distributed between a central and several local authorities but the local legislative organs are also empowered to make or amend the constitution of their territory. This power may be granted entirely or partially, i.e., within the framework of the norms set up by the central constitution for the local constitutions. This may be described as a more or less far-reaching constitutional autonomy of partial communities. It is possible also, at least to a certain degree, in the so-called *Länder* (as was the case in the Austrian monarchy). In order that the members may be designated as "states," it is further necessary that they participate in the central legislative or even executive process. Technically, this increase of decentralization is carried out by constituting the organ of central legislation in two bodies. One body is elected by the entire nation as a national chamber or "house of representatives" — an organ which is centralized also in the dynamic sense. The other body is composed of members elected or appointed by local parliaments or local governments — a "chamber of states," or "senate" — and therefore a centralized organ in the static, a decentralized organ in the dynamic, sense. The second chamber may also participate in the central executive power. In such a federal state each member-state through the "chamber of states" is normally conceded the same influence in the formation of the central will of the state: each member-state, without regard to its

size, is given the same number of votes or representatives
in this chamber. Exceptions to this rule are possible. The
same is true as to the relation between the two chambers.
In the normal federal state they have equal powers, yet the
"national chamber" may be privileged over the other, as
by having its legislative resolutions open to a suspensive
veto only by the other chamber.

Only if the essence of the so-called federal state is conceived as a particular degree and specific form of decentralization is it possible to recognize a concrete positive
constitution by its mere content as a federal state. Consequently the mode of its creation becomes irrelevant:
whether it has come into existence by an international
treaty (comprising the federal constitution) between
hitherto "sovereign states," i.e., states subordinated only
to the international legal order; or by statutory act of a
unitary state in the process of transforming itself into a
federal state. Likewise the problem of sovereignty, the
question whether the member-states or the union (i.e., the
local orders, or the central order) is sovereign — or both together — is a fictitious problem which has created wholly
superfluous difficulties in the old doctrine.

21. *Federal State and Confederation of States as Different Degrees of Decentralization*

If the federal state is understood as a type of decentralization, there is no difference in principle between the
federal state and the confederation of states. Here again
there is a difference only in degree, for in the latter form we
have a still higher degree of decentralization. Like the federal
state, the confederation of states shows a distribution
of legislative and executive power between central and
local authorities. In the federal state the most important
powers are vested in the central order, or at least there is a

certain equilibrium between the powers of the central and local authorities, foreign affairs in particular being ordinarily an exclusive function of the union, i.e., the central order. In the confederation of states, on the other hand, accordance of jurisdiction to the central order is exceptional, as to both extent and importance. In principle, the member-states claim jurisdiction, but certain matters may be assigned to the confederation, even exclusively, as is usually the case with foreign affairs. The member-states, however, may also retain a certain concurrent power over foreign affairs. Further, the central legislation is entrusted to an organ not based on direct election by the people, but composed of delegates appointed by the governments of the confederated states. All members are, at least in principle, equally represented. Resolutions on certain important matters, particularly constitutional amendments, require unanimity; for others, a majority of votes suffices. It is particularly significant that the norms created by the central organ have only indirect validity for the subjects, because the statutes of the confederation must be promulgated by the individual states before they become binding on the individuals whose behavior they regulate.

With regard to the central norms, the process of legislation is, therefore, only partially centralized; significantly enough, the act of promulgation which makes them binding on the citizens is under local jurisdiction. As compared with that of the federal state, the organization of the executive branch is little developed in the confederation of states. While the federal state has not only a legislative but also an executive organ, generally also a head of the state of its own, as in the unitary state, the central legislative organ of the confederation of states — either directly or through a committee — takes care also of the executive functions which come under central jurisdiction. Executive acts, too, have in principle only indirect validity; but exceptions are more frequent here than in the domain of legislation. We may give as an example executive acts concerning military affairs for which the individual states retain authority. In the typical confederation, each state, in case of war, provides a certain military contingent; but all the contingents are under a commander-in-chief of the confederation, either elected by the central organ or directly designated by the constitution of the confederation. The expenditures of the confederation are covered by so-called "immatricular" contributions of the member-states. The federal state normally has the power to create and execute tax laws which are directly binding upon the subjects. In case a member-state does not comply with the duties imposed by the confederate constitution the confederation may resort to a so-called federal execution (a military coercive act, warlike in nature) against the state violating its obligations. In the federal state collective responsibility for the result may be replaced by individual responsibility for a fault of that state organ to which the federal constitution attributes the fulfilment of the member-state's corporate duty. In this case, the establishment of the fault and the rendering of a decision may lie with an objective court.

22. *The Unions*

The associations of states known as "unions" have a still smaller degree of centralization. No general norms at all, but only individual norms, no legislative, but only executive, acts can be brought into being with a validity for the entire union. We speak of "unions" especially in the case of monarchical states united by the fact of having the same monarch. If these states are constitutional monarchies in which the acts of the monarch require the

countersignature of a responsible minister, common ministers must be provided for the affairs concerning which
executive acts, valid for the union of states, are possible,
normally foreign affairs and war: a common foreign minister, a common minister of war. Or these acts must be done
by the common monarch with the countersignature of the
authorized ministers of both states of the union. If foreign
affairs and war in their entirety are common, as regards
executive acts, it follows that the other organs of these departments of administration are common also: a common
diplomatic representation abroad, a common army. But
apart from the common army there may be an independent
army of each of the two states of the union. The common
executive acts are taken on the basis of union member-state
statutes, which are not common, but identical in contents.
Insofar as there must be arrangements to bring about this
identity of contents, parliamentary committees which
meet in common or exchange their resolutions appear —
the beginnings of an organization which makes the union
approximate a confederation of states or even a federal
state. In this case, we speak of a "real union." If there is
only a common monarch but no possibility of executive
action with common validity for the two states of the
union, we speak of a "personal union"; then, for example,
no common treaty valid for both states of the union can be
concluded with third states; but in order to accomplish
this, the monarch has to conclude a treaty for each of the
two states whose common monarch he is. In this case
the union is based on the sole fact that only the bearer of
the organ-function of "head of the state" is common, but
not the function and therefore not the organ.

A union of states in the larger sense of the term is finally
constituted by each international treaty by which two or
more states bind themselves to observe reciprocally a cer-

tain behavior with regard to a certain end. The degree of their centralization is decisive for the classification of such unions: whether or not the treaty which constitutes the union authorizes the creation of general or individual norms with validity for the entire territory of the union of states. Because of the extent and importance of the matters for which such creation of norms is possible, other forms of organization may come into existence which more or less resemble the ones known as composite states in a more restricted sense of the term, such as the federal state, the confederation of states, and the real or personal union.

23. The International Community

The international community, too, is a union of states. The customary norms of the so-called general international law are the general norms valid for the entire territory of the international community. Its constitution according to which new general norms may be created by a conscious act is expressed in the rule: *pacta sunt servanda*. This means that general norms for the territory of two or more, or even all the states, may be created on the basis of unanimity by an organ constituted by representatives of the states for whose territory the intended norm shall be valid. The constitution of international law leaves the determination of their representatives to the constitutions of the individual states. In concluding a concrete international treaty the organs of these states (heads of states, ministers of foreign affairs, parliaments) together form the organ of the international community, an organ creating particular or, if all the states conclude the treaty, general international law. The representative of each contracting party is a partial organ of the entire organ which creates the treaty-norm. The international community is, therefore, typical of a partially decentralized legal order. More closely organized partial communities can be created by treaty within the international community — partial communities which, so to speak, stand between the international community and the legal orders of the individual sovereign states.

24. Centralization and Decentralization as Principium Individuationis

The idea of centralization and decentralization is, therefore, the fundamental structural principle in the different communities of law: the very *principium individuationis* which constitutes the variety of legal formations as contrasted with the idea of unity, the *principium unitatis*, the basic norm. It is the law according to which all legal formations may be arranged as a continuous line of formations gradually passing into one another. This continuous line starts with the contractual community of private law, leads to the association, the municipality, the country, the member-state, the federal state, the unitary state, unions of states, and treaty communities of international law, and ends in the universal international community.

NOTE

1 Cf. my study, *Reine Rechtslehre* (Vienna, 1934), with detailed bibliography. In English, see: Kelsen, "The Pure Theory of Law," *The Law Quarterly Review*, 1934–35, pp. 474 ff. and pp. 517 ff.; Kunz, "The 'Vienna School' and International Law," *New York University Law Quarterly Review*, 1934, pp. 1 ff.; Lauterpacht, "Kelsen's Pure Science of Law," in *Modern Theories of Law* (Oxford, 1933); Voegelin, "Kelsen's Pure Theory of Law," *Political Science Quarterly*, 1927, pp. 268 ff.; Wilson, "The Basis of Kelsen's Theory of Law," *Politica*, 1934, pp. 54 ff.

THE PROBLEM OF AUTHORITY AND THE CRISIS OF THE GREEK SPIRIT*

WERNER JAEGER, PH.D., LITT.D.

Professor of Classical Philology, University of Chicago
(formerly of the University of Berlin)

THE theme of authority and individual freedom, although one of the burning questions of our day, is yet as old as higher civilization itself; and the series of lectures which has just been delivered on this subject would be incomplete without some attempt to trace the influence of this problem upon the intellectual development of Greece. The Greeks are the authors of individual liberty; and as one cannot speak of authority, in any sense relevant for us, except where the level of a free individual mind has already been attained, the problem of authority has its historical origin only with the Greeks, although in a different sense the Oriental civilizations were highly authoritarian. The Greek solutions of this question as of many others possess that happy combination of theoretical consistency and typical ideality which gives them an immediate significance for our life despite all changes of outward circumstance.

Out of the unlimited profusion of features I choose a certain sector from the curve of Greece's intellectual development, the social and spiritual crisis which coincides, in point of time, with the great war among the Greek states

---

* Translated from the German by Mrs. W. L. Langer, Cambridge, Mass.

in the last third of the fifth century. This is the classical age of the great fundamental conflict between authority and the individual.

The historian cannot begin, like the philosopher, by defining his concepts. The discourse itself must endow them with life and content. None the less it may be possible to elucidate what I mean by authority, and by its critical period in the intellectual history of Greece, by contrasting the Greek with the Roman spirit in order to illuminate a characteristically Greek situation.

Authority is in itself a Roman concept. It might seem like a misuse of the term to apply it to Greek affairs at all. The absence of a real equivalent in the Greek language for the Latin *auctoritas* is, of course, in itself no proof that the same or a similar condition might not have prevailed among both peoples; but the Romans, just by virtue of their contact with Greek philosophy and science, have given the notion a very peculiar turn, and its perpetuation in the Roman Catholic Church makes this directly important to our own intellectual life. The mind of Rome opened very readily to the influence of rational thought as embodied in Greek science, but among the Romans this type of thinking loses its radical, transforming power; it does not penetrate to the depths of the Roman mind.

In Cicero's dialogue on the Nature of the Gods, the Roman Pontifex Maximus Cotta, a man of excellent philosophical education, refuses to base the truth of the established religion on the Stoics' rational proofs of God, and accomplishes the neat trick of being a skeptic in his private philosophy while as Pontifex he finds support for his faith in the *auctoritas* of the Roman cult and its tradition. So we may see that this Roman, when faced with the naïve self-confidence of Greek criticism and science, has a feeling of reserve, indeed of superiority; in his conception of authority lies a strain of super-intellectual, one might say historical, reason.

It is inconceivable that the Greek mind should have recognized such a distinction even though the argument is not entirely unknown to Greek thinkers. For the Greek, the discovery of a contradiction between tradition and reason, νόμος and φύσις, would itself involve normally a decision in favor of reason. For to him reason represents Nature, the only truth and necessity. Whereas Roman conservatism rejects the uninhibited use of this criterion, because that would require the sacrifice and devaluation of some piece of long-established experience, the Greek, on the contrary, takes his cognition of natural fact as a legislative norm. He feels and evaluates natural knowledge as essentially constructive, not destructive; in fact, reason is his true cosmic organon.

In this light we may view the whole history of Greece — political as well as intellectual — as one superb struggle for the dignity and authority of a true norm of life. Of course there was, in Greece as elsewhere, before and beside the authority of reason, an authority of mere tradition or of divine sanctions, especially in those quarters where rational science had not yet penetrated or where people sought to barricade themselves against such influences. But those are not the places or the circles which have formed Greek civilization. The latter are characterized by their faith in rational insight and a tendency to replace the authority of mere social growths by the authority of reason. In contrast to the Roman feeling for *collective* reason, embodied in historical tradition, Greek authority is most visibly incarnate in the works and acts of *creative individual personalities*, the poets, sages, and law-givers, the pioneers of new knowledge. These all have some aureole of intellectual prophethood, they are the teachers and educators of their nation. Such creativity presupposes an amazing mental freedom, and leads others toward that freedom. But it must be remembered that every one of these men regarded his insight as an obligation in the deepest sense, a civic function within the community. Without that freedom to which human individuality rises in these creative geniuses, Greek civilization could not have come into being. Without it, moreover, the Greek spirit could never have attained that supreme authority, in the highest sense of the word, which binds us by its law even to the present day.

In the field of politics the same reciprocity of heightened individual initiative and conscious inner obligation is exhibited by the life of the average Greek citizen in the great first period of the Athenian democracy. In this state, according to its conception, Law itself was to be king. Protagoras' theory of education made the law the true mentor of the man who had outgrown his schooling. The ideal of this constitution, as Pericles formulates it in his eulogy of the dead warriors in Thucydides, consists of combining the authoritative power of any healthy administration with the greatest scope of personal freedom for the individual in speech, thought, and action, even in matters of private taste and pleasure; and the real measure of a statesman is the degree to which he can carry out this ideal. But freedom, for Pericles, is not synonymous with mechanical equality of all individuals; he ranges their worth and corresponding political standing in three categories. The great mass of citizens enjoy, above all, equal rights before the law, full respect for every individual, though he be of ever so modest means. Within certain limits the average man is to have, besides his professional training, some education to participate in the tasks and problems of civic life. Persons of higher ability are recognized as such and form a sort of natural aristocracy. The government of the state lies in the hand of one ruler, the "foremost man." Pericles could not, of course, say that himself in his speech, but Thucydides presents him thus. The Athenian state in its Periclean form is the prototype of the so-called mixed constitution, designed to bring the democratic, the aristocratic, and the monarchical principle into harmonious combination. That this ideal was the inspiration to Thucydides' eulogy cannot be doubted, as he explicitly refers to it himself in another connection.

It might seem as though the statesmanship of Pericles, with its skillful balance of all social elements, must have found the solution of our problem once and for all. But the classic form is always just one irretrievable moment in the crescendo and equilibrium of conflicting forces. The fatally long war which broke Hellas in its fullest flower was indeed not the cause, but only a hastening factor in precipitating the insidious disease that was wasting the national organism. Likewise the sophistic philosophy which is often held responsible for the fall of Greece is greatly overestimated if we take it for anything more than the conscious expression of that process which in fact pervaded everything. In one respect the Greek mind remains true to form in its destruction as in its growth; namely, in that it still measures all things by a criterion derived from Nature itself. But whereas formerly the recognition of an all-equalizing justice of Being had served as a foundation whereon the sovereignty of Law could be erected, a later age gathered from its natural insights a very different picture: self-preservation seemed the only law which all creatures naturally followed. Even mind appeared to be nothing more than a convenient implement in the unrestricted war of each against all; the state, a tool in the hands of a temporarily ruling caste for the exploitation of all other men; and the Law merely the expression of the will of the strongest. Moral ideals were taken to be a reflection of what society deemed expedient, or accepted as a necessary fiction, a formidable screen behind which it could cater without restraint to the egoistic demands of its own self; political freedom was regarded as simply an organization of the weaker to counterbalance the dangerous superiority of the few that were truly capable, and religion as a fabrication of clever statesmen, by which they gave their laws mandatory power even in the absence of witnesses. Such is the philosophy of Nature portrayed in variegated, scintillating colors by the poets and Sophists of the time. Thucydides, the great historical realist, describes this transvaluation of all values from the depth of his own suffering under the fate of his generation, the unbearable burdens of war that enervate and sap the moral organism: the general dislocation of all ethical concepts. The State itself, spurning no means for its outward defense, defying all rights, sets its citizens an example of that mock-morality which presently governs even business and private relations: the right of the stronger. This is the only law that can maintain itself in the face of that consistent, unreluctant naturalism.

It is an impressive spectacle how the Greek spirit, with inner strength yet unbroken, strives throughout that whole fourth century that followed the collapse of its greatest constructive feats in state and society to make way for a new authority. The struggle took three different directions: intellectually, it produced the Socratic and Platonic philosophy; politically, the return to tyranny, which, though diametrically opposed to the Platonic doctrine, yet had one point of contact with it, and even of mutual attraction: the attempt to set up a new authority by denying personal freedom in the community. The third direction may be seen in the restoration of democracy after it had been deeply shaken by the fall of Athens, especially in its classical home and stronghold, Athens itself, where a radical breach with the traditional forms of democracy proved to be impracticable.

The Platonic philosophy is sprung entirely from the tragic historical conditions of that fall, which in its eyes was not merely an overthrow of an external power, but the collapse of a long-tottering moral and intellectual world. That is why Socrates, despite his abstinence from active political life which made him an object of suspicion to his democratic fellow men, appears in the Platonic writings as a political figure, and indeed as the only political figure of his time. Thus, Plato has sought consistently to deduce the construction of an ideal state from the Socratic pursuit of the good; a state whose aim is to set up new norms of life, and to train its future leaders according to these norms. The Platonic philosophy is the greatest instance of the belief in the authoritative power of knowledge. We are able to understand this belief at that point where the philosophical mind first aspires to the Idea and the Universal. That is a new, all-controlling sort of truth, and at this point science becomes the highest form of education. Plato's aristocratic antipathy against excess of freedom, which in most communities of his day had turned into its very opposite, together with his deep admiration for Sparta, led him to conceive a state which one might describe as an intellectualized Spartanism. In this state, the authoritarian principle is carried to very great lengths; in the Laws, even to the extent of an Inquisition against those who do not believe in gods. The general sentiment of Greece is better reflected in the criticism of Aristotle, who brands Plato's ideal state as exaggerated and revolutionary. Yet obviously the best minds of the time tended very strongly to sacrifice the prize of individual liberty, which had been the goal for centuries of struggle, for the sake of a stable order and universally valid standard. Of course one must not forget that the Platonic philosophy deemed itself capable of creating such an order on a basis of eternal truth, and that that authority to which Plato entrusts the supreme command was to have its roots in a transcendental realm.

In practical politics, the demand for a more authoritarian government arose from purely mundane motives. The mechanics of a democracy as great as Athens, which Thucydides still regarded as the high-water mark of political construction, proved too complicated to maintain itself in the universal struggle for power. Especially in Syracuse and in Cyprus, where the tradition of personal liberty was neither so old nor so strong, and the Greeks were constantly on the defensive against foreign nations such as the Carthaginians and the Persians, it was not hard for an improvised dictatorship to develop along militaristic lines and to maintain itself for several decades. Plato would have been ready to recognize it, had only Dionysius of Syracuse been ready, for his part, to organize the Sicilian states against the aspirations of the Carthaginian power, on the basis of Plato's notions of political reform. The demand for authority had sprung from entirely different sources in the two respective systems: in one from practical, in the other from ethical, considerations. The pure Machiavellian could never follow the way toward that ideal of kingship which was the peak of Plato's ethico-political program.

Dionysius was fond of composing tragedies, and perhaps he was himself a tragic figure. In politics he ruthlessly went the way of force and national interest. Yet he did it consciously, with a sense of tragic conflict between the cynical policy of power and the ideal of justice, which for

Plato and for all traditional Greek sentiment was the true soul of the state.

This form of tyranny, commonly referred to as the second tyranny, must have harbored some deeper historical necessity, since the general trend of the times supported it, and it arose in several places in rapid succession. Even in Sparta this age produced a Lysander and an Agesilaus, who sometimes approach very close to dictatorship; but their state, in the long run, proved to be incapable of carrying on the modern politics of power without serious damage to that social and moral structure so greatly admired by the philosophers. Athens maintained its democratic form to the end. In spite of all its shortcomings, which philosophical criticism and the course of history had amply revealed, it was the best form of government for a population of such intellectual independence and individuation, and in its way it was irreplaceable and unforgettable. Here too there was, to the end of the Peloponnesian War, no dearth of attempts to resurrect the authority of the law, now internally shattered, which had been the heart of the old democracy, and to combine it with the tradition of personal liberty. The authority of the state was an essential prerequisite even for the reconstruction of economic credit, as an unknown Sophist wrote directly after the war, but most of all for the sake of education and moral discipline. Of course he cannot base it on any absolute truth, as Plato claimed to do, and this remains the weak point in his scheme, if Plato's requirements are to be realizable at all. But this democratically-minded Sophist proves that disregard for the law, frequently advocated by his own school, is practically equivalent to dictatorship. Here, finally, lawfulness is recommended for the very sake of personal liberty. Isocrates, who represents the wealthy and politically most experienced upper class of Athens, tends in his

comments on domestic policy to limit the excessive freedom of individuals and proposes the formation of a new
Areopagus, which is to serve as an independent authority
and give the state a moral center of gravity. In foreign
policy, the most hotly debated question was whether the
state, weakened by reverses, could best protect the freedom
and welfare of its citizens by holding aloof from world
politics, or by gradually increasing its outward activities,
especially since its conflict with Philip's Macedonian monarchy in the North Aegean. In this encounter, Demos-
thenes once more made liberty his clarion call to arms
against the foreign danger, and combined it with the national cause. It was spiritually a strong program, but
behind it stood no adequate vital force, despite all heroic
spirit of sacrifice. After the battle of Chaeronea, the day of
political individualism was over. The age of great world
monarchies began. But this was no solution of the *inner*
problem of authority which had confronted Plato. To his
mind a solution of this problem was not possible except in
an ideal state. This ideal state which Plato had at first
intended to realize, soon appeared to belong to the same
transcendental world as the Platonic ideas which were its
models. According to Plato's original intention, his philosophical state was to picture an ideal community in which
individualism would have no justification any longer, and
everybody would attain his happiness in devoting himself
to the service of the whole. This was a strict confession of
the value of a real political authority in the midst of social
dissolution. But practically the distinction between the
real and the ideal state means the *withdrawal* of the more
highly organized individual from political life into a merely
spiritual sphere inaccessible to the command of force.
Thus historical events as well as the inner development of
the individual contributed to his retirement from the pub-

lic scene. But not even then could individual autarchy exist without authority, and whereas originally the authority of the state had been based on its divine sanction, in post-classical times state and religion become separated from one another and the individual finds the norm of his life immediately in God. It is a most paradoxical fact, but it is a fact, that in a certain sense the spiritual development of the human individual has made its greatest progress since the external world of liberty — which it had built up in the state of the classical time — broke down, and has escaped into the new freedom of the philosophical and religious world within the human soul.

AUTHORITY AND THE INDIVIDUAL DURING THE DIFFERENT STAGES OF THE EVOLUTION OF NATIONS

Corrado Gini, Dr.Jur., Econ.D., Soc.D., S.D.

Professor of Statistics and Sociology, University of Rome

THERE is perhaps no subject of more immediate concern, in the field of social science, than that of "Authority and the Individual," which the Tercentenary Committee has invited me to treat. At the same time, there is none which requires a broader view of the facts, past and present, for reaching some scientific conclusion. Some light may be cast on this problem by examining the relations between authority and the individual during the different stages of the evolution of nations.

That a minimum of authority is necessary for the preservation of the social order is evident; but above that level there are, from population to population and from time to time, tremendous differences. State or civic authority ranges from regimes in which even sexual duties of consorts are in some way regulated by the central power, as was the case in the Jesuit missions of South America, to regimes in which the central power has no other function than defense against exterior enemies. Not less fundamental are the differences in the power of family and religious organization, the two other great sources of authority over the individual; in these fields we may say indeed that the authority ranges from practically all to nothing.

Is it possible, then, to find, among such tremendous variety, some regularities deserving the name of scientific laws? This is the basic problem which confronts us tonight.

It is certain that in the better-known periods of history we may recognize some definite tendencies, dynamic in character, in the relations between authority and the individual. Thus in the modern age as well as in later epochs of ancient Greece and ancient Rome, a gradual disintegration of familial authority is apparent. As for religious authority, we may note a progressive decline from a period of deep mysticism in medieval times till the prevalence of materialistic philosophy in the last century, this in turn having been succeeded by a revival of mysticism in recent years. In the field of political authority, a cycle has long been perceived: the power, concentrated at one time in one or few hands, gradually becomes more fractional and diffused until reaching a regime of democracy, from which more or less suddenly an autocratic regime is rebuilt. In the internal economic field, there has been a distinct transition from corporativism to individualism, and now we observe the contrary movement towards a corporative or syndicalist state. Similarly, in international economic relations history shows the prevalence of paternalistic and mercantilistic conceptions giving place to more and more liberal programs, until a reprisal of protectionism develops and gradually leads to state control of foreign trade, which is more or less pronounced today in all the nations.

It is difficult to deny that those tendencies constitute laws of sequence. But, proceeding a bit further, we may inquire whether there is a consistent correspondence between such regularities and external circumstances or internal conditions of populations, and if these circumstances or conditions may be identified so as to establish in this field laws of dependence or interdependence, which constitute the highest aim of scientific research.

That the various relations between authority and the individual represent adaptations to different external and internal conditions is strongly suggested by the observation that it is not always the same system or regime of relations which meets with success. On the contrary, at times it is one regime and at others another regime; and generally it is the regime most typical of the age which is highly successful, precisely as if it represented the best adaptation. So, in the last century, the triumphant age of individualism, materialism, and laissez-faire policy, England, where this regime was most strongly manifested, attained the greatest achievements; the Roman and Byzantine empires, on the contrary, like the empires of the Aztecs and Incas, provide clear examples of centralized organizations standing as high plateaus in the midst of a plain of political bodies apparently rendered ineffective by the shortcomings of other regimes.

But what are the external and internal conditions which cause an authoritative or an individualistic regime to be better adapted to the age and thus destined to prosper? Moreover, is it possible to discover, among such conditions, some evolutive or cyclical tendencies which may explain the secular trends that we recognize in the history of relations of the individual with the family, the state, and religious authority?

It is clear that an individualistic regime involves a maximum of advantage and a minimum of shortcomings in a population generally endowed with strong personal initiative, confident in its abilities and in collective progress, and simultaneously self-controlled and self-consistent. Where, contrariwise, the people are frivolous and readily deluded, or indolent and pessimistic, where they are traditionalistic, or inconstant and erratic, where the impetus of the passions can be restrained only with difficulty, or apathy is general, there an authoritative regime appears indispensable for stimulating appropriate behavior or for curbing natural excesses.

Homogeneity of physical characteristics, interests, and feelings, which leads to reciprocal sympathy and conformity in behavior, or mutual tolerance, which smooths out existing differences, permits the spontaneous realization of social consensus. But this cannot be attained without the pressure of authority if the people are heterogeneous in respect to race or social position, with contrasting interests and divergent feelings, and, moreover, uncompromising.

Likewise, in the field of intellectual abilities and of artistic and moral ideals, a general average level is more favorable to an individualistic and democratic regime than a condition of marked disparity, which creates a natural hierarchy, facilitates the advent and increases the advantages of a government by the more intelligent and energetic elements. Finally, the presence of a strong personality contributes to the establishment and maintenance of an autocracy.

If the people are enlightened by a system of general education, obviously they are more apt to provide for their own interests; whereas ignorance of the masses and their backwardness, especially in matters of technique and hygiene, demand direction of some sort. On the other hand, the most advanced developments of social science, inasmuch as they enable the prediction of social trends and reveal the existence of a mechanism of self-regulation in the social body, also demand a central agency which may take advantage of such knowledge for directing the national activities.

The hedonistic and rationalistic conception of life, basing society on personal interest, is in keeping with an individualistic order, especially if, as often happens, it is rather epicurean or materialistic in character; while the strength of instincts, of myths, of religious feelings, may act as a good substitute for personal interest in stimulating economic production and social progress and, at the same time, constitute fruitful ground for the development of an authoritative regime.

In many societies the psychology of labor, regulating productive efforts for the attainment of a decent standard of living, constitutes an automatic guarantee against crises of shortage or surplus; while the fundamental instincts of reproduction and accumulation, seconded by scientific curiosity, need of artistic expression, philanthropy, effectively establish co-ordination between the welfare of present and future generations. But if an over-rationalization or a weakness of genetic instincts leads the people to place their own satisfactions above all else and to neglect the generation and welfare of future citizens, authoritative intervention for protecting the collective interests becomes imperative. Similarly, intervention may become necessary to compel assiduity in labor — as for centuries it was done through slavery — if the tendency of the people is to work solely for sheer subsistence; or, on the contrary, to avoid the danger of over-production if the pleasure of laboring — rooted in human psychology through selection and education — leads the captains of industry to push production beyond the absorptive capacity of the market.

Not less important than the intrinsic qualities of population in determining the relations between authority and the individual are the economic conditions of the environment.

In a country with abundant resources and adequate capital, the principal characteristic and aim is the rapid progress of production. Compared with this, problems of distribution or concern with economic cycles are quite secondary in character. A quick response is necessary in order to take full advantage of the multifarious and ever-changing conditions. Individual initiative, stimulated by high compensation of labor and capital and by intensive competition, expands fully and with notable success. A mass of private enterprises of all forms and dimensions, which freely arise, develop, combine, and disappear, originates a spontaneous condition of moving equilibrium. But, when progress slackens, economic cycles, no longer submerged by the upward trend, become more dangerous. Problems of economic stability and distribution of wealth take the ascendancy over those of production and require centralized regulation. In time of crisis the people appeal to the government, which can only with difficulty refuse intervention. From the social point of view, intervention, even if not economically profitable to the nation, may be more advisable than no intervention at all. When remuneration of capital falls below the level of natural interest which compensates the difference between the evaluation of present and future satisfactions, the system of private capital can no longer function, and it is inevitable that the state take in hand the task of production.

This critical point may be hastened by high taxation on capital, necessary to cover heavy fiscal requirements. Uniformity of needs and a consequent rigidity of demand may be a favorable condition for the collectivization of production, inasmuch as production becomes stationary and consumption uniform and standardized. Another favorable circumstance is the territorial concentration of production, which facilitates management by a central agency. Favorable also is the diffusion of giant corporations which accustom employees to work efficiently without the stimulus of personal interest in the undertaking. Great public works which exceed the capacity of private enterprises and whose utility will mature only in the distant future are the natural tasks of public bodies; but these may be called upon to stimulate, integrate, or create large enterprises in other branches of production when private capital is scarce or timid.

Without causing the extreme solution of state capitalism, a strong and increasing inequality of distribution of wealth, or of some special categories of wealth such as land ownership, may well call for redistributive provisions by central authorities, in order to eliminate the economic and social dangers of an all-powerful plutocracy. Similarly, coalitions of employers or employees may become so efficient as to succeed in absorbing, at the expense of the antagonist, all gains derived from production; in which case state intervention is justified for the purpose of re-establishing a more equitable situation. Military conquest, colonization, and control of foreign populations inevitably lead to widespread interference of the state in the individual affairs.

On the other hand, there are special occupations and conditions which are appropriate for the exercise of individual qualities. This is the case for the commercial activities, in which personal initiative and adaptability to particular circumstances assume decisive importance, and consequently for populations largely engaged in such activities. This is, par excellence, the case for scientific research.

Personal qualities are of special importance in sparse populations, where the central power is distant and the individuals must daily face the harshness of nature and the hostility of dangerous animals. With the increase of population, the contacts with other men and with civic authority expand and intensify; competition and co-operation develop hand in hand; social solidarity asserts itself; there arises an increasing interest in the actions and possessions of others, and opportunities for the intervention of central authority correspondingly multiply.

Population may be important, not only in an indirect way, inasmuch as its increase promotes economic relations and social solidarity, but also as a direct objective of state interference.

Where there is an equilibrium between population and available resources, as well as between their respective growths, the state has no basis for interfering with demographic development; but where the population is sparse relative to the territory, or declining, or, on the contrary, where it is superabundant and threatening through an excessive increase to lower the general standard of living, a demographic policy naturally arises and develops.

The qualitative composition of population may also provoke the reaction of authority, as when an undue proportion of youth impresses the trait of impulsiveness upon the nation, or, on the contrary, when the preponderance of aged people induces timidity and indecision, or when heterogeneity of race and tradition makes advisable a policy of amalgamation, or when the burden of degenerate stocks and the weakness of natural selection endanger the biological heritage of the nation.

Having considered the characteristics of populations over which authority must be exerted, we may turn to consider the qualities of the authoritative bodies themselves.

Efficiency, rapidity, adaptability, honesty, sensitivity

to the general needs, and spirit of co-operation with the public are qualities which may or may not be found among officers and leaders, qualities which depend partly upon the characteristics of the people, partly upon the selection, the tradition, and the training of the administration, partly upon circumstances which appeal more or less strongly to social solidarity. These qualities are of paramount importance in deciding the practical advisability of the interference of authority with individual behavior when it is theoretically justified. Another condition is the public confidence, which evidently depends largely upon the previously mentioned qualities, but may also be influenced by other circumstances, such as racial differences between officers and the masses.

The state is, in modern civilized countries, the chief source of authority; but this has not always been the case, and also at present this is true in very different measure in different countries. Family and church are generally the two other leading sources of authority, but political parties, occupational unions, athletic associations, philanthropic and other organizations aiming at social welfare and progress, may also have a very important function in supervising, directing, and checking individual activities.

There is generally a compensation between the development and efficiency of such sources of authority and the practice of power by the state. When those sources are feeble or divergent in their action, the central political authority is naturally driven to substitute its own control for theirs, thus giving rise to what is commonly called the "totalitarian" state. When, on the contrary, state authority is not highly developed, the family, church, private associations, local bodies, increase in power. Herein, perhaps, we may seek the explanation of the great role played by associations in American life, as well as that of the organization of the American universities, which strike the European as singularly autocratic in character.

Up to this point we have considered the internal conditions of the state independent of international relations. It is, however, evident that the kind and intensity of relations with foreign nations may be decisive for the extent of governmental interference with individual behavior.

The more isolated a country, either because of geographical situation or sparsity of surrounding population, the fewer are its international relations. Independent of the geographical situation, the relative importance of international exchanges, material and intellectual, increases with the decrease in the size of the state, with the territorial diversification of natural resources, with the increasing division of labor, with accentuated variety of consumption. Supposing such relations equally intense, the concern of the state is more or less strong according to the economic sensitivity of the population. Great concern of the state does not, however, necessarily involve governmental interference if international relations develop in keeping with the general interest. Only when it seems that the collective advantage demands an intensification or some other modification of the relations between nationals and foreigners does the government intervene. When individuals of different political groups are mutually suspicious so that commercial exchange between them occurs only with difficulty, or when on the contrary the government, for political or other reasons, suspects their contacts, international trade may become a state function. Without adopting such an extreme measure, the state may intervene during difficult times in order to reduce the risk of foreign commerce through a participation in the enterprises or through the concession of credits. Governmental intervention in the promotion of foreign trade is especially marked when commerce is particularly important for exploitation or domination of colonies or other territories. Highly justified is concern over the continuation of exchange once established, because commerce increases the division of labor, and this may change from an advantage to a hindrance upon suspension of commercial relations. Hence, the state endeavors to maintain a national fleet and to assure the continuous supply of raw materials and foodstuffs necessary for national consumption.

There are situations in which the government seeks, on the contrary, to restrain international relations — when the free exercise of relations would in the long run create a condition of comparative inferiority by affording the foreign countries a disproportionate advantage in exchange, or when exchange, for the purpose of meeting temporary difficulties, would compromise the future sources of national income, or when it would prevent the progress of industry by crystallizing its backward conditions, which are due to historical rather than to contemporary factors, or when exchange would jeopardize the development already attained, by preventing adaptation to sudden changes in the cost of production or in the demand of the market.

Similar observations may be made concerning the international movements of population. These may also attain a higher or lower intensity, according to the geographical situation of the country, the development of means of transportation, and the disequilibrium between the various nations in respect to their economic resources, social security and freedom, or demographic density. Here also, however, intervention of authority occurs only when movements resulting from individual interests and preferences stand in contrast to the national advantage and hence require control.

State regulation of commodity exchange and of population movement necessarily reacts upon national economic production and human reproduction and, if radical, may result also in a more or less widespread interference with national activities. Moreover, an international authority is often required for co-ordinating governmental regulations and for enforcement of the agreements between states.

What has been said previously refers essentially to normal international relations. When these become abnormal and a struggle is pending between the states, authority extends and intensifies. Dictatorship, as is well known, is an outgrowth of war. As a matter of fact, it has long been recognized that imminent danger demands quickness of decision, determination of action, co-ordination of all available resources, subordination of the individual to authority to a degree which can only be attained through the rule of a single and powerful will. Not only is a refusal to act in accordance with the orders of authority inadmissible under such circumstances, but also a critical attitude or the expression of disagreement or even pessimistic predictions may be prohibited and repressed as manifestations which may weaken the solidarity and determination indispensable for overcoming the danger.

War is, however, not the only form of international struggle. In critical epochs the destiny of the nation may be felt to depend upon the success of international competition in economic, political, demographic, or religious fields. At such times the maximum expression of authority through an autocratic regime is the necessary result; we may then observe restriction of individual action and thought, similar to that during periods of war. Such restriction, not only of action but even of thought, is moreover present also in the most peaceful times in all matters considered essential to social stability. Through education and tradition, however, such restriction often becomes so customary that we are no longer aware of it. Thus Europeans may be shocked upon learning that in some states of North America teaching the theory of evolution is prohibited, just as Americans may be shocked in hearing that in some European states it is prohibited to teach democratic theories, but both Americans and Europeans find natural the prohibition of advocating vendettas, flagellation, cannibalism, incest, or sodomy, which we now consider as contrary to the fundamental principles of society, but which in other times or places have been the object of recognized institutions and sometimes the very basis of the social organization. The truth is that when authority achieves general consent the burden of restrictions vanishes and all conflict between authority and individual disappears. It often occurs that we lament the condition of certain people whom we regard as crushed under the heel of authority — for example, this is frequently the attitude towards the position of women in many past and present societies — and they, on the contrary, acknowledging the necessity of their social order, accept their position without any feeling of sacrifice and regard themselves as completely free.

We must now turn to the central problem in this lecture. Is it possible to discover among the multifarious variety of factors previously discussed any which, changing regularly with time, may explain the uniformity in the evolution of the relations between authority and the individual?

Certainly, several factors are not associated with the passage of time. Physical factors, such as geographical

situation, climate, territorial distribution of natural resources, available supply of certain raw materials, fall in
this category. This is likewise true in part for the biological factors which determine the character of the populations. Although there are good reasons for thinking that the
character of peoples also changes during their evolution, as
we shall see later, it may be recognized that throughout
their existence they conserve certain special traits which
may be important for the relations in question. Thus personal initiative and pronounced individualism have always
been characteristic of Anglo-Saxons, which may explain the
fact that autocratic systems and collectivistic programs
have never been very successful among them and that even
modern socialistic parties have softened and transformed
themselves into labor parties easily adjusting to the bourgeois regime. Opposite traits of docility, discipline, and
passive submission to group authority are common among
American Indians, who with the Inca empire and the
Jesuit missions furnished the best examples of successful
communistic organization. These traits also seem prevalent in Russia, where, as a matter of fact, communistic elements were always present in rural organization and where,
in contrast to all other countries, the bolshevist ideal might
consistently take root. A mystical conception of authority
appears quite in keeping with the character of the Japanese, and has survived the radical changes in their political
and social organization. It is evident that among such
peoples the influence of secular trends or of cyclical tendencies on the relations between authority and the individual must be less pronounced than among others not
endowed with such persistent characteristics.

There are other factors, among those previously examined, which may have a considerable influence on the
policy of the government and which do not present regular

variations through time, either because, like the dimensions of the state and the prevalence of certain occupations, they depend principally upon geographical conditions or the character of the people and are therefore fairly constant, or because, like the appearance of exceptionally strong personalities, they are fundamentally a matter of chance, even though not completely independent of cyclical tendencies.

One important group of factors is, however, clearly progressive in character: it is the group dominated by the accumulation of knowledge and improvement of technique. Certainly there have been, in the past, many hiatuses in the progress of civilization, the Dark Ages which followed the barbarian invasions being the last of them. But it is difficult to believe that such an event will be repeated in the foreseeable future, because social interrelations between the different stocks of mankind have already become so close that the decline and disappearance of a civilization will not occur without leaving its cultural heritage to other stocks. It may be, as some indications suggest, that the white civilization is doomed to disintegration and extinction, and we must remember that history knows of no everlasting civilization. But in any case the seeds, transplanted and already developing in Japan, will continue to flourish among the yellow race, and we may even now perceive that when, in a more distant future, this race will also have described the parabola of its life, other races, such as the Eur-American mestizos, or the populations of India, or those of Malaysia, will be apt to carry over the heritage of world civilization.

Accumulation of knowledge and progress of technique provoke an improvement of means of communication, an increase of production, which raises the upper limit set by subsistence on population, an accentuation of the division of labor and of diversification of consumption. Through all these effects they enhance the economic and intellectual interdependence among individuals and nations. Moreover, increasing welfare and diffusing a comfortable standard of living, they have the effect of generalizing the demand for the essentials of civilized life, while through abundant information and refined scientific devices they improve the reliability of social prediction. All these are circumstances, as we have seen previously, which demand intervention by centralized authority or international agency, or facilitate their task. So that we may observe, with the development of civilization, a progressive tendency towards an increase of governmental or international interference with the behavior of individuals and of nations.

It is certain that this tendency has been one of the factors leading to the abandonment of the *laissez-faire* policy which constituted a characteristic of the past century.

Another not less important group of factors, periodical in character, is connected with the cyclical evolution of nations.

The cycle of national life sometimes develops from an initial stage of colonization; other times from the conquest by a more powerful stock of a relatively depopulated country. In the first case the population of the colony is under the rule, generally inspired by authoritative principles, of the mother country; in the second instance, the country is governed by the conquerors, generally organized in the absolutistic form appropriate to a warrior nation. Population is in both cases scarce, public services limited or totally absent, life hard and dangerous. So individuals, for the sake of personal security and attainment of elementary social aims, group themselves into minor units —

family, clan or village, tribe, county, or province — generally ruled with an iron hand by an energetic chief. Especially the family and parenthood have not only reproductive but also basic economic and political functions. Parental authority is under such conditions almost unlimited. Precarious existence and general ignorance predispose toward widespread mysticism. Even though it cannot penetrate remote sections of the country, there is ample opportunity for governmental action to be exercised. Population is numerically insufficient; new immigrants are wanted and sought for; at their arrival they must be established or directed to appropriate sections. Population is heterogeneous, different in extraction and feelings. It is qualitatively inadequate. Education is lacking; hence prejudice flourishes and a most powerful check upon the passions is missing. Add to this the limited experience and hot temper of youth, which in this stage generally constitute a disproportionate part of the population. The new generations have not yet been molded by long collective action to the exigencies of social life. During my contacts with as yet incompletely developed populations belonging to different races, I have had the opportunity to observe similarities between them in respect to some shortcomings, for example, lack of punctuality, of sincerity, of consistency, generally of reliability, absence of sensitivity to the economic misfortunes of others, lack of willingness to work more than is necessary to satisfy daily needs. The corresponding positive qualities, indispensable to the efficiency of the social mechanism, are acquired only after the prolonged action of education, tradition, and selection, and must often be supplemented by governmental measures. Other shortcomings, as the backwardness of technique, the scarcity and timidity of capital, are consequences of economic conditions and are the source of a whole series of governmental provisions with a twofold design, on the one hand to stimulate internal development and on the other to protect it from the crushing competition of other countries. Thus, in spite of considerable differences between nations, we may recognize in their development a first stage characterized by strong authority of family and church and by marked governmental exercise of paternalism.

All such conditions are, however, destined to be superseded more or less rapidly.

Population increases in number and improves in quality. Education becomes more and more general. Technique advances. Nature is completely dominated. The hardship and danger of pioneer life are over. Personal security is assured. Division of labor prevails. The family loses its economic and political functions. The necessity of unlimited parental authority ceases. Mysticism withdraws before rationalism. Church authority confines itself more and more to matters of conscience. The minute prescriptions and bonds of the paternalistic epoch lose their utility and fall rapidly into desuetude. Biological and cultural fusion ensues from prolonged contacts, and the heterogeneity of race and customs is smoothed and suppressed, generating a conspicuous conformity in feelings and in behavior. Under the continued pressure of education, competition, tradition, natural and social selection, the previously mentioned defects of character, peculiar to the undeveloped people, are gradually overcome. Solidarity, efficiency, confidence in self and in collective progress, "drive" and "pep" (to use terms characteristic of one such stage), become common endowments. It is probable that biological factors also contribute to this result, factors which lead to the improvement of innate physical and psychical qualities in successive generations. Demographic factors likewise contribute. The proportion between the various age groups renders society a balanced system in which the experience of the eldest corrects the impulsiveness of youth. The differential natural increase of the social classes provokes the ascent of the best elements from the lower strata and thus keeps the directing classes in contact with the needs and ideals of the masses. And finally the economic conditions greatly contribute to the changes defined above. An equilibrium is established between natural resources and human forces of production; not a stationary but an evolutive equilibrium in which each advance contains the elements of further progress. Accumulation furnishes abundant capital, promptly available even for the most risky and the most slowly maturing enterprises. Large profits and high salaries constitute an incomparable stimulus. In spite of reduced natality, increase of population is maintained at a rate higher than ever; this assures a progressive expansion of the internal market for staple products, while the multiplication, diversification, and refinement of needs constantly open new possibilities to the manufacturers, stimulate inventions, evoke a complete exploitation of natural resources and of intellectual endowments. New enterprises arise almost magically; many flourish, many fall in fierce competition. Demand and supply of labor, saving and investment, production and consumption, are so diversified that it is easy for every right man to find his right place, for every need to find appropriate satisfaction, for capital to find the most profitable application. Economic cycles appear with the development of industry, but they do not halt the general progress and act rather as a supplementary means of selection, and consequently, in the long run, of further progress. Accumulation reaches impressive figures and largely outruns the growth of population. Inequalities in the distribution of wealth increase; but the increase is not felt in the general rise of the standard of living. Moreover, it facilitates the concentration needed by certain industries, swells the yield of taxes and so enables a reduction of the fiscal burden.

Public administration cannot keep pace with such rapid progress and, once left behind, it is ever more outdistanced by the tendency of the more intelligent and energetic people to apply themselves to private enterprises. The contact of poorly paid functionaries, dilatory and incapable, with wealthy business men pressed for time and accustomed to overcome all obstacles, leads inevitably to bribery and corruption. The people look at governmental action with suspicion and distrust, as an unavoidable evil which it is wise to circumscribe as much as possible. Moreover — it is asked — cannot private associations, easily formed and easily financed, more efficiently and economically take in their own hands many of the governmental functions? In the meantime, political authority is subdivided and distributed among the entire population. As a matter of fact, when external constriction fails, there is a social tendency to equalize the exercise of authority, a sort — it may be said — of political entropy.

So much for internal organization. As for international relations, manufacture, having attained the full development permitted by the internal market, looks for foreign outlets and, feeling strong enough to overcome foreign competition, demands freedom of trade. Freedom is likewise demanded for movements of population in order to obviate the scarcity of labor, manual or skilled, if the country is underpopulated; in order to assure territories for settlement or exploitation if the country is overpopulated.

Dominated by the events, but with the illusion of dominating them, scholars rationalize the interests of the people and, from a temporary situation of their country, construct an ideal theory universal and everlasting.

It is the age of rationalism, of liberalism, of democracy, of *laissez-faire* policy, of the triumph in all forms of the individual over authority.

The age may last a more or less long time, according to circumstances, but gradually shades into a quite different epoch.

Rationalism — after having invaded business, science, philosophy, government — invades the family, already enfeebled by the loss of political and economic functions. The reproductive function, which subsisted, was based upon the instinct of reproduction and secondarily upon the traditional pride in the family name; and implied a submission of the individual personality to the advantage of the species. Rationalism, leading to the subordination of instincts, to the criticism of tradition, to a hedonistic conception of life, undermines the very basis of the family. It is probable that a weakening of the genetic instinct itself, through economic, social, and biological causes, contributes to the result. Births decline in number, while the improvement of the death rate becomes continuously less significant, both because the progress of hygiene approaches a limit and because the reduced action of natural selection has its inevitable contrary effects. The immediate result is the prevalence of the adult classes, and this is temporarily useful from both the economic and the demographic viewpoints. Later, however, the older age groups become disproportionately large. Then the decline of population follows and — no less important — its character becomes profoundly modified. The nation assumes the traits of old age: prudence, thrift, peacefulness, love of the *status quo*, traditionalism, reverence for authority, attachment to hierarchy, inability to forget antagonisms and differences.

Certainly to the change of the national character contribute greatly the diffusion of wealth and the preponderance of capitalistic feelings and interests, especially those of the petty capitalists. Weakening of natural selection, determined by advances in medical technique, as well as weakening in social selection due to the general well-being, also plays its part. Other consequences follow. Racial improvement is held to warrant a rational control of marriage and births, and state intervention is demanded for its enforcement, sometimes with provisions directly antithetical to the traditional rights of the individual. Such rational control — which practically means limitation — of reproduction usually begins among the upper classes and so increases their need of replenishment by the lower strata, which can hardly meet the great demand with their best elements. The consequent alarm over a degeneration of the directing classes often provokes governmental intervention aimed to reduce or even to prevent social ascent. Later, as birth control spreads among the masses, the dangers of the progressive depopulation become manifest. The state is then called upon to adopt a policy encouraging population growth, restraining emigration, favoring immigration, taxing bachelors, according the married people preferential treatment in matters of employment, lodging, and inheritance, establishing allowances and tax exemptions for large families, providing for the care of children of employees, attempting to revive reverence for motherhood and to substitute for the family and ancestral cult that of nation and race as a stimulus for reproduction. Unable to halt the progressive disintegration of the family, the state endeavors to take over its last function.

The necessity of governmental intervention is not less marked in the economic field. The wealth of the directing class weakens the rational stimulus to produce. At this time, production continues unabated because of instinctive impulses, such as desire for economic and social power, pleasure in great achievements, and especially an instinct of activity which has resulted from a long process of education and selection and is strongly favored by social disdain of the idle rich. Under the rule of instinct, however, production can hardly be commensurate with consumption, and the economic cycles become more and more pronounced and more frequently degenerate into crises. The problem of stability, rather than that of progress, occupies the foreground. Governmental intervention is asked for by the public. Entrepreneurs do not fail to engage in direct action as well, forming giant corporations, combining into trusts and cartels, and promoting general agreements between the various branches of production. The collective form of production gradually prevails over individual enterprise. But the temptation of exploiting the monopolistic machinery for increasing profits at the expense of consumers and workers is too great to be resisted in times of difficulty, and the mass of consumers and workers react. The reaction is stronger as the democratic conception of life is extended from the political to the economic field and the masses look with envy upon great fortunes and large enterprises. The problem of distribution supplants that of production in importance, and political authority cannot but second the people's demand for regulation. On the other hand, the workers, under the influence of labor leaders, bind themselves into unions and succeed in obtaining substantial increases in wages. Moreover, they succeed in obtaining acknowledgment of the principle that the remuneration of labor must not fall under a certain level, necessary for a decent standard of living, irrespective of the condition of the enterprise. Sooner or later, interference of the state follows for fixing minimum wage scales. Systems of compulsory arbitration in case of conflict, or more radical systems for avoiding the open conflicts through a corporative regime, may be initiated. But the acknowledgment of the principle of minimum wages, however much in keeping with the social conscience, has badly wounded the private capitalistic system, and the cost of treatment falls upon the government. During economic depression, the entrepreneurs cannot but close their doors or at least reduce their activity, and the unemployed, numbering millions, fall in the lap of the public treasury. The alternative measure, sometimes adopted, of subsidizing industry is equally expensive. At the same time, the public expenses for other social services increase continuously. Treasury expenses naturally must be met with receipts; thus the taxes rise to an unparalleled level. Industry can no longer withstand foreign competition. At least the basic industries, and above all agriculture, and the key industries, must be protected; and the need of protection soon becomes general. The state is gradually obliged to intervene more and more in foreign commerce, aiding the exporter by extending credits, promoting exporting and importing combines, introducing into commercial treaties systems of compensation which imply its continuous action or supervision, transforming itself in a marked degree into a seller or a buyer in behalf of the nation, sometimes ending with the control of all foreign trade. But all these devices, though preventing the national enterprises from immediate ruin, cannot substantially increase their profits. Capital is even more impeded, not only through taxes but also through a governmental fixing of the rate of interest, and is periodically confiscated through inflation. Under such conditions, private accumulation practically ceases and the national capital can then be reconstituted only through accumulation by the state. Often, however, before this point is reached, a regime of state capitalism is attained in another way. In time of crisis, the government, in order to avoid social disturbances, was obliged to assume the exercise of those large industries which were operating with a deficit. But the government must sustain the losses thus suffered. Why not also take over the large and profitable industries as well? Individual production is thus confined to small undertakings, often satellites of the larger ones, and the national economy ends in a regime of practically complete state control.

Several circumstances render this result possible. The existence of large corporations has already accustomed people to work efficiently without an immediate personal interest in the success of the enterprise. Uniformity of consumption leads to rigidity of demand and standardization of production, which render superfluous the adaptability of the private entrepreneur. In the meantime, the organization of the public administration has equaled, if indeed not overtaken, that of private business. Centuries of experience bear fruit. The increased power of the government is reflected in higher prestige and in higher salaries of functionaries, from which derives honesty in administration. Public confidence follows. The myth of the nation appeals strongly to its high priests. A tradition of rigidity and devotion is established in the bureaucracy. Civil service, in its various forms, now attracts the most capable and energetic people, who prefer stability and prestige of public office to the mediocrity of private employment and the incertitude of business and professional life. It may well be that great men are not more numerous in the last stage of the evolution of nations than in the preceding one; but they are now increasingly attracted by public life, so that, when the time is ripe, a strong hand is more readily available to take control of the state.

Thus, according to the successive stages of the evolution of nations, the relations between authority and the individuals also evolve, passing from a stage of paternalism to one of liberalism to that of progressive centralization of authority which tends to a regime of complete autocracy. Those who are acquainted with the modern neo-organicistic theories will not be surprised by this result. In the nation, as in the individual, we recognize an initial period of development and a final period of decline, in which the body requires more regulation and control, and an intermediate period in which the organism, in the fulness of its power, may be permitted relative freedom. This analogy is useful for illuminating the error characteristic of many supporters of *laissez-faire* policy, who, because the two are generally associated, conclude that progress is the result of freedom. This is just as tenable as maintaining that the absence of restraint enjoyed by adults, as compared with children and the aged, is the cause of their superior strength. The crucial test is provided, as we have previously indicated, by periods of decline, like those of the Hellenistic and late Roman epochs, for not those nations which continue their attachment to liberalism, but those which have adopted a policy of centralized authority, are the more prosperous and successful.

At this point I should like to make clear that the previous description represents only a theoretical scheme. The division into three stages of the life-history of peoples and of the relations between authority and the individual is of course only methodological; in fact the evolution is a continuum. Nor may one expect an exact correspondence between the concrete history of any one people and this abstract scheme. So immeasurably varied is reality that one can hope only to describe its general tendencies. In fact many disturbing factors intervene. There are no two peoples, as there are no two individuals, for which life development is identical, and for many nations, as for many individuals, the cycle of life is cut off, at various points, before its full course is run. Moreover, disturbing factors probably influence the life of nations more profoundly than that of individuals. Other factors interfere with the regular correspondence between stage of evolution and relations between authority and the individual. I have already suggested some of these factors: the physical condition of the country, the permanent characteristics of the populations, various accidental occurrences. But another factor deserves discussion: the reciprocal influences obtaining between populations in different stages of evolution.

The prestige which emanates from the stronger nations leads to the diffusion of their regime. Imitation is a social force also in matters international, and at times a fashion prevails in the sphere of authority and the individual. Thus the fashionableness of liberalism in the last century may explain the adoption of free-trade policy, often contrary to their own interests, by some nations of the second rank.

Occasionally a people's solidarity of interest and feeling with another nation may disturb the expected relations, especially in the international field, between authority and the individual. This frequently occurs in the case of colonies and mother country or of allied nations.

Competition and actual or threatened retaliation constitute another source of disturbance. Free-trade countries have sometimes been obliged to adopt a protective tariff for purposes of retaliation, and contrariwise protectionist countries are generally induced to mitigate the duties demanded by national industry in order to avoid foreign retaliation. The control of foreign commerce by the Soviet government has proved to be a strong weapon in international competition and has provoked some other governments to interfere with commodity exchange. Similarly the devaluation adopted by some great nations with the purpose, or at least with the result, of favoring export has induced other states to follow suit, while others were obliged to introduce rigid control of foreign exchange and commerce in order to preserve parity.

When international competition becomes general and acute and the menace of war impends and spreads, the autocratic system tends to be adopted by all nations, whatever their stage of evolution. The occurrence of such an international situation is, however, not independent of cyclical factors. In addition to the demographic-economic cycle which we have described, another longer cycle, biological in character, probably exists, involving not single nations but an entire race. Plutarch reports that the Etruscan sages had recognized the existence of such a long cycle, called the "Great Year," at the end of which one of the great races of mankind, previously hegemonic, declined and another took its place on the stage. During such stormy periods of transition, dictatorship, an institution historically originated by contingent emergencies and undoubtedly best fitted for temporary tasks, may nevertheless prove permanently necessary and establish itself as a predominant system, in spite of the sacrifices imposed, at least initially, upon the individual. In such circumstances, struggle between nations indeed assumes preponderance over competition between individuals: success and free expansion of nations become of greater import than individual freedom and welfare. We may say that on the shifting scene of history, nations, not persons, are the actors in such periods. Someone may add that consequently the free behavior of nations and abandonment by international bodies of paternalistic restrictions upon state initiative constitute the policy most in keeping with the interest of mankind.

The substitution of races naturally is not instantaneous; it may cover an entire epoch during which the retreating race is not at all doomed to an inglorious life; it may even, taking advantage of the past accumulation of wealth, power, and knowledge, attain some of its greater achievements. Plutarch tells us that the diviners had recognized infallible signs of the approaching end of the Great Year during the first Civil War. Roman civilization, however, subsequently lasted, not without troubles and almost constantly under autocratic control, for some centuries in Rome, and continued for many other centuries in its offshoot, Byzantium.

I have always had a distinct antipathy for prophecies, and, besides, I have not Plutarch's good fortune to write two centuries after the event — a circumstance that usually improves the reliability of divinations or the ability to select successful ones — but, standing on purely scientific ground, which I prefer not to abandon, I believe that the considerations raised in this lecture may help us to appreciate the present world situation. I should be especially glad if they contributed to the mutual understanding between our Old Europe and your younger America.

IV
CLASSICISM AND ROMANTICISM

KLASSIZISMUS, ROMANTIZISMUS UND HISTORISCHES DENKEN IM 18. JAHRHUNDERT

FRIEDRICH MEINECKE, PH.D., DR.JUR., LL.D., LITT.D.

Professor of History, Emeritus, University of Berlin

ÜBER Klassizismus, Romantizismus und historisches Denken im 18. Jahrhundert habe ich übernommen zu sprechen, um einen Beitrag zu dem uns gestellten Generalthema Klassizismus und Romantizismus zu liefern. Man hat es uns gewiss in der Hoffnung gestellt, grössere Klarheit über diese beiden viel erörterten und umstrittenen Begriffe zu bekommen. Auch ich werde mich von meinem besonderen Thema aus darum bemühen, möchte aber gleich bemerken, dass ich den Versuch zu einer endgültigen Klarheit und Bestimmtheit dieser Begriffe zu gelangen, für aussichtslos halte. Allein schon die endlosen, immer wieder neue Kritik erregenden, immer wieder neue Anläufe hervorrufenden Bemühungen, das Wesen dessen, was "romantisch" ist, exakt festzulegen, deuten darauf hin. Die Geisteswissenschaften können es nun einmal nicht zu der Exaktheit der Naturwissenschaften bringen. Sie dürfen es aber, so wage ich zu sagen, auch nicht. Denn das Feinste und Wertvollste des geistigen Lebens würde dabei in Gefahr stehen, verloren zu gehen im *caput mortuum* einer Definition. Ich lehne darum die Bemühungen, geistige Phänomene auf Begriffe zu bringen, nicht etwa ab. Denn das würde heissen, die Geisteswissenschaften in ein formloses Chaos zu stürzen. Aber nur einen annähernden, nur einen vorläufigen Wert dürfen solche Definitionen beanspruchen. Denn das Leben des Geistes und der von ihm hervorgebrachten geschichtlichen Gebilde ist derart fliessend und beinah proteusartig wandlungsfähig, dass es nur in immer neuen Aspekten und Anläufen erkannt werden kann.

Wir werden darüber einig sein, dass Klassizismus die ältere, Romantizismus die jüngere Richtung im 18. Jahrhundert darstellt, die sich dann erst im frühen 19. Jahrhundert zu dem, was man Romantik schlechthin nennt, entwickelt hat. Ich würde den Romantizismus des 18. Jahrhunderts deshalb auch lieber als Präromantik bezeichnen. Und ich bin auf Grund langjähriger Studien zu dem Resultat gekommen, dass diese Präromantik eine wesentliche und notwendige Vorstufe des modernen historischen Denkens gewesen ist. Aber nicht die einzige Vorstufe. Vielmehr hat auch der Klassizismus in einer der besonderen Formen, die er im 18. Jahrhundert annahm, zur Entstehung dieses modernen historischen Denkens mit beigetragen. Der Klassizismus wieder hing vielfach zusammen mit der Aufklärungsbewegung, der mächtigsten geistigen Richtung des 18. Jahrhunderts. Diese brachte die grosse Aufklärungshistorie der Voltaire, Hume und Gibbon hervor. Das moderne historische Denken und Geschichteschreiben aber ist von dieser so tief verschieden, dass Lord Acton (1861) sagen konnte, der Unterschied zwischen der Geschichte zur Zeit Gibbons und heute sei so gross, wie der zwischen der Astronomie zur Zeit des Kopernikus und nach ihm. Und dennoch hat auch diese Aufklärungshistorie dem modernen historischen Denken in wichtigen Dingen vorgearbeitet und darf ebenfalls als eine Vorstufe zu ihm gelten. Ja, es gibt noch weitere, noch ältere Vorstufen und geistige Richtungen, die auf die Entstehung des modernen historischen Denkens tief

eingewirkt haben. So ergibt sich ein ungeheuer reiches
und verschlungenes Gewebe geistiger Tendenzen, die dazu
beigetragen und das hervorgebracht haben, was wir heute
in Deutschland als Historismus im guten, positiven Sinne
bezeichnen. Und was ist dessen Wesen? Nichts anderes,
als die historischen Erkenntnisprinzipien, auf die ich mich
im Eingang berief, nämlich der Sinn für Individualität
und Entwicklung in der Geschichte, der Sinn für das ste-
tige Fliessen und sich Wandeln aller menschlichen Gebilde, den Sinn aber auch dafür, dass diese Gebilde nicht
nur wiederkehrende Typen sind und allgemeinen Gesetz-
mässigkeiten entsprechen, sondern jedes für sich auch
einen ganz individuellen und eigenartigen Charakter
tragen, wie denn auch jeder einzelne Mensch sowohl dem
allgemeinen Typus Mensch entspricht, als auch für sich
ein von allen Anderen unterschiedenes und deshalb unver-
gleichliches Individuum darstellt.

Das Erwachen dieses Sinnes für Individualität und
Entwicklung in der Geschichte ist eine der grössten geistigen Revolutionen, die das Abendland erlebt hat. Wohl hat
man auch schon vorher, wenn man Geschichte schrieb,
mit frischer Naivität Individuelles sehen und Entwick-
lungen darstellen können. Von Herodot und Thucydides
an ist das geschehen. Aber diese Sehweise drang nicht
völlig und grundsätzlich durch. Der antike, vor allem der
griechische Geist war mehr darauf gerichtet, feste, bleibende Normen des menschlichen Lebens zu suchen, als die
ewigen Wandlungen und Neugestaltungen desselben zu
verstehen. Gewiss, man suchte sie auch zu verstehen, aber
eben durch feste Normen, nämlich durch die Annahme,
dass die menschliche Natur zu allen Zeiten die gleiche
geblieben sei und dass die geschichtlichen Verläufe sich
also wiederholten. Ich erinnere an die Kreislauftheorie des
Polybios, die Machiavell später erneuert hat. Man hielt

auch die menschliche Vernunft, insofern sie sich nur
reinige von Unwissenheit und Leidenschaft, für identisch
in allen Menschen, für stabil, für zeitlos immer dasselbe
aussagend. Man setzte Natur und Vernunft einander
gleich, und so entstand, durch die Stoiker vor allem, der
Glaube an ein Naturrecht als ein Inbegriff ewiger ver-
nünftiger Wahrheiten. Dies Naturrecht wurde auch vom
Christentum, wie Ernst Troeltsch gezeigt hat, übernommen und mit dem Glauben an die übernatürliche Offenbarung amalgamiert. Es wurde zu einer geistigen Macht
von ungeheurer Bedeutung, von stärkster historischer
Wirkung. Wer wollte verkennen, dass der Glaube an un-
veräusserliche ewige Menschenrechte Millionen von Menschen Halt und Kraft gegeben hat. Das Volk, als dessen
Gast ich hier spreche, hat seine Freihiet damit begründet.
Es gibt einen bleibenden Kern des Naturrechts, es gibt
aber auch Auswirkungen des Naturrechts, die der modernen historischen Kritik als schwerer Irrtum erscheinen
müssen. Natur und Vernunft des Menschen sind sehr viel
wandelbarer und entwicklungsfähiger, als die naturrechtliche Denkweise annimmt. Die entwicklungsgeschichtliche
Betrachtungsweise, verbunden mit dem Sinn für den
individuellen Charakter des Menschen und der menschlichen Gebilde, hat dem alten dogmatischen Naturrecht
den Boden entzogen. Aber geherrscht hat dieses bis in die
Aufklärung des 18. Jahrhunderts hinein, ja diese Aufklärung kann sogar als die höchste Steigerung des alten, aus
der Antike stammenden Naturrechts gelten. Denn der
Glaube an die zeitlose menschliche Vernunft gewann jetzt
eine Kraft und Sicherheit wie nie zuvor, weil er bestätigt
zu werden schien durch die grossen naturwissenschaft-
lichen Entdeckungen des späten 17. und des 18. Jahrhunderts und weil die christlich-religiösen Einschränkungen,
mit denen er bisher behaftet gewesen war, in Misskredit

kamen durch das Ende der Religionskriege, durch das
Erlöschen der religiösen Fanatismen. Die autonome
menschliche Vernunft fühlte sich fortan berufen, sowohl
das gegenwärtige Leben neu zu gestalten, als auch das
vergangene Leben, die Geschichte im weitesten Umfange,
Kultur and Staat alles mit eingeschlossen, neu zu beurtei-
len und universale, den ganzen Erdkreis umspannende
Geschichte zu schreiben, wie sie nie zuvor geschrieben war.
Von Voltaire an begann sie diesen historiographischen
Siegeszug.

Aber in demselben Jahre, 1769, in dem Voltaires
berühmter Essai sur les mœurs et l'esprit des nations seine
endgültige Form erhielt, schrieb der junge Herder auf der
Seefahrt von Riga nach Frankreich umwälzende Gedanken
nieder, die nun die Aera von Sturm und Drang in Deutschland eröffneten und die dem Naturrecht, der Aufklärung
und der Aufklärungshistorie den gewaltigsten Stoss ver-
setzten. Der Kern dieser Gedanken aber war der in ihm
neuerwachende Sinn für Entwicklung und Individualität
in der Geschichte. Ein geistesgeschichtliches Drama von
höchster Wucht und Steigerung, dieses Aufeinander-
prallen zweier geschichtlicher Denkweisen innerhalb desselben Jahrhunderts. Ich nehme die Frage wieder auf:
Wie ist die neue Denkweise, d. h. der Sinn für Individualität und Entwicklung nun eigentlich entstanden? Ich
versuchte die Antwort zu geben in einem Buche über die
Entstehung des Historismus, das in kurzem erscheinen
wird, und will nun versuchen, aus dieser Antwort, die na-
turgemäss von sehr mannigfaltigem Inhalte ist, diejenigen
Fäden herauszunehmen und hier vorzulegen, die den
Klassizismus und Romantizismus betreffen. Unter Klassizismus versteht man eine Richtung in der Kunst und
Kunstlehre, die eine feste und bleibende Norm der Schönheit kennt, nämlich diejenige Norm, die in der Blütezeit

der antiken, vor allem griechischen Kunst und Dichtung
geherrscht hatte. Der Künstler und Dichter hat also
Muster und Vorbilder zu befolgen. Ist das etwas Anderes,
als die Anwendung der naturrechtlichen Denkweise auf
das Gebiet der Künste? Steht hier nicht auch der Glaube
an eine ewige, zeitlose Vernunft im Hintergrunde, die für
alle höheren menschlichen Betätigungen, für das Schöne
nicht minder, als für das Wahre und Gute bleibende, un-
verrückbare Gesetze und Normen gibt? Besteht nicht, so
wird man zunächst vermuten, darum auch eine tiefe Kluft
zwischen Klassizismus und Historismus? Denn dieser
wird, angewandt auf das Gebiet der Kunst, auch hier das
Feste in Fluss und Entwicklung bringen, auch hier die
Individualität der künstlerischen Hervorbringungen und
der aesthetischen Empfindungen beachten und so zu dem
Ergebnis kommen, dass es keine bleibende Norm des
Schönen gibt, dass es in mannigfachen immer neuen
Gestaltungen auftritt. Er wird einem Rembrandt hoch-
schätzen, obwohl er der klassischen Schönheitsnorm nicht
entspricht. Ein Goethe aber, als er 1787 in Italien und
ganz in den klassischen Schönheitsgeschmack versunken
war, hat seinem Herzoge Karl August lebhaft zugestimmt,
dass man auf die Rembrandtsammlung in Weimar keinen
besonderen Wert mehr zu legen brauche, denn die reine
Form der Kunst, die er hier in Italien suche, sei doch viel
interessanter.

Und doch hat gerade Goethe den Sinn für Individualität
und Entwicklung wie kein Anderer wecken helfen. Er hat
1780 einmal an Lavater die denkwürdigen Worte gerichtet: "Habe ich dir das Wort Individuum est ineffabile,
woraus ich eine Welt ableite, schon geschrieben"? Und im
Alter 1826 gesagt: "Wie sehr wir uns auch mit Geschichte
von Jugend auf beschäftigen, so finden wir doch zuletzt,
dass das Einzelne, Besondere, Individuelle uns über

Menschen und Begebenheiten den besten Aufschluss gibt."
Den Entwicklungsgedanken aber hat Goethe auf der
italienischen Reise sich zum vollen Bewusstsein und
Eigentum gemacht. Er entdeckte die Entwicklung, die
Metamorphose der Pflanze und erklärte 1787: "Dasselbe
Gesetz wird sich auf alles übrige Lebendige anwenden
lassen." Er bemerkte sogar von der Kunst, die er doch
gleichzeitig klassizistisch ansah: In diesem Felde "sei
kein Urteil möglich, als wenn man es historisch entwickeln
kann."

So lässt uns Goethe vermuten, dass es am Ende doch
eine Brücke, eine innere Vermittlung zwischen dem normativen Klassizismus und dem individualisierenden Historismus gab. Es gehört ja zum Wesen geschichtlicher Entwicklung überhaupt, dass auch das einander Entgegen-
gesetzte, obwohl logisch unvereinbar, doch geschichtlich
aufeinander wirkt und einander zu befruchten vermag.
Und oft werden die grossen Gegensätze einer Zeit in ein
und derselben Brust ausgekämpft. Will man wissen, was
der normative Klassizismus trotz seines prinzipiellen
Gegensatzes zum Historismus doch als Wegbahner für
diesen zu leisten vermochte, so muss man das Lebenswerk
des Mannes anblicken, dessen kunstgeschichtliche Lehren
ein Leitstern für Goethes klassizistische Kunstbegeister-
ung in Italien wurden, — Winckelmanns Geschichte der
Kunst des Altertums 1764. Von diesem epochemachenden
Buche hat Winckelmanns grosser Biograph Justi mit
vollem Recht gesagt: "Die Gesinnung, die sein grosses
Werk beherrscht, ist eher eine antihistorische." Denn mit
dogmatischer Strenge und Bestimmtheit wurde hier das
Schönheitsideal der hohen griechischen Kunst als Kanon
und Masstab aller übrigen Kunst gelehrt. Wohl lehrte
nun Winckelmann gleichzeitig auch, dass diese hohe
griechische Kunst sich erst *entwickelt* und in einer Folge

verschiedener Stile von archaischer Härte an sich vervoll-
kommnet habe, um dann stufenweise wieder zu sinken und
zu verfallen. Entwicklung kennt also auch schon Winckelmann, und seine Entdeckung der Stilfolgen hat ohne
Frage auch die entwicklungsgeschichtliche Behandlung
aller Kunst aufs stärkste angeregt. Aber es ist noch nicht
geschichtliche Entwicklung im Sinne des Historismus, die
Winckelmann vor Augen hat. Denn es fehlt ihm noch der
volle Sinn dafür, dass die griechische Kunst und das
Griechentum überhaupt eine ganz einmalige, ganz singu-
läre, gewiss wundervolle, aber auch unvergleichliche und
unnachahmliche *Individualität* war. Als Norm vielmehr,
als höchste Vervollkommnung und Verwirklichung eines
absoluten, zeitlos gültigen *Ideals* sah er die griechische
Kunst an. "Es gibt nur Ein Schönes, wie es nur Ein
Wahres gibt" sagt er einmal, und der ganze Geist des
Naturrechts weht uns daraus an.

Es gibt also verschiedene Begriffe von Entwicklung.
Der deutsche Geschichtsphilosoph Heinrich Rickert hat
einmal deren sieben unterschieden! Ich will nicht darauf
eingehen, sondern nur das Eine betonen, dass derjenige
Entwicklungsbegriff, den Winckelmann vertrat, auch derjenige war, den die naturrechtliche denkende Aufklärung
von Voltaire an überhaupt vertrat. Man kann ihn auch
den Vervollkommnungs-, den Perfektionsgedanken der
Aufklärung nennen. Man misst am absoluten Masstabe
der Vernunft die Aufwärts- oder Abwärtsbewegung eines
geschichtlichen Gebildes, und wenn der nötige Optimismus
sich einstellt, glaubt man sogar an den stetigen Fortschritt
der menschlichen Kultur und steigert so den Perfektionsgedanken zum Fortschrittsgedanken. Von einem solchen
Glauben an den allgemeinen *Fortschritt* der Kunst war nun
freilich Winckelmanns Klassizismus weit entfernt. Im
Gegenteil, er sah auf die hohe griechische Kunst wie auf ein

verlorenes Paradies. Und so kam er in einen merkwür-
digen Widerspruch zu sich selbst. Auf der einen Seite
glaubte er, dass man sie nie wieder erreichen oder gar
übertreffen könne, hielt sie also doch für etwas Einmaliges,
Singuläres, fast möchte man schon sagen, Individuelles, —
auf der anderen Seite sah er in ihr eine absolute Norm, ein
festes Ideal für alle Zeiten und riet darum den Künstlern
seiner Zeit, sie nachzuahmen, — aber ohne den Glauben,
dass die Nachahmung sie je werde erreichen können. Da
sieht man nun, in welche verzweifelte Situation der Klassizismus hineinführen konnte. Man sieht aber auch im
Hintergrunde schon eine erste leichte Brücke vom Klassizismus zum Historismus hinübergeschlagen. Je stärker
nämlich man die Einzigkeit und Unerreichbarkeit der
griechischen Kunst empfand, um so mehr näherte man
sich der neuen, wahrhaft historischen Einsicht, dass die
griechische Kunst ein besonderes, individuelles, unver-
gleichliches, von bestimmten historischen Bedingungen
abhängiges Gebilde sei, das seinen Masstab in sich selber
trage und nicht zu einer absoluten Norm für alle Zeiten
erhoben werden könne. Diese Einsicht ist erst im späteren
19. Jahrhundert durch die moderne Archäologie und Phi-
lologie im vollen Umfange gewonnen worden. Bis dahin
gingen die normative und die historisch individualisier-
ende Betrachtungsweise der griechischen Kultur, so oder
so gemischt, mit einander her, und gerade Goethes
Kunstbetrachtung zeigt dies Nebeneinander auf Schritt
und Tritt. Und nun ist noch eine weitere Brücke zu bemerken, die bei Winckelmann und Goethe vom Klassizismus zum Historismus, von der normativen zur individualisierenden Betrachtung hinüberführte. Individualität kann
ja nicht bloss mit dem logischen Verstande erfasst werden.
Es ist etwas begrifflich Unfassbares in ihr. Eben das ist ja
der Sinn jenes wunderbaren, aus der Scholastik und Mystik

des Mittelalters stammenden und von Goethe so hoch gehaltenen Wortes Individuum est ineffabile. Empfindung
und Gefühl müssen mitarbeiten, ja die ganze Seele des
Menschen muss mitschwingen, wenn wir das Individuell-
ste an unseren Freunden verstehen wollen. Und dasselbe
gilt von den Individualitäten der Geschichte. "Man lernt
nichts kennen, als was man liebt," hat Goethe einmal
gesagt. Und nun muss man feststellen, dass diese ver-
stehende Liebe für das Menschliche, diese seelische Einfühlung in fremde Gebilde sowohl der rationalistischen
Aufklärung, wie dem mit ihr wesensvervandten Klassizismus bis dahin in hohem Grade gefehlt hat. Verstandes-
mässig, intellektualistisch stellten sie ihre Normen fest und
massen daran die menschlichen Werke. Und hier ist nun
der Punkt, wo in und durch Winckelmann der Klassizismus
mit einem Male anfängt, sich zu beseelen und die neue
Sprache innerlichster Empfindung zu sprechen. Sein
grosses Wort von der "edlen Einfalt und stillen Grösse"
der griechischen Kunst floss aus der Seele. Die Schönheit
ist, sagt er auch noch, eines von den grossen Geheimnissen
der Natur, deren Wirkung wir alle sehen und empfinden,
von deren Wesen aber ein allgemeiner deutlicher Begriff
unter die unerfundenen Wahrheiten gehört. Diese Ehr-
furcht vor dem Geheimnis der Schönheit, vor ihrem
Ineffabile, diese Verachtung magerer Verstandesbegriffe,
diese religiöse Andacht vor dem hohen Kunstwerke als
Symbol und Offenbarung des Göttlichen — das ist das
Neue und Epochemachende, was vor allem diesen Winckel-
mannschen und Goethe'schen Klassizismus zu einer unmittelbaren Vorstufe des individualisierenden Historismus
erhebt. Denn die seelische Einfühlung in das geschichtliche Leben ist das eigentliche Erkenntnismittel des Historismus. Und hier ist nun auch ferner der Punkt, wo antike Gedanken, diemal aber nicht hindernd, wie im

Naturrecht, sondern fördernd und belebend in die geistige Entwicklung eingreifen. Winckelmann war Platoniker, es war platonischer Eros, den er im Angesicht der höchsten Kunstwerke empfand. Darum sprach er von "der von Gott ausfliessenden und zu Gott führenden Schönheit." Darum konnte er schliesslich, vom Sinnlichen der Kunst zum Übersinnlichen aufsteigend, mit Platon sagen: "Das Höchste hat kein Bild."

Und Goethe war Neuplatoniker und hat ähnlich empfunden. Ich widerstehe der Versuchung, die Bedeutung platonischen und neuplatonischen Denkens und Empfindens für die Entstehung des Historismus hier weiter zu verfolgen. Sie ist ausserordentlich gross, und ich habe in meinem Buche versucht, sie genauer nachzuweisen. Ich habe aber hier die Aufgabe, ausser vom Klassizismus nur noch vom Romantizismus des 18. Jahrhunderts in seiner Bedeutung für das historische Denken zu sprechen.

Während der Klassizismus von Hause aus eine Abzweigung des normativ-naturrrechtlichen Denkens auf das Gebiet der Kunst war, hat der Romantizismus, oder wie ich lieber sage, die Präromantik des 18. Jahrhunderts in ihrem Wesen mit Naturrecht nichts zu tun, sondern entsprang aus unmittelbaren, naiven Bedürfnissen des Geschmacks und der Phantasie, hier und da darf man auch schon sagen, des Gemüts, der Empfindung, der Seele. Das Charakteristische nun ist, dass diese neuen Regungen, die sich vom Beginn des 18. Jahrhunderts an in England vor allem zeigen, dem herrschenden Klassizismus und der Aufklärungsbewegung nicht etwa feindlich entgegentraten. Zu einem förmlichen Kampfe hat es erst die eigentliche Romantik des frühen 19. Jahrhunderts gebracht. Sondern in derselben Brust konnten klassizistische, aufklärerische und präromantische Tendenzen friedlich — naiv nebeneinander hausen. Von Pope, dem klassischen

Dichter des englischen Aufklärungsgeschmackes hat Crane
Brinton gesagt, dass auch in seinem Geiste Raum für
Zweifel, Mysterium und Unendlichkeit gewesen sei.
Pope hat selbst 1716 bekannt: The more I examine my
own mind, the more romantic I find myself. Und Pope
hat auch mit die Anregung zur Schaffung jener englischen
Gärten gegeben, in denen die Freude an den Reizen der
einfachen, ungekünstelten Natur neben dem klassizistischen Gartengeschmack der Franzosen und Italiener sich
ihr Recht eroberte. Und nun dauerte es nicht lange und es
tauchten etwa seit der Mitte des Jahrhunderts in und
neben den englischen Gärten Gebäude im gotischen
Geschmack auf, — keine echte Gotik, sondern Rokokogo-
tik, oft sehr spielerisch und willkürlich, aber auch ein
Zeichen, dass man neben der eigentlich für korrekt und
normal gehaltenen Baukunst gern noch etwas Anderes zur
Abwechslung geniessen möchte. Das Mittelalter, dem die
Gotik enstammte, galt nach wie vor dabei noch als roh und
finster, aber man entdeckt jetzt seine kleinen Reize, seine
efeubewachsenen Ruinen, die sentimental stimmen, seine
romantischen Rittergeschichten und Balladen, die man
nun sammelte. Simplicity and sentiment suchte man in
diesen Balladen, als Percy, der erfolgreichste dieser Samm-
ler, 1765 sie herausgab. Aber um diese Balladen für den
Zeitgeschmack geniessbar zu machen, mussten sie charak-
teristischer Weise erst korrigiert und modernisiert werden.
Es war viel Mode, viel Spielerei mit diesen präromantischen Regungen verbunden, noch nichts von der leiden-
schaftlichen Sehnsucht, von den idealisierenden Träu-
mereien, die dann in der echten vollen Romantik des
frühen 19. Jahrhunderts erwachten. Aber diese war auch
der Gegenschlag gegen die furchtbaren Erschütterungen
der französischen Revolution, während die Gesellschaft

des ancien régime und Rokoko mit ihren geistigen Neigungen noch vielfach spielen und tändeln konnte.

Das volle Recht, von einer präromantischen, nicht nur englischen, sondern europäischen Bewegung des 18. Jahrhunderts zu sprechen, gibt erst die Tatsache, dass hinter Spiel und Tändelei sich zuweilen schon etwas Tieferes regte, etwas was wirklich als Vorspiel der echten Romantik gelten kann: — nämlich die Reaktion der irrationalen Seelenkräfte gegen den auskältenden Rationalismus und die verfeinerte, raffinierte Zivilisation der Zeit. Rousseau in Frankreich durch seine beiden Discours von 1750 und 1754 und Sturm und Drang in Deutschland unter Herders Vortritt seit etwa 1765 sind die Wetterzeichen einer neu heraufziehenden Epoche. Man wurde irre an den Errungenschaften der eigenen aufgeklärten Zeit, man spürte, dass bei aller Verfeinerung des äusseren Lebens und allen Fortschritten des Wissens die ursprüngliche Natur, die Seele des Menschen nicht zu ihrem Recht gekommen sei. Man warf den Blick zurück auf Zeiten und Völker, die noch ein ganz naturfrisches und ungebrochenes Menschentum gehabt zu haben schienen. Die Naturvölker Amerikas und die Urzeiten der eigenen Völkerwelt, der man angehörte, erregten in einer Weise, wie nie zuvor, das Interesse. Einen ersten wahrhaft genialen Blick auf die Urmenschen hatte schon der grosse Italiener Vico in seiner Scienza nuova (in den 3 Ausgaben 1725, 1730 u. 1744) geworfen, aber mit der Mentalität eines tiefgründigen Barockmenschen, noch nicht aus einer Frontstellung gegen die Aufklärung. Die Aufklärungshistoriker selbst, ein Voltaire bereits, ein Hume namentlich, ein Robertson später, hatten ebenfalls schon mit gespanntem Interesse die geistige und gesellschaftliche Verfassung der Urzeiten und Naturvölker zu studieren begonnen. Aber ihr Motiv war ausschliesslich die kausale Wissbegierde, wie die untersten Stufen des grossen Perfektionsprozesses der Menschheit beschaffen gewesen seien. Wesentlich anders waren nun die Motive, die in der präromantischen Bewegung des 18. Jahrhunderts hervortraten. Sie waren mannigfach gemischt und accentuiert. Aber man kann wohl durchweg sagen, dass sie aus einem Ungenügen an der eigenen Zeit stammen, aus einem komplementären Bedürfnis nach Ursprünglichkeit, aus einem echten Bedürfnis der Seele, sich zu erweitern und zu vertiefen, zurückzukehren in eine verlorene schönere Heimat. Man idealisierte nun freilich oft übermässig diese Urzeiten und Naturzustände. So vor allem Rousseau, der dabei neben seiner präromantischen Seele auch noch eine aufklärerisch-rationalistische Seele in sich trug. Aber sein Irrtum gehörte zu den produktiven Irrtümern der Geistesgeschichte. Er hat, obwohl sein Denken bis zuletzt ganz unhistorisch blieb, in unzähligen Menschen seines Jahrhunderts die Fähigkeit geweckt, das Vorurteil der eigenen Zeit, als sei sie die vollkommenste aller Zeiten, abzustreifen und sich umzuschauen in anderen Zeiten und Welten, ob dort nicht ein besseres und edleres Menschentum zu finden sei. Von Rousseaus unhistorischem Romantizismus führt ähnlich wie von Winckelmanns unhistorischem Klassizismus dennoch ein Weg zu tieferem Verstehen der geschichtlichen Welt, zum Historismus, — weil in beiden die ganze Seele es war, die ein neues Land für sich suchte. Wohl war es ein Weg, der namentlich bei Rousseau, zuerst zu Illusionen führte. Der reine, unverdorbene Naturmensch, den er pries, war ja nur der umgestülpte Normalmensch der Zivilisation, der nie und nirgends vorhanden gewesen war. Aber gleichzeitig und neben ihm gab es noch andere Regungen des präromantischen Bedürfnisses in Europa, die zwar auch noch zuerst durchweg mit rationalistischen Elementen versetzt waren, aber zum Teil auch schon mit wirklich wissenschaftlichen Mitteln es vermochten, bisher missachtete geschichtliche Welten neu und sympathisch anzuschauen, ja sogar seelisch zu verstehen. In Frankreich versuchte seit 1746 schon De la Curne Sainte Palaye eine Ehrenrettung des mittelalterlichen Rittertums, die zwar sehr rokokohaft anmutet, aber auf einer nicht geringen Kenntnis der Quellen beruhte. Dann hat, um manches Andere zu übergehen, der junge Genfer Mallet 1755 in seiner Introduction à l'histoire de Dannemarc die Wunder- und Riesenwelt der Edda und des altnordischen Heldentums erschlossen. Er war zwar noch völlig unkritisch in der Behandlung der tatsächlichen geschichtlichen Zusammenhänge der nordischen Völker, aber merkwürdig schöpferisch in der lebendigen Vergegenwärtigung des altnordischen Menschen mit seiner Mischung von Indolenz und Leidenschaft, Grossherzigkeit und Brutalität. Er weckte eine Begeisterung für den Norden, eine Septentriomanie, zwar nicht in Frankreich, aber in der Literatur und Dichtung Englands und Deutschlands.

In Frankreich führten diese präromantischen Regungen nur ein Nebendasein neben der herrschenden Aufklärung. In England eroberten sie sich neben dieser seit der Mitte des Jahrhunderts ein fast gleichberechtigtes Dasein. Sie brachten zwar nicht, wie die Aufklärungshistorie dies tat, so grosse Erscheinungen wie Hume und Gibbon hervor, aber eine Anzahl mittlerer wunderschöner Talente, die nun mit Lust und Liebe, mit Phantasie und Gemüt die schon vorhandene modische Tändelei mit Vergangenheitswerten vertieften. Schon 1735 hat Blackwell sein Buch über Homer veröffentlicht, das Winckelmann "eines der schönsten Bücher in der Welt" genannt hat. Denn es zeigte die homerischen Menschen, naturfrisch und elementar, wie sie wirklich waren, und lehrte, dass Schicksale,

Sitten und Sprache eines Volkes lebendig zusammen-
hingen. Noch farbenreicher hat dann Robert Wood 1769
aus eigener Anschauung Griechenlands und Kleinasiens
die heroische und patriarchalische Welt Homers gemalt
und in Homer den faithful mirror of life einer jugend-
lichen Menschheit gezeigt.

Vielleicht die bedeutendste Leistung innerhalb der präromantischen Bewegung Englands war das Buch des
Oxforder Professors Robert Lowth De sacra poesi Hebraeo-
rum 1753. Hier wurde nun die Bibel, obwohl sie für ihn
nicht aufhörte heilige Schrift im strengsten Sinn zu sein,
mit einem Male auch historisiert. Ganz individuell liess er
die prachtvolle Poesie der Hebräer erblühen aus einem
Bauern- und Hirtenvolke im steinigen Lande Palästina
und verband dabei, wie es der Historismus verlangt,
seelische Einfühlung mit genauer Einzelforschung.

Die Bibel und Homer, diese Grundbücher abendländi-
scher Bildung, erhielten so durch diese Engländer einen
neuen leuchtenden, einen historischen Sinn. Neben der
Antike und dem Christentum aber war die mittelalterliche
Welt der dritte Grundfaktor in den Fundamenten des
abendländischen Kultur. Ich habe schon von der modi-
schen Spielerei mit der Gotik in England gesprochen.
Auch hier setzte vertiefende Betrachtung ein, und des
Bischofs Richard Hurd Letters on chivalry and romance
1762 stellten zum ersten Male, soweit ich sehe, das
grundlegende historische Prinzip auf, dass die gotische
Baukunst eine Kunst sei, die nicht an dem klassizistischen
Masstabe griechischer Kunst gemessen werden dürfe,
sondern ihre eigenen Regeln in sich trage, ein besonderer
geschichtlicher Wert also für sich sei.

England war, bis 1765 etwa, schlechthin führend und
bahnbrechend in der präromantischen Bewegung Europas.
Von da ab, genau mit dem Ende des 7 jährigen Krieges

und in Zusammenhang mit dem nationalen Selbstgefühle,
das er schuf, beginnt die deutsche Bewegung stärker
einzusetzen und von England wie von Frankreich her
befruchtet die präromantischen Tendenzen weiterzutrei-
ben. Herder und Goethe treten nun auf als die eigent-
lichen stärksten Wegbahner des Historismus. Sturm und
Drang ist von präromantischen Regungen durchwirkt,
aber nicht von ihnen nur allein. Es tritt hinzu ein neuer
mächtiger subjektivistischer Lebensdrang, aber er wird
auch genährt durch alte, sogar uralte Quellen. Der seelen-
erweckende mystisch angehauchte Pietismus und der das
ganze Weltall beseelende Neuplatonismus waren solche
Quellen, für den jungen Herder, wie für den jungen Goethe.
Und als Sturm und Drang sich ausgetobt hatten, kam die
Zeit, wo Goethe auch dem Klassizismus die Hand bot und
von Winckelmann lernte. Ich habe gezeigt, wie auch vom
Klassizismus Winckelmanns neues geschichtliches Verstehen und Erleben ausstrahlen konnte.

Viele Wege führten nach Rom, viele Wege führten auch
zum Historismus. Goethe hat in der Epoche seiner Vollen-
dung dann dessen Grundgedanken, Individualität und
Entwicklung, auch auf die geschichtliche Welt in grossem
Umfange angewandt, und Ranke hat, von Goethe befruchtet, das ganze geschichtliche Leben der Menschheit
nach diesen Principien verstehen gelehrt. Klassizismus
und Romantizismus des 18. Jahrhunderts konnten sich in
Goethe auch zuletzt völlig verschmelzen, weil die Seele des
Menschen, die Totalität aller Innenkräfte einer Individualität, zum gemeinsamen Movens geworden war.

Soll ich nun am Schlusse auf die Frage des Eingangs
zurückkommen und in Definitionen zu bannen versuchen,
was ich gezeigt habe von der Entwicklung des Klassizismus wie des Romantizismus des 18. Jahrhunderts? Ich
denke, man wird mir das ersparen. Die unmittelbare

Anschauung und das Mitgefühl für eine sich entwickelnde
Individualität lässt sich nicht in eine logische Definition
umsetzen. Aber das geschichtliche Leben zerfliesst auch
nicht durch Verzicht auf solche Definitionen in eine form-
lose Masse. Wohl ist es in stetigem Flusse, aber auch in
stetiger Hervorbringung von Formen und Gestalten, von
zuweilen sehr festen und anscheinend deswegen auch wohl
definierbaren, zuweilen sehr lockeren und wolkenartigen
Gestalten. Der Klassizismus scheint eine sehr feste Form
darzustellen, weil er von einer festen Norm getragen
wurde. Und doch sahen wir ihn in Winckelmann und
Goethe in Bewegung geraten und durch die treibende
Kraft der Seele zum Historismus hinüberwirken. Der
Romantizismus erscheint dagegen als ein ursprünglich
sehr wolkiges Gebilde, das aus allerlei dunklen Bedürfnissen allerlei neue menschliche Werte abseits von der
klassischen Norm aufstöbert. Aber bei diesem Suchen
und Tasten entdeckt er mit einem Male auch Form und
Gestalt, Sinn und Zusammenhang in bisher missachteten
Erscheinungen der Vergangenheit und öffnet auch dadurch
einen Weg zum Historismus. Klassizismus und Romantizismus ergänzten sich in ihrer Funktion für die Entstehung des Historismus. Jener entwickelte sich von fester
Norm zu seelischer Bewegtheit hinüber. Dieser von einem
unfesten, suchenden Verlangen der Seele zur Erkenntnis,
dass das, was man sucht und findet, Form und Gestalt hat.
In beiden war es die Liebe zum Menschlichen, die in die
Tiefe führte. Und so ist das, was beiden gemeinsam ist,
ausgedrückt in den Versen des Goethischen Faust:

> Das Werdende, das ewig wirkt und lebt,
> Umfass' Euch mit der Liebe holden Schranken,
> Und was in schwankender Erscheinung schwebt,
> Befestiget mit dauernden Gedanken.

UN ROMANTIQUE DE 1730:
L'ABBÉ PRÉVOST

PAUL HAZARD, DR. ÈS LETTRES

Professor of Comparative Literature, Collège de France

PARMI les spectacles qui s'offrent à la curiosité de l'historien des lettres, il n'en est guère de plus passionnant que de voir se produire, dans la série des types représentatifs que l'Europe a choisis tour à tour — le saint, le chevalier, le courtisan, l'honnête homme, le philosophe — un personnage nouveau. Une époque le forme d'abord de ses désirs secrets, de ses aspirations, et de ses rêves; il naît, il brille, il s'impose comme un modèle; et l'époque suivante lui obéit comme à un maître, heureuse de suivre son exemple et de subir sa domination. Vers quel temps le héros romantique, le cœur gonflé de passion, l'âme lourde d'ennui, fatal et pathétique, orgueilleux et faible, toujours prêt à chanter sur le mode lyrique ses rares délices et sa longue peine, est-il apparu sur notre horizon?

Pour marquer sa venue, il ne suffit pas de noter, chez tel écrivain du passé, tel trait particulier que l'on trouve, il est vrai, chez Werther ou chez Lélia, mais qui n'est qu'une des composantes éternelles de l'âme humaine. La première génération romantique, nous dit-on, fut celle de Job: Adam n'aurait-il pas lieu d'être jaloux? L'appétit du fruit défendu, les nostalgies, les révoltes, les désespoirs, les malédictions contre la vie, datent de toujours: mais il n'y a pas toujours eu des Manfred, fils de Byron. Ce que nous cherchons ici, c'est un ensemble de caractères qui, à un moment donné, concourent à former une psychologie unique,

telle qu'on ne l'avait jamais vue auparavant et telle que les
années la dissocieront à son tour. Heureux de profiter des
travaux de nos prédécesseurs, et de leur exprimer notre
reconnaissance,[1] nous voudrions montrer que cette psychologie se manifeste, confuse encore, contradictoire, mais
déjà spécifique, aux environs de 1730, dans les romans de
l'abbé Prévost.[2]

Considérons d'abord les principes sur lesquels le classicisme se fondait: stabilité; ordre social; ferme croyance
dictant la conduite de la vie; et voyons ce qu'ils sont
devenus.

De la stabilité, les personnages de l'abbé Prévost ont
horreur: sans cesse ils changent de maison, de ville, de
pays, de continent; ils quittent la province pour Paris, et
Paris pour la Hollande, l'Allemagne, l'Autriche, la Serbie
où l'on se bat, la Turquie où ils s'introduisent au sérail.
D'un mouvement fébrile, ils parcourent l'Italie des ruines
et des miracles, l'Espagne des guitares et des sanglantes
amours, l'Angleterre qui croit les retenir parce qu'ils
l'aiment, et qu'ils abandonnent cependant.[3] L'Europe ne
leur suffit pas; ils s'engagent dans une poursuite effrénée
qui les emporte à la Martinique, à l'île de Cuba, dans les
Florides, dans la Caroline et jusqu'au cœur de l'Amérique
sauvage, chez les peuplades dont les géographes n'ont
jamais retrouvé le nom.[4] Tantôt ils errent sur les eaux
méditerranéennes, autour de l'île de Malte;[5] tantôt ils s'en
vont trafiquer sur les côtes d'Afrique, aux Indes orientales,
aux Indes occidentales: à peine arrivés au port, ils repren-
nent le large:[6] car rien n'arrête leur humeur vagabonde.
Partir; aller vers le nouveau, vers l'incroyable, quel plaisir!
Cette longue *Histoire des voyages*, des voyages par terre
et par mer qui ont été publiés jusqu'à présent dans les
différentes langues de toutes les nations connues, en quinze
volumes in folio,[7] est autre chose qu'une entreprise de

librairie: c'est l'épopée de l'inconnu, de la surprise, et du mouvement.

Insatisfaits, inadaptés, rebelles à leur milieu, ces êtres passionnés s'évadent — comme avait fait l'abbé Prévost lui-même. Il a passé du couvent à l'armée, et de l'armée au couvent; il a reçu la marque de la prêtrise, la marque éternelle, *tu es sacerdos in aeternum,* pour jeter le froc aux orties; il a fait scandale en Hollande et en Angleterre, où il a risqué d'être pendu; et c'est une chose étrange à penser, que l'auteur de *Manon Lescaut* soit un Bénédictin. S'il s'est amendé par la suite, il n'a pas cessé d'être, au fond de son âme, un aventurier. Aussi ses personnages seront-ils des aventuriers, comme lui-même. Il les choisit volontiers en marge de la vie régulière, rois sans royaumes, réfugiés politiques, ministres tarés, seigneurs désinvoltes que la police recherche parce qu'ils ont innocemment passé leur épée à travers le corps d'un ennemi ou d'un rival, fils de famille en rupture de ban, veuves consolables, filles perdues. Demandons au chevalier des Grieux sa conception de l'ordre social. Les puissants de ce monde, nous dira-t-il, seraient trop heureux, s'il étaient intelligents par surcroît. La Providence a sagement agi, en voulant qu'ils fussent presque toujours des imbéciles. Ainsi les petites gens peuvent les duper à leur aise: "c'est un fond excellent de revenu pour les petits, que la sottise des riches et des grands." [8]

L'abbé Prévost n'est pas de ceux qui estiment que

> De la foi des chrétiens les mystères terribles
> D'ornements égayés ne sont pas susceptibles;

au contraire, il n'hésite pas à mettre la croyance au premier plan de ses histoires profanes, puisque la vie est dominée par le problème religieux, et que le roman se confond désormais avec la vie. Mais vers quelle croyance va-t-il nous

mener? — Il hésite; quelquefois il est pour les accommode-
ments qui rendent moins pénible la voie du salut, comme
les Jésuites; quelquefois il pense, comme les Jansénistes,
que sans la grâce octroyée par un Dieu qui ne doit compte
à personne de ses dons, l'homme adresse vainement ses
prières au ciel inexorable. Ce qui est sûr, c'est qu'il perd
la notion d'un dogme impérieux; son plan n'est pas celui du
ciel, mais de la terre, d'une terre où la religion apporte des
promesses et des consolations. L'histoire de Cleveland, le
philosophe anglais, est celle d'un long examen de conscience, entrecoupé, il est vrai, de quelques occupations
moins austères. Ce héros soucieux fait le tour de toutes les
opinions possibles; et lorsqu'il se laisse ramener enfin au
christianisme, son convertisseur invoque trois raisons dé-
terminantes: la religion est la nécessité la plus juste; elle est
la vérité la plus réelle et la mieux établie; mais d'abord, elle
est le bien le plus désirable. Telle que certains protestants
l'enseignent, elle est âpre et rude; et donc, triste et rebu-
tante; elle n'inspire que du dégoût. Telle que Cleveland
l'adopte, elle offre une face riante, et dont les charmes seuls
sont d'abord un soulagement pour l'imagination; elle com-
porte des grâces intérieures, des secours invisibles, des
faveurs constantes qui n'ont besoin que d'être demandées
pour être obtenues; une liaison anticipée de l'esprit et du
cœur avec un ordre supérieur à la nature; et elle présente
pour dernière perspective une éternité de bonheur et
d'amour.⁹ On ne reconnaît pas, dans de telles paroles, la
rude voix de Bossuet, affirmant la valeur transcendentale
de l'universel et de l'éternel, *quod ubique, quod semper*; mais
on croît entendre les balbutiements d'une apologétique
qui, trois quarts de siècle plus tard, justifiera la foi par sa
valeur émotive: "ce n'était pas les sophistes," dira-t-elle,"
qu'il fallait réconcilier à la religion, c'était le monde qu'ils
égaraient. . . . Il fallait appeler tous les enchantements de

l'imagination et tous les intérêts du cœur au secours de cette même religion contre laquelle on les avait armés." [10]

La morale, enfin, cesse d'être un commandement impérieux, une obligation sans recours. Les personnages de l'abbé Prévost ne se sentent jamais tellement liés par une loi, par un serment, par une promesse, qu'ils ne se délient sans trop de peine; suivant en cela l'évolution d'un siècle qui va de la rigueur aux facilités. L'autorité, qu'elle émane de l'état, du maître, du père de famille, ou de la conscience, est un mot qu'ils n'entendent plus. L'héroïsme que comportait l'esprit classique, et qui exigeait un constant sacrifice de soi-même à l'intérêt ou seulement au plaisir d'autrui, fait place à l'affirmation de caractères qui ne souffrent plus d'entraves, et s'acceptent tels qu'ils sont. Le devoir est une ombre qui s'attire encore des regrets et des désirs, mais qui est trop faible pour exiger des efforts; [11] et son souvenir vient quelquefois ajouter à la faute le plaisir secret d'un faible remords. Être moral, c'est seulement s'examiner et se connaître, non plus pour se dominer, mais pour se complaire, ou, suivant les propres termes de notre auteur: "il entend par le côté moral certaines faces qui répondent aux ressorts intérieurs des actions, et qui peuvent conduire par cette porte à la connaissance des motifs et des sentiments." [12]

Ainsi l'abbé Prévost répudie l'héritage du dix-septième siècle. Non pas tout l'héritage: [13] les fils qui attachent ce qui devient à ce qui était, nous le savons de reste, sont innombrables; et les novateurs les plus impérieux sont encore chargés de chaînes. Il n'a même pas conscience d'être novateur; et cette espèce d'ingénuité rend plus remarquable le travail d'un esprit qui ne s'attaque pas aux apparences du passé, mais qui détruit ses principes profonds. Encore n'est-ce que la partie négative de son œuvre; la partie positive, la voici maintenant.

L'affirmation, l'exaspération du sentiment, caractérisent Cleveland aussi bien que Fanny, Cécile aussi bien que Gelin, Rose aussi bien que Patrice. Celle de nos facultés qui porte le moins notre marque individuelle, la raison qui égalise tout, qui prétend tout soumettre à des règles générales et à des lois uniformes, perd sur eux son empire. La sensibilité, au contraire, qui semble révéler à notre être particulier des puissances inconnues, en multipliant ses joies, ses souffrances et ses délires, les agite et les emporte depuis leur jeunesse jusqu'à leur dernier jour. Leur Moi tumultueux, enrichi de tant de richesses troubles, loin de leur paraître haïssable, est l'objet de leurs préoccupations attendries; ils découvrent, étonnés et ravis, cette masse de sentiments qui palpitent en eux, ces forces dont ils ne sont plus maîtres, et leur souci le plus cher est de pénétrer dans leur impénétrable cœur. [14]

Ils sont tous les victimes de l'amour. Ils s'installent sur le devant de la scène, et toujours sur le mode personnel, ils racontent qu'un beau jour, ils ont rencontré l'amour: et tout de suite, ils ont cédé à cette puissance souveraine, contre laquelle leur volonté s'est trouvée si débile qu'elle n'a pas résisté. La passion s'est emparée de leur cœur et de leurs sens; et ils sont partis sur la route semée d'obstacles, de déconvenues, de malheurs, de violences et de crimes, qui est pourtant la seule qui conduise au bonheur. Les événements qu'ils rappellent au cours de leur confession ne valent qu'en fonction de leur amour, suivant qu'ils le favorisent ou s'opposent à lui. Souvent ces êtres de désir avouent qu'ils ont manqué leur vie; mais ils ne regrettent rien, puisqu'ils ont aimé.

Les traits qu'on ne manque jamais de signaler, quand on veut définir la psychologie romantique, se trouvent rassemblés chez eux. L'ennui: car déjà les grands premiers rôles sont atteints de cette maladie, qu'ils transportent inutilement sous d'autres cieux pour essayer de la guérir, qui ruine leurs raisons de vivre, et qui les pousse à chercher l'apaisement dans la mort. La mélancolie; le dégoût du présent, le désir d'un bien inconnu.

Il ne trouvait rien qui fût capable de le satisfaire, et de lui faire goûter un véritable sentiment de plaisir. Les plus fortes occupations n'étaient pour lui qu'un amusement, qui laissait toujours du vide à remplir au fond de son cœur. . . . Sous un visage enjoué et tranquille, il portait un fond secret de mélancolie et d'inquiétude qui ne se faisait sentir qu'à lui, et qui l'excitait sans cesse à désirer quelque chose qui lui manquait. Ce besoin dévorant, cette absence d'un bien inconnu, l'empêchaient d'être heureux.[15]

Qui parle ainsi? Ce n'est pas René, comme on pourrait le croire; c'est le doyen de Killerine, qui nous peint le caractère du sombre Patrice. Ils ont le goût du mystérieux, ces personnages toujours attentifs aux messages qui leur viennent de la partie de l'âme que ne gouverne pas la raison; ils croient aux pressentiments, aux présages, aux rêves, aux apparitions, aux miracles. Ils ont le goût de la solitude; ils ont le goût du lugubre. Lorsque l'Homme de qualité a perdu sa très chère Sélima, il fait ouvrir son tombeau pendant la nuit et dérober son cœur, qu'il enferme dans une boîte d'or.

Après cela [nous explique-t-il], mon premier soin fut de faire couvrir les murs et le pavé de la chambre que j'avais choisie pour ma demeure, d'un drap noir. Les fenêtres furent bouchées, n'ayant plus envie de revoir la lumière du soleil, mais de me servir seulement de celle de quelques flambeaux. Je fis suspendre aux murailles les habits de Sélima, afin qu'ils pussent frapper continuellement mes yeux. Je posai son cœur sur une table, couverte d'un grand tapis noir, au-dessus de laquelle était un tableau qui la représentait au naturel et dans toute sa beauté. Aux deux côtés de la table étaient les guéridons qui soutenaient les flambeaux dont ce triste lieu devait être sans cesse éclairé. Quelques livres, un lit, et une robe de couleur noire, composaient le reste des meubles. Telle était la disposition de cette espèce de tombeau dans lequel j'avais résolu de m'ensevelir tout vivant. [16]

En fait d'invention mélodramatique, Guilbert de Pixeré-court lui-même ne trouvera rien de plus affreux.

Jusqu'où peut aller cette sensibilité maladive? Au delà du connu, au delà du permis. Le marquis dont l'Homme de qualité est le précepteur fait la connaissance d'un jeune Turc, Memiscès, pour lequel il éprouve un penchant irré-sistible. Il multiplie les attentions à son égard, le couve des yeux: il ne peut plus vivre loin de sa présence. Et nous aurions lieu d'être inquiets, si nous n'apprenions à temps que ce Turc est, en réalité, une jeune fille qui voyage en habits d'homme.[17] Cleveland aime Cécile; et il l'épouserait d'aurant plus volontiers que Cécile l'aime en retour; or voici qu'elle est sa propre fille. Même après cette dé-couverte, Cécile ne peut se délivrer de l'amour impur qui la brûle: elle en fait l'aveu, et elle meurt. Mais elle ne meurt que pour qu'elle puisse enfin se rassasier d'amour: "Déjà moins semblable à une créature mortelle qu'à ces bienheureux esprits dont la substance est toute composée d'amour, son dernier soupir n'avait été que l'élan pas-sionné d'une amante qui se précipite dans le sein de ce qu'elle aime, pout y rassasier à jamais la fureur qu'elle a d'aimer et d'être aimée." [18] Ainsi l'amour, même incestu-eux, est encore d'essence divine. L'amour excuse les vile-nies, les vols, les meurtres; l'amour réhabilite les courti-sanes;[19] l'amour peut être condamné dans certains de ses effets, mais jamais dans son principe;[20] le sentiment, c'est la vertu.

Êtres excessifs, qui ont perdu la notion de la mesure: ils crient, ils s'exclament, ils poussent des soupirs; ils pleurent, ils versent des ruisseaux, des torrents de larmes; ils s'éva-nouissent. Caractères orgueilleux, qui croient porter la marque d'une fatalité qui leur a fait l'honneur de s'attacher

spécialement à les perdre: aucun malheur n'est pire que
leur malheur, aucune souffrance n'égale leur souffrance, le
ciel les a choisis pour montrer en leur personne, par un
illustre exemple, jusqu'où peut aller la fureur du destin.
Caractères qui savourent leur chagrin, qui trouvent une
volupté dans leur tristesse; créatures d'exception, heu-
reuses de sentir en elles une capacité de souffrir qui les met
au-dessus du vulgaire:

> Le commun des hommes n'est sensible qu'à cinq ou six pas-
> sions dans le cercle desquelles leur vie se passe, et où toutes leurs
> agitations se réduisent. Ôtez-leur l'amour et la haine, le plaisir
> et la douleur, l'espérance et la crainte, ils ne sentent plus rien.
> Mais les personnes d'un caractère plus noble peuvent être
> remuées de mille façons différentes; il semble qu'elles aient plus
> de cinq sens, et qu'elles puissent recevoir des idées et des sensa-
> tions qui passent les bornes ordinaires de la nature. Et comme
> elles ont un sentiment de cette grandeur qui les élève au-dessus
> du vulgaire, il n'y a rien dont elles soient plus jalouses.[21]

Héros romantiques. . . .

À la confession pathétique, procédé favori de l'abbé
Prévost, il faut ajouter l'effusion imaginative. Il n'est pas
l'homme qui se borne, qui cent fois sur le métier remet son
ouvrage, qui porte en lui un critique de lui-même, et qui
peine jusqu'à ce qu'il ait atteint la plus haute perfection:
il est, au contraire, trop dégagé, trop facile, et trop abon-
dant. Une seule fois il a su se limiter: et cette exception-
nelle sagesse nous a valu *Manon Lescaut*. Une seule fois il
a corrigé son style; et ce fut encore pour rendre *Manon
Lescaut* plus parfaite. Mais d'ordinaire sa plume court sur
le papier, noircit page après page, avec une intrépidité
qu'aucun scrupule n'arrête. "Pour le *Doyen de Killerine*, mon
intention est de donner la seconde partie dans six semaines,
et de continuer ensuite d'en faire paraître une tous les mois.

J'ai assez d'avance pour être exact à suivre cet arrange-
ment. Tout l'ouvrage consistera en douze parties, qui com-
poseront à la fin de l'année six volumes." [22] Quand ses
ennemis l'accusaient d'écrire ses romans à la diable, sur
une table de cabaret, au milieu des conversations et du
bruit, ils n'avaient peut-être pas tout à fait tort.

Dans ces conditions, sa fantaisie n'a pas de frein. Il invente aventure sur aventure, multiplie les évènements,
entasse les péripéties, insère une histoire dans une autre
histoire, une intrigue dans une autre intrigue: c'est une
débauche d'imagination. Il est d'un sans gêne admirable.
Tel personnage, laissé pour mort à la fin d'un chapitre, cin-
quante pages plus loin ressuscite, paisiblement. Du côté
des monts Apalaches, les féroces Rouintons font rôtir
l'infortunée Madame Riding, pour la dévorer. Elle n'en
réapparaît pas moins un jour, dans une rue de Chaillot,
comme si de rien n'était; elle racontera que les sauvages
l'ont épargnée, qu'elle s'est échappée à travers la forêt
vierge; qu'elle a mangé des poissons qu'elle avait pêchés
à la main, sur lesquels elle s'était couchée une heure ou
deux pour adoucir leur crudité par la chaleur naturelle de
son corps; qu'elle a abreuvé de son sang la petite Cécile, sa
compagne; et qu'en fin de compte, elle a pu regagner
l'Europe. Jadis elle était grasse et blonde: elle est devenue
maigre et brune, ou plutôt noire, tant elle a été brûlée du
soleil, et changée par d'affreuses souffrances. . . .[23] L'abbé
Prévost ne s'embarrasse pas pour si peu; il méprise les
gens qui font les difficiles et les dégoûtés devant les belles
histoires;[24] le merveilleux l'attire, et peu s'en faut qu'il ne
croie l'incroyable, parce qu'il l'aime.

Mais que devient, à ce compte, le naturel dont il se vante?
Ici s'engage un débat essentiel.

L'esprit classique recherche la vérité profonde du cœur
humain. Peu lui importe le décor; et l'histoire, grecque ou

romaine, n'est que le cadre commode qui lui permet de localiser dans le temps des observations éternellement vraies. Au besoin il l'altère sans trop de scrupule, puisque son dessein n'est pas de restituer le passé dans son exactitude, mais de peindre des passions qui n'ont jamais changé et jamais ne changeront. Pour lui, le vrai est moins historique que psychologique.

Pour l'abbé Prévost, le vrai n'est pas l'adhésion donnée par le modèle à un portrait parfaitement réussi. Le vrai ne consiste même pas dans la cohésion logique d'une affirmation avec elle-même: car ce n'est encore là, dit-il, "qu'une preuve de simple raisonnement." Le vrai est garanti par le témoignage historique.

Un de vos arbres a produit des feuilles au milieu de l'hiver; j'en doute malgré vos assurances. Croyez-vous me convaincre, en m'expliquant par quelle voie la nature a pu se développer avant le retour de la belle saison? Vous me forcerez peut-être à convenir que la chose est possible. Mais faites-moi confirmer cette merveille par des témoins sages, qui l'aient vue comme vous, et qui n'aient pu s'accorder pour surprendre ma crédulité; faites-moi voir quelques unes de ces feuilles, avec la verdure et la fraîcheur qu'elles doivent avoir en naissant; j'ajoute foi à votre récit, sans m'embarrasser un moment de votre examen.[25]

Ainsi l'écrivain peut donner sans crainte dans l'exceptionnel et dans l'invraisemblable, si la vérité de cet invraisemblable est assurée par des faits. Le jeune marquis de Rosambert court à Paris les aventures les plus étranges. Il faut cependant les croire, puisque le récit qu'en donne le marquis s'appuie sur des faits incontestables. Il a lié amitié avec Charles de Sévigné, lequel l'a mené chez une actrice qui avait joué la veille le rôle d'Iphigénie. Ils ont assisté à la réception de Racine à l'Académie française; et le soir, ils ont prié à souper Racine en personne, ainsi que Boileau, Molière, le chevalier de Méré, l'abbé Genest. Boileau, qui

était de fort bonne humeur, a raconté une plaisante que-
relle qu'il venait d'avoir avec M. Mocolieri, envoyé de
Venise, au sujet du clinquant du Tasse.²⁶ Ces grands noms,
ces souvenirs connus, ces dates — Racine a été reçu à
l'Académie le 12 Janvier 1673 — donnent à l'ensemble un
air de sérieux et d'authenticité.

Seulement, comme l'abbé Prévost n'est pas historien;
comme il est toujours pressé, et ne vérifie jamais rien;
comme en matière de roman il n'a pas d'esprit critique, et
qu'il se contente de l'à peu près, ces témoignages impo-
sants ne sont qu'un tissu d'erreurs. Comment une actrice
aurait-elle pu, en 1673, jouer un rôle dans *Iphigénie*, qui est
de 1674? Comment Molière, malade et mourant, aurait-il
assisté au souper qui a suivi la réception de Racine à l'Académie? Et comment le chevalier de Méré, qui n'était pas à
Paris? Et comment Boileau se serait-il disputé avec Mocolieri, envoyé de Venise, qui n'a jamais existé? ²⁷

Cette pseudo-vérité tombe du coup. Telle sera, pourtant,
l'attitude mentale d'un Chateaubriand, lorsqu'il décrira
des paysages qu'il n'a pas vus, mais qui sont vrais, puisqu'ils sont garantis par le témoignage de Charlevoix, de
l'abbé Barthélemy, ou de Chandler. Tel Victor Hugo, qui,
pour faire taire les critiques appliqués à lui reprocher ses
invraisemblances et ses inexactitudes, se justifiera par ses
références, généralement empruntées au Dictionnaire de
Moreri, et transcrites avec quelques erreurs supplémen-
taires et quelques inventions personnelles. Tel, et davan-
tage encore, Alexandre Dumas. Par l'histoire, ils préten-
dront légitimer les jeux de leur fantaisie, et donner une substance à leurs rêves: et de l'histoire elle-même, ils feront un
rêve et un jeu.

C'était le temps où l'esprit triomphait: *Le Jeu de l'amour
et du hasard* est de 1730. C'était le temps où la raison pré-
tendait dissiper toutes les ombres, projetant ses lumières

sur le mystère de la vie: les *Lettres philosophiques* sont de
1734. L'abbé Prévost n'est pas pour l'esprit, pour le jar-
gon, l'affectation, les réflexions sophistiquées.[28] L'abbé
Prévost n'est pas pour la raison abstraite. L'abbé Prévost
n'est pas pour Locke, dont ses contemporains se sont en-
goués: et même il les met en garde, à plusieurs reprises,
contre une doctrine qui conduit tout droit au matérialisme
et à l'athéisme.[29] Comme si l'on pouvait prétendre que
l'esprit est une table rase; et comme si les Anglais eux-
mêmes, tout férus qu'ils soient de sa philosophie, n'étaient
pas de tous les peuples du monde celui qui se conduit le
plus généralement par les premières impressions de la
nature! L'abbé Prévost n'est pas pour les facultés qui con-
trarient les forces spontanées, les émois, les élans de l'âme.
L'abbé Prévost, quand il exprime le tréfonds de lui-même,
dans de rares et délicieux moments, est lyrique.

Quelquefois, en effet, il renonce à son fatras; ses récits
éperdus se ralentissent et s'arrêtent; le lieu n'importe plus,
ni le temps; les trop nombreux comparses rentrent dans
l'ombre; quelques notes servent de prélude, et une voix
s'élève, si belle qu'elle émeut moins encore par les mots
qu'elle prononce que par la qualité unique de son chant.
Non pas qu'elle s'exprime en vers: elle invente une musique
plus subtile que celle des alexandrins régulièrement coupés,
que celle des rimes résonnant chaque fois à leur place fixe,
et chaque fois attendues: elle crée sans cesse ses rythmes
et ses tons; elle fait de la prose l'instrument le plus parfait
de la poésie; et ainsi elle accomplit ce miracle de ressusciter
le lyrisme dans un siècle qui en avait perdu jusqu'à la
notion, jusqu'au souvenir. Celui qui l'a entendue, cette
tendre voix plaintive, ne peut plus l'oublier; elle résonne
au fond de son cœur, qu'elle remplit de ses charmes et de
ses enchantements:

Ah! Manon, Manon,
il est bien temps de me donner des larmes
lorsque vous avez causé ma mort.
Vous affectez une tristesse
que vous ne sauriez sentir.
Le plus grand de vos maux
est sans doute ma présence
qui a toujours été
importune à vos plaisirs.
　Ouvrez les yeux,
　voyez qui je suis;
　on ne verse pas
　des pleurs si tendres
　pour un malheureux
　qu'on a trahi
　et qu'on abandonne
　cruellement.[30]

Dans ces exceptionnels passages, Prévost atteint la beauté souveraine. Il traduit la qualité d'un amour qui prend une valeur absolue. Nous l'avons dit ailleurs: [31] la passion de Des Grieux, sensuelle et égoïste d'abord, aboutit à un état psychologique où l'individu ne se considère plus comme sa propre fin, et se subordonne entièrement à l'objet de son culte. Que s'il y a, dans le romantisme, entre tants d'éléments impurs qu'il renferme, un transport vers l'idéal; s'il est exaltation, abandon à un objet conçu comme surhumain, offrande de soi-même, sacrifice, immolation: ici encore, l'abbé Prévost fait figure d'initiateur.

Certes on trouve avant lui, autour de lui, des expressions de l'individualisme passionné dont le développement transformera la littérature et la société.[32] Mais ce qu'il offre, et ce qu'il offre seul à son époque, c'est l'ensemble que nous cherchions; c'est le talent qui était nécessaire pour donner une forme à cette psychologie en devenir; le talent, et même le génie, le jour où il a composé *Manon Lescaut.*

Si ces observations sont exactes, il faut, en premier lieu,

avancer d'un quart de siècle la manifestation avérée de
l'état d'esprit romantique; et ne plus dire que Rousseau est
le premier, mais le second. Rousseau est plus âpre et plus
fort; Rousseau anime et vivifie les arbres et les eaux, les
plaines et les montagnes, que Prévost n'avait pas encore
appris à aimer; [33] Rousseau commande, et Prévost bavarde;
Rousseau concentre, et Prévost dilue; Rousseau possède,
suivant l'expression d'un critique allemand, une *Radikali-
tät* [34] qui confère à chacun de ses livres, à chacun de ses
chapitres, et presque à chacune de ses phrases, une puissance inégalée. Reste qu'avant lui, Prévost déchaîne la
sensibilité et l'imagination; exempte l'individu des disciplines qui le réfrénaient; et en conséquence, charge le
roman de procéder à un nouvel examen de conscience, à un
reclassement de valeurs qui n'épargne ni la politique, ni la
pédagogie, ni la philosophie, ni la religion. Reste qu'avant
lui, Prévost affirme sa confiance dans la nature. Lorsque
Cleveland la découvre dans sa simplicité primitive chez les
sauvages Abaquis, il constate que ses droits sont les premiers de tous les droits; qu'avant d'être corrompue par
l'habitude du vice, elle inspire l'innocence et la vertu;
qu'elle suffit à fonder une société heureuse et une religion
bienfaisante; et qu'il convient non pas de la réprimer, mais
de la régler seulement. [35]

C'est sans doute moins théâtral que les affirmations solen-
nelles: *Tout est bien, sortant des mains de l'auteur des choses*; ou
encore: *L'homme est naturellement bon*; mais c'est d'une presque
aussi ferme assurance. Jean-Jacques a compris de bonne heure
la portée de ces principes de Prévost; et c'est à travers *Cleveland*
que ce jeune homme de vingt-sept ans a, pour la première fois
peut-être, pressenti son système:

 ... Dans Cleveland j'observe la nature
 Qui se montre à mes yeux touchante et toujours pure.

(Verger des Charmettes, VI, 6)[36]

Il n'est même pas impossible de soutenir que sur deux points, l'auteur de *Cleveland* est plus près des romantiques que l'auteur de *La nouvelle Héloïse*. Le premier: Rousseau, après avoir détruit la société par l'avènement d'un Moi tumultueux qui fait éclater ses cadres, éprouve le besoin de la reconstruire; Julie redevient bourgeoise et finit par faire des confitures. L'abbé Prévost n'a pas ce souci. — En second lieu: la vie morale des romantiques implique une contradiction profonde: ils proclament la bonté de la nature et en même temps, ils n'arrivent pas à abolir en eux le sens du péché. Dans le moment où ils exaltent les droits de la passion, ils ont conscience d'une force obscure qui la condamne: ils sont incapables de chanter librement l'hymne payen à la vie. Tel n'est pas Rousseau, pour qui la nature n'a pas d'autre ennemie que la civilisation; et tel est Prévost, âme encore chrétienne qui ne peut abolir en elle l'angoisse secrète du problème du mal.[37]

Mais au changement de dates que nous proposons, et qui tend à substituer 1730 à 1760, la littérature française n'est pas seule intéressée. C'est une opinion communément reçue, en effet, que le triomphe de la sensibilité s'affirme avec Richardson; Pamela et Clarisse, frémissantes et pathétiques héroïnes, ont fait pleurer les Anglais d'abord, puis les Allemands et les Français, puis les Italiens et les Espagnols, puis toute l'Europe. Seulement, *Pamela* est de 1740, et *Clarisse Harlowe* de 1748; or *Cleveland* est traduit en anglais dès 1734, en allemand dès 1736; un avant-goût des *Mémoires et aventures d'un homme de qualité* est donné aux Allemands dès 1730, et l'ouvrage entier est offert aux Anglais dès 1738. Dès lors, il est hors de doute que l'influence de l'abbé Prévost s'est exercée en France, en Angleterre,[38] en Allemagne,[39] avant celle de Richardson, et d'ailleurs après elle; de sorte qu'il faut nuancer, maintenant, la progression autrefois établie: le drame sentimental anglais, Richardson, Rousseau; et en proposer une autre, plus nuancée: le drame sentimental anglais, l'abbé Prévost, Richardson, Rousseau; et puis le Goethe du Sturm und Drang; et puis Chateaubriand. . . .

Ainsi le passé dont nous sommes les gardiens doit être retouché sans cesse. C'est notre rôle que d'essayer de lui conférer toujours plus de précision, d'exactitude, et de vérité. Historiens, nous devons défendre le patrimoine de l'humanité contre les causes d'altération qui le menacent, si lointain déjà, si pâle, et si près d'être effacé. Les présentes fêtes n'auraient pas tout leur sens, si l'Université Harvard ne nous avait invités d'abord à rappeler, par l'exemple et par le symbole de ces enquêtes menées dans tous les ordres du savoir, à la fois la difficulté de notre tâche, et sa grandeur. Chercher; chercher encore. Regarder de plus près, pour remplacer, s'il est possible, les approximations par des certitudes. Ne pas jurer sur les paroles des maîtres; mais revenir aux faits, et à la critique des faits. Ainsi nous arriverons à restituer les vies que nous avons traversées quand nous n'existions pas encore; les vies que nous n'avons pas vécues, et dont nous sommes si lourdement chargés.

NOTES

1 Citons en particulier l'étude de B. Woodbridge, "Romantic Tendencies in the Novels of the Abbé Prévost," *Publications of the Modern Language Association*, vol. XXVI (1911), riche d'indications utiles sur le même sujet.

2 Nous utilisons de préférence les romans de l'abbé Prévost qui ont paru avant la *Pamela* de Richardson: *Mémoires et aventures d'un homme de qualité qui s'est retiré du monde* (tomes I et II, 1728; tomes III et IV, 1728; tomes V, VI, et VII, 1731 — tome VII, *Histoire du chevalier des Grieux et de Manon Lescaut*); *Le philosophe anglais; Histoire de Cleveland, fils naturel de Cromwell, écrite par lui-même et traduite de l'anglais* (tomes I et II, 1731; tomes III et IV, 1731; tomes V et VI, 1738). *Le doyen de Killerine, histoire morale, composé sur les mémoires d'une illustre famille d'Irlande, et ornée de tout ce qui peut rendre une lecture utile et agréable* (première partie, 1735; deuxième et troisième partie, 1739; quatrième, cinquième et sixième partie, 1740). Les romans postérieurs à ces dates ne seront invoqués qu'à titre de confirmation.

Nos citations seront faites d'après les *Œuvres choisies de l'abbé Prévost* (Amsterdam, 1783, 39 vols.).

3 *Mémoires et aventures d'un homme de qualité.*

4 *Histoire de Cleveland.*

5 *Mémoires pour servir à l'histoire de Malte, ou Histoire de la jeunesse du Commandeur de XXX* (1741).

6 Voir J. Ducarre, "Une supercherie littéraire de l'abbé Prévost: Les voyages de Robert Lade," *Revue de littérature comparée*, Juillet 1936.

7 *Histoire générale des voyages, ou Nouvelle collection de toutes les relations de voyages par mer et par terre, qui ont été publiés jusqu'à présent dans les différentes langues des nations connues* (1741).

8 "La Providence, ajoutai-je en réfléchissant sur les différents états de la vie, n'a-t-elle pas arrangé les choses fort sagement? La plupart des grands et des riches sont des sots; cela est clair à qui connait un peu le monde. Or, il y a là-dedans une justice admirable. S'ils joignaient l'esprit aux richesses, ils seraient trop heureux, et le reste des hommes trop misérables. Les qualités du corps et de l'âme sont accordés à ceux-ci, comme des moyens pour se retirer de la misère et de la pauvreté. . . . C'est un fond excellent de revenu pour les petits, que les sottises des riches et des grands" (*Histoire de Manon Lescaut; Œuvres*, III, 290–291).

9 *Histoire de Cleveland; Œuvres*, VII, 425.

10 *Génie du christianisme*, première partie, I, 1.

11 "Ce fut dans ce moment que l'honneur et la vertu me firent sentir encore les pointes du remords, et que je jetai les yeux, en soupirant, vers Amiens, vers la maison de mon père, vers Saint Sulpice, et vers tous les lieux où j'avais vécu dans l'innocence. Par quel immense espace n'étais-je pas séparé de cet heureux état! Je ne le voyais plus que de loin, comme une ombre qui s'attirait encore mes regrets et mes désirs, mais trop faible pour exciter mes efforts" (*Histoire de Manon Lescaut; Œuvres*, III, 313).

12 *Le monde moral, ou Mémoires pour servir à l'histoire du cœur humain* (1760), Avertissement.

13 Nous avons nous-même marqué la part de classicisme — ou, pour mieux dire peut-être, d'humanisme — qui revient à l'abbé Prévost, dans nos *Études critiques sur Manon Lescaut* (University of Chicago Press, 1929, pp. 29 et suivantes).

14 "Pénétrer dans le cœur qui passe pour impénétrable! Oui, si, malgré le préjugé commun, des routes secrètes, ménagées par la nature, en ouvrent l'accès à ceux qui peuvent les découvrir. Je les ai cherchées pendant quarante ans, et j'abandonne au lecteur le soin de mes découvertes. Cyrano s'est promené dans le monde lunaire, Kirker dans le monde souterrain, Daniel dans le monde de Descartes, Bekker dans un monde enchanté; et moi, j'ai pris pour objet de mes courses et de mes observations le *Monde Moral*; carrière aussi vaste, moins imaginaire, plus riche, plus variée, plus intéressante et, sans comparaison, plus utile . . ." (*Le monde moral; Œuvres*, XXIX, 1–3). On se rappelle l'expression de Chateaubriand, qui cherche à expliquer son inexplicable cœur.

15 *Le doyen de Killerine; Œuvres*, VIII, 20–21.

16 *Mémoires et aventures d'un homme de qualité; Œuvres*, I, 264–265.

17 *Mémoires et aventures d'un homme de qualité; Œuvres*, II, 180 et suivantes.

18 *Histoire de Cleveland; Œuvres*, VII, 379.

19 *Mémoire d'un honnête homme; Œuvres*, XXXIII, 62 et suivantes.

20 *Histoire de Cleveland; Œuvres*, IV, 145: "Il me parut, après un sincère examen, que les droits de la nature étant les premiers de tous les droits, rien n'était assez fort pour prescrire contre eux; que l'amour en était un des plus sacrés, puisqu'il est l'âme de tout ce qui existe; et qu'ainsi tout ce que la raison ou l'ordre établi parmi les hommes pouvaient faire contre lui était d'en interdire certains effets, sans pouvoir jamais le condamner dans sa source."

21 *Histoire de Manon Lescaut; Œuvres*, III, 324.

22 *Le doyen de Killerine; Œuvres*, VIII, préface, p. 16.

23 *Histoire de Cleveland; Œuvres*, VII, 109 et suivantes.

24 *Ibid., Œuvres*, IV, préface, p. 11.

25 *Ibid.*, pp. 10–11.

26 *Mémoires et aventures d'un homme de qualité; Œuvres*, I, 97 et suivantes.

27 F. Neri, "Disputa di Boileau e di un Italiano," *Revue de littérature comparée*, 1933, p. 487. Voir, pour des procédés analogues, Jean Hankiss, "Secrets d'atelier de l'abbé Prévost," *Séances et travaux de l'Académie des sciences morales et politiques*, Juillet-Août 1933.

28 *Le pour et le contre*, III, nombre 36.

29 *Ibid.*, III, 38; IV, 55; V, 44; IX, 130; XIII, 183. C'est à IV, 55, que se trouve la critique la plus développée des idées de Locke.

30 *Histoire de Manon Lescaut; Œuvres*, III, 404.

31 Dans les *Études critiques sur Manon Lescaut*, pp. 45–46.

32 Gustave Lanson, *Nivelle de la Chaussée et la comédie larmoyante* (2e édition Paris, Hachette, 1903), troisième partie, chap. IV; Paul Hazard, *La crise de la conscience européenne* (Paris, Boivin, 1935), quatrième partie.

33 Prévost ignore encore le sentiment de la nature. Voici, en effet, ce qu'il trouve à dire devant les montagnes d'Innsprück: "Nous demandâmes en grâce à voir sa prison. C'était une chambre honnête, d'où il n'avait que la vue d'une affreuse chaîne de montagnes" (*Le monde moral; Œuvres*, XXIX; avant-propos, p. xi). Notons toutefois une fraîche et charmante impression de nature, à l'aube d'un jour de mai, par contraste avec l'atmosphère d'un souper que la débauche a prolongé jusqu'au matin (*Mémoires d'un honnête homme; Œuvres*, XXXII, 49–50).

34 Hugo Friedrich, *Abbé Prévost in Deutschland: Ein Beitrag zur Geschichte der Empfindsamkeit* (Heidelberg, Carl Winter, 1929; Beiträge zur neuen Literatur-geschichte, XII).

35 *Histoire de Cleveland*, tome V, livre IV, passim. L'idée d'une nature foncière-ment bonne revient à maintes reprises dans les premières œuvres de Prévost. Par exemple: "Sans affecter d'être insensible au mouvement de la nature, il avait trouvé l'art de la régler" (*Histoire de Cleveland; Œuvres*, VII, 409). "Je sais qu'un juste penchant anime les deux sexes l'un pour l'autre; il est établi pour la douceur autant que pour la conservation de la société; et les atteintes du sort ou de la malignité des hommes qui peuvent en troubler les charmes ne doivent point être reprochées à la nature" (*Ibid.*, pp. 419–420).

36 Pierre Maurice Masson, *La religion de Jean-Jacques Rousseau* (Paris, Hachette, 1916), I, 114-115. Voir Servais Étienne, *Le genre romanesque en France depuis l'apparition de la Nouvelle Héloïse jusqu'aux approches de la Révolution* (Paris, Colin, 1922) — cet ouvrage s'attache particulièrement à montrer le grand rôle que joue l'abbé Prévost dans le développement du roman euro-

péen——; Daniel Mornet, *Introduction à Jean-Jacques Rousseau, La nouvelle Héloïse* (Paris, Hachette, 1925, tome I); A. Monglond, *Histoire intérieure du préromantisme français de l'abbé Prévost à Joubert* (Grenoble, Arthaud, 1929); Pierre Trahard, *Les maîtres de la sensibilité français au dix-huitième siècle* (Paris, Boivin, 1931).

37 *Mémoires et aventures d'un homme de qualité*, I, 7: "Personne n'est plus persuadé que moi de la réalité d'un premier crime, qui a rendu tous les hommes coupables, faibles et malheureux. C'est le fondement du christianisme, et je ne vois rien de mieux établi. . . ."

38 Voir James R. Foster, "The Abbé Prévost and the English Novel, "*PMLA*, vol. XLII (1927).

39 Hugo Friedrich, *Abbé Prévost in Deutschland*.

THE DRIFT TO LIBERALISM IN THE AMERICAN EIGHTEENTH CENTURY

HOWARD MUMFORD JONES, A.M., LITT.D.

Professor of English, Harvard University

THE topic before us is "Classicism and Romanticism"; and ranged as this topic is under the larger heading of "Authority and the Individual," it suggests that in the conflict between authority and the individual, classicism and romanticism have their part. I propose to inquire how far the terms in question are applicable to American literary history.

I shall not attempt to define either term,[1] though it is important that no literary historian has spoken of a classical age in American literary history, those portions of the seventeenth and eighteenth centuries which are elsewhere known as classical, neoclassical, or Augustan being called the Colonial and Revolutionary periods. As for romanticism, recalling Professor Lovejoy's warning that we should discriminate among romanticisms,[2] I shall begin by touching upon the confused uses of the word by American literary historians.

In the first place, it is notable that a number of histories of American letters having considerable philosophical weight, published between 1887 and 1936, do not find it necessary to discuss or distinguish a "romantic period."[3] Other books formally recognize a "romantic period" under a variety of names, but do not agree as to the extent of the era involved. Thus Parrington entitled his second volume

The Romantic Revolution in America: 1800–1860; Leisy entitles his third chapter "The Romantic Impulse," and discusses literature from Irving to the metropolitan poets; Blankenship believes that "America of the early nineteenth century accepted" the ideas of the romantic school "as if they were of unquestionable validity," and extends romanticism from the early 1770's to the Civil War; Dickinson thinks the romantic period runs from 1789 to 1855; McDowell confines the "romantic triumph" to the years 1830–1860; Miller tells us that the literature of romantic America extends from 1800 to 1850; and Taylor extends "romantic art in an agrarian republic" to 1870.[4] These authors are not so generous as the late George Edward Woodberry, who, though he told his readers on one page that American literature "has been sundered from the great movement of romanticism abroad," told them elsewhere that "America was romantic from the first," that "romance has been our genius," and that American literature has been controlled "by the academic, artistic, and romantic spirit."[5]

Such is the chronological perplexity; what may be called the geographical confusions of American romanticism are also noteworthy. There is general agreement that romantic literature was written sometime in New England; but one writer says that this movement democratically "emphasized the worth of human nature"; another, that on the whole "the aristocratic tradition persisted more strongly in literature than in most other fields of life"; a third, that Unitarianism accomplished a "wide dissemination of eighteenth-century French liberalism" in New England; a fourth, that this writing exhibits "reactionary tendencies of thought, Utopias, and a refuge in history and mediaevalism"; a fifth, that a wave of Wordsworthianism "swept gently over New England and here and there found a mind which was . . . refreshed"; a sixth, that if "Emerson and Whitman were pure Romanticists, then none of the various definitions of Romanticism so far formulated is adequate"; and a seventh dubs the whole thing an "Augustan age" when "gentlemen pursued litera-ture in a seemly fashion."[6] As for the South, the inquirer will find it asserted that the Southern planters cherished "a romantic dream," and that classicism is "a distinctly Southern trait"; that, "landing first in Virginia in the early seventeen-seventies, [French romantic theories] met with a hospitable reception from the generous planter society," and that "the heritage of the pre-Civil War South from feudal mediaevalism by way of the eighteenth century was inevitably expressed in reactionary thinking"; that the favorite reading of the South was Scott, Bulwer, Byron, and Moore, its lyrical poets being "disciples of the romantic poets of England," and that early nineteenth-century Virginia writers were anti-romantic, and Charles-ton, that influential intellectual capital, was a place domi-nated by the Addisonian essay, the heroic couplet, and a classical education. Not unnaturally, in view of these con-tradictions, one historian concludes that "in literary ad-vancement, the South stood in 1860 where America as a whole stood at the beginning of the century"![7] In the earlier nineteenth century New York or Philadelphia is variously described as romantic or conservative, depend-ing on the book one consults;[8] and the frontier is alter-nately a source of romanticism and a mistaken adopter of it.[9]

What are the inciting causes, origins, beginnings, initial impulses, or backgrounds of American romanticism? In other words, what started it? There is a rich variety of theories. One may learn that American romanticism is due to French rationalism, [10] mysticism,[11] Puritanism,[12] the revolt against Puritanism,[13] a belief in the innate goodness of man,[14] a Puritanical absorption in sin,[15] post-Kantian idealism,[16] travel, [17] closeness to nature in America,[18] the search for foreign themes,[19] an interest in the American rather than in the European past,[20] industrial expansion,[21] the fact that we were not an industrial but an agrarian society,[22] optimism,[23] an unconscious return to Jonathan Edwards,[24] a slavish following of Wordsworth, Coleridge, and others,[25] pride in our new-found independence,[26] the frontier,[27] the romantic charm of Spain,[28] the fact that Channing visited Virginia,[29] a thirst for greater culture,[30] primitivism,[31] and the absence of primitivism from American literature[32] — they all had something to do with it! A movement thus heterogeneously "founded" is necessarily equipped by scholars with a wild disorder of qualities, but these I shall not pause to enumerate.[33]

Since by "romanticism," "the romantic revolt," "the romantic triumph," "the romantic impulse," and similar phrases, historians of American literature mean so many things, we can clarify the situation by discriminating among meanings. One may pass over such naïve confusions as that of "romance" in the sense of a form of fiction with "romanticism" as a literary philosophy and such vague generalized uses of the term as appear in phrases like "the romantic New World"; one may note in passing that if Fichte, Schelling, Coleridge, and the like are to be denominated romantic philosophers, the same adjective can not be consistently applied to rationalists, sceptics, and materialists like Voltaire, Diderot, Holbach, Helvétius, and D'Alembert; and one may find the literary historian referring to some one or other of the following meanings of American romanticism:

1. *Generalized Romanticism.* He may mean that American writers, especially poets, frequently adopt the literary

themes and the literary rhetoric of European romanticism (usually British) without at the same time adopting or expressing any philosophy or system of ideas significantly or primarily romantic.

2. *The Romantic Treatment of History.* He may refer to writing which sets forth real or imaginary events in the American past, so narrating or describing these events through a more or less romantic rhetoric as to emphasize their ideal, colorful, "poetic," dramatic, melodramatic, or heroic qualities at the expense of historical or psychological realism in the contemporary sense of realism.

3. *Romanticism as Escape.* He may refer to "escapist" literature written by Americans, mainly in the nineteenth century, who, dissatisfied with the actual conditions of American existence, sought aesthetic or emotional satisfaction in the contemplation of lands and cultures, real or imaginary, remote in time or space from the actual United States and interpreted by these writers in terms primarily conditioned by their dissatisfaction with the actual conditions of American life.

4. *Romanticism as Philosophy.* He may refer to a phase of American intellectual development primarily theological in its origins, centering in New England, supposed to begin as a revolt against Calvinism and to culminate in the transcendental writers, and influenced to an undetermined degree in the later phases of its history by German transcendental philosophy, French eclecticism, and the philosophical outlook and aesthetic standards of such British writers as Wordsworth, Coleridge, and Carlyle. Writers associated with this movement do not customarily express themselves in the same rhetorical fashion as those in group one.

5. *Romanticism as Political or Economic Theory.* He may refer to a movement in political and economic theory

primarily libertarian in character, expressive of political and economic individualism, supposed to have its intellectual bases in the polemics of the American Revolutionary period, and presumed by some historians to be influenced to a degree not ascertained by a group of eighteenth-century French theorists vaguely denominated the French radical, revolutionary, or romantic philosophers. For some theorists other bases of this movement are supplied by the Newtonian world order, deism, rationalism, primitivism, and a "return to nature" in the sense of a cosmic order benevolently directed towards economic abundance.

6. *Romanticism as Nationalism.* He may refer to the expression in literature, usually through a romantic rhetoric, of a nationalistic spirit in one or more of the following senses: (a) American "democratic" life poetically, or at any rate unrealistically, conceived as *per se* superior to life in the Old World; (b) the American landscape conceived as unspoiled, wild, grandiose, sublime, strange, or beautiful, and fertile in plants, animals, and, I may add, Indians; (c) "pioneer" life poetically, or at any rate unrealistically, conceived as the resultant of the interplay between democratic existence and the natural setting of that existence, the absence of European and of urban culture making for the release of primary or elemental virtues, and therefore, in a somewhat unusual sense of the word, primitivistic. The origins of this phase of American literary expression are left chronologically indefinite, but its ending is usually placed in the 1870's.

Though these categories are neither exhaustive nor mutually exclusive, one may confidently say that American romanticism in senses one, two, and three offers little difficulty. We should agree, I think, that in style and substance American lyricists of the last century are romantic rather than classical in the main; that a poem like "Paul

Revere's Ride," a novel like *The Last of the Mohicans*, and a play like *Shenandoah* offer romantic versions of historical events; and that "escapist" literature is romantic. But senses four, five, and six — romanticism as philosophy, romanticism as political or economic theory, and romanticism as nationalism — offer greater problems because it is precisely to these more intellectualistic concepts that the terms "romantic revolt" and "romantic triumph" are applied. If there was a revolt, against what was it directed? If there was a triumph, in what respects was it a victory? In older literatures, the romantic movement is conceived as a departure from classicism; but the failure of literary historians to distinguish a classical movement in American letters robs us of this easy dichotomy. And yet one writer assures us that at the turn of the last century the romantic revolution

laid hold of men's minds [in America], consuming the stubble of eighteenth-century harvests, sweeping away the drab realisms of a cautious past, and offering in their stead more alluring ideals;[34]

a second, that "the romantic revolution,"

affecting everything from our verse form to our conception of man's place in the universe, was probably the most influential and widespread intellectual force ever liberated in the United States;[35]

and a third, that

Freneau's religion, the religion of nature and humanity . . . illustrates the neglected transition from Puritanism to deism and from deism to Unitarianism and pantheism [and] motivates . . . [the] political and . . . poetical interests[36]

of the "father of American poetry" and therefore presumably serves as the focal point in a revolution wrought for subsequent American verse.

Now my objection to language of this sort is that it is not

justified by the facts of American intellectual development and that it gives a distorted and over-dramatized picture of what actually occurred. The scholar who describes a romantic revolution "consuming the stubble" of the eighteenth century places Thomas Jefferson in the center of the stage and makes much of the influence upon him of French "romantic philosophy," so called, despite the fact that the most careful biographer of Jefferson's intellectual development assures us, not once, but over and over again, that Jefferson owes almost nothing to the French. "The Jeffersonian democracy," Chinard says picturesquely, "was born under the sign of Hengist and Horsa, not of the Goddess Reason."[37] But passing over these aberrations, I should like to examine the idea of nature as set forth in Freneau in order to illustrate the difference between the concept of a literary revolution and the concept of a slow, organic growth in the American mind.

Since "nature" in the sense of the cosmos, however interpreted, is on the whole for the transcendentalists by some historians supposed to be "good,"[38] and since "nature" in the sense of created nature is by some historians supposed for the Calvinists to be "bad," it has seemed necessary to explain this reversal in point of view, and the deism of Paine, Freneau, and Jefferson has been put forward[39] as a middle term of the "revolution" wrought. Thus we are told that deism

found congenial soil on the American frontier, an environment inculcating freedom, self-reliance, and optimism in place of determinism, passivity, and gloom; [that] Freneau reverently tells us that the "Great Frame of the Universe" — its "exact design," a "structure complete in itself" — teaches "the reasoning human soul" to infer an "author of the whole."

in contrast to the deity of this "good" universe our author places the New England Primer, the bloody deity

of Increase Mather, and Jonathan Edwards' deity con-
templating sinners in hell.[40] "One can understand," says
this scholar, "how this sort of thing would annoy Presby-
terians."[41] I can understand that deism annoyed Presby-
terians, and it is regrettable that Jonathan Edwards' God
was not more gentlemanly, but it seems odd that if frontier
conditions in the eighteenth century produced "freedom,
self-reliance, and optimism," analogous conditions should in
the seventeenth century have inculcated "determinism,
passivity, and gloom"; and I am compelled to point out
that there is little in Freneau's interpretation of the universe as rational order which Calvin could not approve and
which was not a commonplace in American thought long
before Freneau.[42]

Calvin, it is true, says that Adam "ruined his posterity
by his defection, which has perverted the whole order of
nature in heaven and earth,"[43] but this does not mean that
the glorious rational order of the cosmos has been warped,
only that man's nature has been fatally affected. As he
tells us at the opening of the *Institutes*:

Of his wonderful wisdom, both heaven and earth contain innumerable proofs; not only those more abstruse things, which
are the subjects of astronomy, medicine, and the whole science
of physics, but those things which force themselves on the view
of the most illiterate of mankind, so that they cannot open their
eyes, without being constrained to witness them. Adepts, indeed, in those liberal arts, or persons just initiated into them, are
thereby enabled to proceed much further in investigating the
secrets of Divine Wisdom. Yet ignorance of those sciences prevents no man from such a survey of the workmanship of God, as
is more than sufficient to excite his admiration of the Divine
Architect. In disquisitions concerning the motions of the stars,
in fixing their situations, measuring their distances, and distinguishing their peculiar properties, there is need of skill, exact-
ness, and industry; and the providence of God being more
clearly revealed by these discoveries, the mind ought to rise to a

sublimer elevation for the contemplation of his glory. But since the meanest and most illiterate of mankind, who are furnished with no other assistance than their own eyes, cannot be ignorant of the excellence of the Divine skill, exhibiting itself in that endless, yet regular variety of the innumerable celestial host, — it is evident, that the Lord abundantly manifests his wisdom to every individual on earth . . . the composition of the human body is universally acknowledged to be so ingenious, as to render its Maker the object of deserved admiration.[44]

"The structure and organization of the world," says Calvin, "and the things that daily happen out of the ordinary course of nature," "bear a witness to God which the dullest ear cannot fail to hear" (*Institutes*, I, v, 1, 3, 7; II, vi, 1); the "light that shines from creation while it may be smothered, cannot be so extinguished but that some rays of it find their way into the most darkened soul" (*Institutes*, I, v, 14); [45] and long before the deistic movement of Freneau, Paine, and Jefferson, seventeenth- and eighteenth-century Americans had taken up with especial ardor those branches of natural science which enabled them to penetrate "further in investigating the secrets of Divine Wisdom." Of the innumerable instances which might be given, I shall cite only one: a sermon or two by that excellent Presbyterian clergyman, the Rev. Benjamin Colman, preached in Boston three-quarters of a century before Freneau's first book appeared. His subject was the incomprehensibility of God.[46] The incomprehensibility of God, he argued, is no reason why fallen man should not try to understand his nature. "The true Pleasure and blessedness of the Intelligent Creature lies in the Knowledge of the Creator," he said. And the learned Presbyterian surveyed "nature" with all the ardor of a deist:

It is the *fixt Opinion* now of *Learned Men*, from what they do see and know of the Creation by *Telescopes*, that there may be and in all probability are many such *Worlds*, as this which our Eyes view, when we take the compass of the Heavens with them. And if it be so, how does it *Enlarge* the Creation to us, and the Greatness of the *Creator*? [47]

Colman admires the great frame of the universe and the "exact design" of the heavens; then he fixes his attention upon the earth, hanging like a ball in the air, and exclaims over the wonders of it:

... the *Living Creatures* in the Air, Earth and Sea are an Inexpressible *Variety* of Divine Workmanship, both of *beauty and use*,

he says, reviewing the furs of beasts, the feathers of birds, and the scales of fishes. The wonders of the microscope are "astonishing," and so is the human body, and he bids his hearers:

Look thro' the Visible Creation, and see the Provision made thro'out it all for the Entertainment of Man, his Soul and Body! Immense Stores from the Divine Fulness and Munificence! What Wonders of Wisdom for our musing *Minds*? What Beauties for our gazing *Eyes*? What Pleasing Sounds for our *Ears*? What Delicacy of Food for our Palates? What a Paradise the Earth. . . . The Law of *Nature* is a very *Sacred* Law, and the Light of Nature a very *great Light*: to *live up* to it is a very great thing; and to *quench* it by Lust, or wilfully to Sin against it is a very *high Guilt*. . . . [God] has given *Man* the *Dominion* over and *Use* of the Inferior Creatures, and puts them under our *Feet*; and it becomes us not to *trample* either in Pride or Carelessness on a very *Worm*. . . . [48]

From this rhapsody by a leading Presbyterian on the wisdom and benevolence displayed in nature, I have omitted one phrase. Colman wrote: "What a Paradise the Earth — if by our Sins we had not blasted it?" — which means, not that the cosmic order is evil, but that man misuses his opportunities for wisdom and happiness offered by a rational and benevolent universe. Calvinist and deist differed as to the nature of man; I am unable to see that they differed importantly as to the order, beauty, and benevolence of the cosmos, *qua* cosmos. And when, on the basis of the theory set forth by Moore that in British poetry the romantic "return to nature" is, to a large degree, based on deism,[49] American scholars argue that Freneau's deism "marks the starting-point in America of this all-important trend toward the concrete in poetry,"[50] I find myself simply bewildered. Was a Calvinist denied the opportunity of calling a thing by its right name? Here is William Morell writing in 1625 of "Deare or Bever, with the hayre-side in"; Anne Bradstreet referring to blackbirds, thrushes, kids, lambs, pears, plums, apple trees, grass, primroses, violets, a "clocking hen" and "chirping chickins," cherries, peas, strawberries, double pinks, roses, honey bees, cowslips, oak trees, elm trees, the grasshopper, and the cricket; here is Benjamin Tompson writing satirically of mud and turf, pick-axes and wagons, pies and tarts, in 1675; here is Nicholas Noyes in 1702 comparing his thoughts to "a swarm of *Bees*, That fly both *when* and *where* they please"; here is Nathaniel Evans, missionary of the S.P.G.A., talking in 1722 of the yellow finch and linnet blue on the banks of the Schuylkill river; here is Joseph Green in 1733 lamenting the loss of his cat; and so on indefinitely.[51] And it is scarcely necessary to say that from the travel books, diaries, histories, letters, and even from the sermons of colonial American literature written by Calvinists and other varieties of Christians, one can cull an indefinite number of passages in which natural objects are referred to specifically because they were the subject of curious admiration and wonder.[52]

If the history of certain themes in the work of Jefferson and Freneau thus suggests a reasonable doubt as to the extent of the intellectual revolution supposed by some to be wrought by the deistic view of nature at the turn of the eighteenth century, one may also note that, although some writers have spoken of transcendentalism as a revolt against Calvinism, an intellectual revolution, or what not, others have, I think more wisely, traced its sources upward to the seventeenth century. Into this vexed problem I shall not enter further than to quote three paragraphs, the authorship of which I shall specify in a moment:

THERE is nothing in the World more clear to ME, than This; That I have in me a *Principle*, which does not meerly *Receive Idea's* (as a Looking-Glass may *Images*,) but also *Perceive* them, and make *Remarks* upon them; and has a certainty of *it self*, and of what *is done* in itself. . . . An *Indivisible Being*, and yet what can Embrace and Contain the *Universe*! No Bounds can be set unto the Number of the *Objects* which it can *successively* take a Cognisance of. . . . The *Body*, which is *Matter* in such and such a *Figure*, cannot Affect the *Immaterial* SOUL, nor can the SOUL, which has no *Figure*, Command the *Body*; But the Great GOD having established certain *Laws*, that upon such and such *Desires* of the SOUL, the *Body* shall be so and so Commanded, HE 'tis, who by His *Continual Influx* does Execute His own *Laws*; 'Tis to His *Continual Influx* that the *Effects* are owing.

Though we suppose, that the existence of the whole material Universe is absolutely dependent on Idea, yet we may speak in the old way, and as properly, and truly as ever. God, in the beginning, created such a certain number of Atoms, of such a determinate bulk and figure, which they yet maintain and always will, and gave them such a motion, of such a direction, and of such a degree of velocity . . . all the ideas that ever were, or ever shall be to all eternity, in any created mind, are answerable to the existence of such a peculiar Atom in the beginning of the Creation . . . God . . . causes all changes to arise, as if all these things had actually existed in such a series, in some created mind, and as if created minds had comprehended all things perfectly. And, although created minds do not; yet, the Divine Mind doth; and he orders all things according to his mind, and his ideas.

Three problems are put by nature to the mind; What is matter? Whence is it? and Whereto? The first of these questions only,

the ideal theory answers. Idealism saith: matter is a phenomenon, not a substance. Idealism acquaints us with the total
disparity between the evidence of our own being, and the evidence of the world's being. The one is perfect; the other, incapable of any assurance; the mind is part of the nature of
things; the world is a divine dream, from which we may presently awake to the glories and certainties of day. . . . Yet, if
[idealism] only deny the existence of matter, it does not satisfy
the demands of the spirit. It leaves God out of me. It leaves me
in the splendid labyrinth of my perceptions, to wander without
end. . . . The world proceeds from the same spirit as the body of
man. It is a remoter and inferior incarnation of God, a projec-
tion of God in the unconscious.

Putting aside obvious differences in style, most readers
would say, I think, that this little essay in three paragraphs is not too bad a sketch of philosophical idealism;
yet the first paragraph was written by Cotton Mather, the
second by Jonathan Edwards, and the third by Ralph
Waldo Emerson! [53]

   The nineteenth century is not the eighteenth; romanticism is not classicism; the universe of the transcendentalist
differs *toto caelo* from the Newtonian world-machine; and
the deistic view of human nature contradicts at every turn
that of high Calvinism. I do not wish to confuse these
clear distinctions. But I submit that our anxiety to equip
American literary history with its complement of "periods" and "factors" has led us to indulge too liberally
that false power by which we multiply distinctions. A sal-
tatory conception of American literature, with its easy
opposition of romanticism to something ever left undefined, its talk of "revolt" and "revolution," its picture of a
libertarian ideology opportunely arriving from Europe to
free the American mind from its theological prison-house
like the angel liberating Paul and Silas — this it is which
has produced the confusions I have sketched. And I suggest that if we are to understand the historic function of

the various American "romanticisms," we must turn to that epoch of American literary history which, since the days of Moses Coit Tyler, has scarcely been explored; we must begin by discovering what the nineteenth century really owes to the colonial period. For it seems obvious that the problem of American romanticism can not be solved merely by enumerating European influences: what is borrowed, after all, is determined by what is wanted; and we can not discover what was wanted until we know what we had. And much penitential reading in the obscurer printed material of the colonial period, especially that of the eighteenth century, leads me to present a simple but suggestive hypothesis — an hypothesis, indeed, implicit in the work of Tyler[54] — which may serve, however tentatively, to place American romanticisms in a more understandable, if less theatric, light.

Our culture is a Protestant, and not a Catholic, culture; it is a Protestant culture begun in dissent and retaining dissent as its chief characteristic for decades, as the failure of either Anglican or Catholic authoritarianism[55] decisively to influence that culture testifies. The essence of dissent lies in the appeal to private judgment, that is to say, to the individual reason; and one of its primary philosophic interests is the problem of the relation of the individual to God. I suggest that the central problem in American thought, at least until late in the nineteenth century, is the problem of the moral order of the universe — a problem so primary as on the whole to subordinate almost all other philosophical and aesthetic considerations to this central question.[56] For the Americans until recent times the metaphysical problem has been characteristically a problem of teleology rather than of ontology, a problem not of being, but of doing — and doing rightly. From their point of view the question of classicism and ro-

manticism is not primarily a metaphysical or an aesthetic
question, but a moral problem; and they have adopted the
patterns of classicism or of romanticism not as aesthetic or
metaphysical absolutes, but as instrumental aids towards
solving the problem of the moral order. Thus it is (to
work for a moment rapidly backward) that in general the
Americans have accepted European romanticisms only as
they have appealed to the moral sense; that American
transcendentalism stresses ethics rather than epistemology
or aesthetics; that American literary criticism between
1810 and 1835 — the only period concerning which we
have sufficient knowledge to judge[57] — owed allegiance to
Kames, Blair, and Alison — that is to say, to critical
principles which fused the question of taste with that of
morality and which led the critic to think of himself as
"the watchdog of society";[58] that the official philosophy of
the period was that of the Scotch school of "Common-
Sense"; and that deism, largely because of its ethical
and theological weaknesses, failed to make any lasting impression on the national mind.[59] Do we not, in fact, in-
stinctively feel, under whatever definition we choose to set
up, that the nearest analogue to American romanticism is
not found among the wits, rebels, and mystics of the
Regency; not among the wild and picturesque young men
of Paris in 1830; not among the Erste Romantische Schule
nor yet the writers of young Germany; but rather among
the earnest idealists of Victorian England?[60] Not rebels,
but reformers, not iconoclasts, but moralists, the American
romantics, with but few exceptions, assumed that the
central problem of thought was the problem of the moral
order of the universe — that is to say, they were men who
subordinated aesthetics to ethical ends and sought to
make their version of reason and the will of God prevail.[61]
Even in their most rebellious moments the appeal is

neither to cynicism, anarchy, nor despair, but always to a higher law.[62]

If then American romanticism, considered as philosophy, as politics, or as nationalism, is best understood as the final phase of a slow evolution in thought beginning in the colonial period, what of the eighteenth century out of which, in a sense, it emerged? In older cultures romanticism was a liberalizing force directed against decadent classicism; but in America, as I have hinted, historians have failed to distinguish a classical period to overthrow. The obvious failure of the colonial centuries to produce a great classical genius, a great classical work of art, or an influential classical aesthetic; the failure of the colonies to create a genuinely classical education — a failure due, on the one hand, to theological preoccupations, and on the other, to a utilitarian misvaluation of "dead languages";[63] the fact that the colonies were never a part of the ancient world and were separated by immense distances from the European heirs of the Roman empire — such were the fatal obstacles to the flowering of a classical culture in colonial America. But if in Europe secular thought was liberalized by a romanticism seeking to overthrow a senescent classicism, in America thought and expression had first to be made secular; and it was the historic mission of that aspect of the classical world-view men call the Enlightenment to liberate American thought and expression from theology in the very decades when the young romantic movement in Europe was seeking to liberate European thought and expression from the Enlightenment! This paradox is, of course, only approximately true; but it becomes understandable when one remembers that there was a cultural lag between the New World and the Old, so that, whereas from 1760 to 1800 the great monuments of a new European literature are to be found in the writings of Rousseau, the *Kritik der Reinen Vernunft*, the earlier emotionalism of Goethe and Schiller, Burns's poems, and the *Lyrical Ballads*, the great monuments of the American intellect in the same decades are the writings of Franklin, of Hamilton and Jefferson, of Otis, the two Adams's, and Tom Paine.

For if one conceives of classicism with Professor Lovejoy as meaning in its widest sense the assumption that, "in each phase of human activity, excellence consists in conforming as nearly as possible to a standard conceived as universal, static[,] uncomplicated, uniform for every rational being," the story of eighteenth-century American development is the story of the slow fusion of a culture founded in Protestant dissent with certain of the secular ideas of classicism. The Lockeian psychology, the contract theory of government, the Newtonian world-view, the theory of progress, experimental science, cosmic optimism, deism [64] — these were some of the forces with which theology had to struggle; the result was, on the whole, a secular, but not a sceptical, victory — that is to say, the transfer of the problem of universal order from the theological to the moral sphere. The documents in this war of liberation are a vast polemic literature in which the remotest village pulpit echoed with contending arguments; until we explore this literature more thoroughly than we have done, we have little right to theorize about a romantic "revolution" or a romantic "triumph."

In sum, the discussion of American romanticism has been extraordinarily confused because of the failure to distinguish terms. In what may be called the rhetoric of belles lettres, this confusion is relatively unimportant; but when it is argued that a romantic movement in America enshrines the monuments of an intellectual revolution in the philosophical or political sphere, closer examination of the evidences does not seem to justify so dramatic an interpretation. In the sphere of political action a romantic revolution in European terms was at once tautological and irrelevant; tautological, since, by the terms of its own "democratic" revolution, America *was*, politically speaking, the romantic revolt;[65] irrelevant, because the return to throne and altar, which is the romantic phase of the European reaction, was meaningless in a Protestant and democratic republic with no medieval past. In the intellectual sphere many of the ideas associated with American romanticisms have roots deep in the national past; and romantic literature in this country for the most part represents but the final phase of a statement of the moral order — final, because the impact of Darwinism ended the older teleologies. In this view emphasis must be given to the struggle between theology and the forces of the classical Enlightenment in the earlier centuries, for the paradox of the American situation is that on the whole the secular phases of classicism served as the original force to liberate the American mind from theological authoritarianism.

NOTES

1 Perhaps the clearest single statement of the classical point of view is that of Professor Arthur O. Lovejoy in his article "Optimism and Romanticism," *Publications of the Modern Language Association*, XLII (1926), especially pp. 942–943: "For two centuries the thought of the Western world, and, above all, the efforts made during those centuries for improvement and correction in beliefs, in institutions, and in art, had been, in the main, dominated by the assumption that, in each phase of human activity, excellence consists in conforming as nearly as possible to a standard conceived as universal, static [,] uncomplicated, uniform for every rational being. Rationality and uniformity were, indeed, commonly assumed to be inseparable notions. . . . 'Nature' was the word oftenest used to designate such a standard of excellence; and nature . . 'is everywhere the same.' The norm . . . of truth or of beauty, was simple and invariant. . . . It was their supposed greater universality, both in content and in appeal, which constituted the essence of the superiority attributed to the classical models. In every domain . . . the program of improvement or reform was one of simplification, standardization, the avoidance of the partic-

ular, the elimination of local variations and individual diversities supposed to have arisen through some ... aberration from the uniformity of the 'natural' order."

Thus deism sought to bring men back to the "simple creed ... supposed to be literally catholic, *i.e.*, to have been understood and accepted *semper, ubique et ab omnibus.*" Ethics was summed up "in the law of nature, of which universality was the distinguishing mark." Political philosophy, conceived of as resting upon natural rights, was concerned with the generic in man. In the aesthetics of literature "the high neo-classical dogma demanded that the subject-matter and emotional content of a drama or epic should be limited to that which is universal in human experience and capable of appealing equally to all men in all times and all lands."

2 "On the Discrimination of Romanticisms," *PMLA*, XXXIX (1924), 229–253.

3 Thus Henry A. Beers, who might be presumed to know romanticism when he saw it, recognizes no "romantic period" in his *Outline Sketch of American Literature* (1887; revised as *Initial Studies in American Letters*, 1895) and says little more about the origins of transcendentalism than that the movement was a restatement of the idealistic philosophy (p. 121). F. L. Pattee's *History of American Literature* (1896) has no section on the "romantic period," does not recognize romanticism in the index, and speaks only generally of romantic poetry. E. P. Whipple's *American Literature and Other Papers* (1896) speaks in like terms of the influence of English romanticism on American writers. C. F. Richardson, *American Literature: 1607–1885* (popular edition, 1898), touches on romanticism in passing. Barrett Wendell, *A Literary History of America* (1900), which, with all its crotchets, is penetrating, discusses English romanticism as a background to nineteenth-century American literature, but distinguishes no separate period. William P. Trent, *A History of American Literature: 1607–1865* (1908), has only brief references. John Macy, *The Spirit of American Literature* (1913), recognizes no "romantic period," though the author talks in general terms of such a subject as Emerson's relation to European thought. Leon Kellner, *American Literature* (trans. by Julia Franklin, 1915), remarks that "spirits of a higher strain followed slavishly in the footsteps of the English [romantic] poets" (p. 57), and says that "an admiration of German philosophy" was common to the transcendentalists (p. 81), but makes no separate division. Though Stanley T. Williams, *The American Spirit in Letters* (1926), makes casual reference to obvious relations with Europe, "romanticism" does not appear in the index or the table of contents. It might be thought that romanticism would be a concept useful to the thesis of Ludwig Lewisohn (*Expression in America*, 1932), but he uses the term only generally. Romanticism appears only infrequently in V. F. Calverton, *The Liberation of American Literature* (1932). Percy H. Boynton's *Literature and American Life* (1936) does not discover a "romantic period" and stresses native elements.

4 V. L. Parrington, *Main Currents in American Thought*, vol. II (1927); Ernest E. Leisy, *American Literature: An Interpretative Survey* (1929); Russell Blankenship, *American Literature as an Expression of the National Mind* (1931), pp. 48–49, 199; Thomas H. Dickinson, *The Making of American Literature* (1932), subdividing the period into two phases: 1789–1830, 1830–1855; Tremaine McDowell, *The Romantic Triumph: American Literature from*

1830 to 1860 (1933): see the introductory essay, pp. 1–8; James McDonald Miller, *An Outline of American Literature* (1934), which subdivides the period into two phases: 1800–1825, 1825–1850; Walter Fuller Taylor, *A History of American Letters* (1936), pt. iii.

5 *America in Literature* (1903), pp. 193, 222, 250.

6 These quotations are, in order, from Taylor, pp. 141–142; C. R. Fish, *The Rise of the Common Man* (1927), p. 255; Parrington, *The Romantic Revolution*, p. 322; Miller, p. 101; Whipple, p. 35; Frederic I. Carpenter, "The Vogue of Ossian in America: A Study in Taste," *American Literature*, II (1930–31), 405; Lewisohn, p. 153, who adds that "even the transcendentalist revolt did not forget what was due to birth and breeding. . . ." Bliss Perry, *The American Spirit in Literature: A Chronicle of Great Interpreters* (1918), remarks that the "Renascence of New England" was due to many causes, but that it "is a good illustration of that law of 'tension and release,' which the late Professor Shaler liked to demonstrate in all organic life" (p. 111).

7 The authors cited are, in order, Miller, p. 90; Woodberry, p. 125; Parrington, *The Romantic Revolution*, p. vi; Grace Warren Landrum, "Notes on the Reading of the Old South," *American Literature*, III (1931–32), 60–71; Leisy, p. 67; Parrington, *op. cit.*, pp. 28 ff., 111; Taylor, p. 215. Landrum notes, however, that economics and politics absorbed a great deal of the intellectual energy of the South, and discovers a marked religious and theological interest among the middle classes. Parrington is especially confused. "French revolutionary theory" is for him "French romantic philosophy" (*The Colonial Mind*, pp. 342–357; *The Romantic Revolution*, pp. vi–vii), but in sections iv and v of pt. i of "The Mind of the South" in *The Romantic Revolution* note that the taste of Wirt was formed by the (older) eighteenth century (p. 31); that Tucker is essentially anti-romantic (p. 70); that Caruthers was a liberal who did not believe in emancipation, elsewhere credited to "French romanticism" (p. 43); and that Kennedy is a Federalist of whom "devout romantic" (p. 49) is used in a sense directly opposite to that in which Jefferson is elsewhere "romantic."

8 To John Macy, Irving as a representative Knickerbocker is no more eighteenth-century than his British contemporaries (pp. 27 ff.); whereas to Leisy, Irving is romantic when, "in conformity with foreign tradition, [the Knickerbocker writers] garbed the landscape of the Hudson in idyllic hue" (p. 67). To Wendell, Irving expresses "romantic sentiment" (p. 179); whereas Parrington, who emphasizes Irving's dislike of the "romantic revolution," cryptically tells us that this "most distinguished of our early romantics" was "immolated on the altar of romanticism" — i.e., "lured . . . away into sterile wastes." He also says that New York had no intellectual revolution corresponding to that in New England (*The Romantic Revolution*, p. 200), and that Philadelphia "remained content with the ways of the eighteenth century, immersed in an old-fashioned culture" (p. 187), whereas Blankenship assures us that Philadelphia was the center of "French and English influence" (p. 206). Miller remarks that the Middle East was materialistic in temper, but "just as romantic as the territorial expansion in the West" (p. 140). Cooper is by a number of writers classed with the romantics because he wrote historical novels and displayed a "love of nature" and of the frontier; but Whipple remarks that "no Hamlets or Werthers or Renés or Childe Harolds" tenant his woods or walk his quarterdecks, and thinks a physician of the mind would

recommend him to "weak and sentimental natures" (p. 47); Wendell remarks that "the old world was looking for some wild manifestation of this new, hardly apprehended, western democracy" and got only Bryant, Irving, and Cooper (p. 203); and Parrington, that Cooper's "romantic impulses are held in check by a growing tendency towards realism" (p. 234). [Had Parrington read *The Crater*?] Although each of these statements may be justified, that fact does not help us to apprehend what is meant by the romantic movement in America.

9 "Two great romantic forces were shaping the economic progress of the country, the brilliant industrial expansion of the East with its attendant influx of new blood from Ireland and Germany, and the great migration to the valleys of the Mississippi and the Missouri." The literary expression of the period (1825-1850) was as a result "extravagantly romantic in temper" and "of course, the literature which such a temper [frontier optimism] produced was romantic" (Miller, pp. 98-99, 133). For Mrs. Hazard, however, frontier "romanticism" is not the result of optimism, but of defeat (*The Frontier in American Literature*, 1927, p. 70). To Dorothy Anne Dondore "this romantic literature . . . does not represent the most distinctive contribution of the prairie" (*The Prairie and the Making of Middle America*, 1926, p. 288), whereas Boynton (*Literature and American Life*) notes that the frontier goes romantic because of nostalgia (p. 600).

10 "The creative influence of the French Revolution upon the western world resulted from the enormous impetus which it gave to the movement to democratize American life and institutions" (Parrington, *The Colonial Mind*, p. 321). "The first stage in the romanticization of American thought resulted from the naturalization of French revolutionary theory" (*The Romantic Revolution*, p. vi). See also Blankenship, pp. 180, 186.

11 McDowell, p. 3.

12 According to Foerster, *The Reinterpretation of American Literature* (1928), the temporal background of American romanticism is Revolutionary idealism and Puritan idealism. According to Williams (p. 136) romanticism is the flowering of Puritan idealism.

13 Pattee, p. 197. This revolt later "drifted into intellectual and humanitarian channels."

14 Harry H. Clark, *Poems of Freneau* (1929), p. xlii; see also his article, "What Made Freneau the Father of American Poetry?" *Studies in Philology*, XXVI (1929), 1-22.

15 Whipple, p. 40, tells us that Dana's novels are romantic and that they deal with "the darker passions of our nature," and on the next page explains that this is due to Dana's "overpowering conception of the terrible reality of sin." The same is true of Washington Allston (p. 42).

16 Macy, chapter on Emerson; and others.

17 Woodberry, p. 222.

18 "In Europe man had to flee from society and seek nature; in America nature came to a man's door and demanded admittance" (Blankenship, p. 202).

19 Richardson, I, 263.

20 Taylor, p. 86.

21 Miller, p. 98.

22 Taylor, p. 87.

23 Miller, p. 74; and others.
24 Whipple, pp. 57, 61.
25 Kellner, p. 57.
26 Dickinson, pp. 259 ff.; and others.
27 Miller, pp. 83, 133; and others; and see note 9.
28 Wendell, p. 177. He finds Irving an inciting force.
29 Parrington, *The Romantic Revolution*, p. 331, who is followed by Blankenship, p. 205. The stress laid by these authors on Channing's twenty-one months in Richmond is remarkable. Because Channing's influence on transcendentalism was important, Parrington seeks to unite him with Jeffersonianism and "French romantic philosophy." He writes that Channing read "French revolutionary thought" in Virginia and that "one can scarcely over-emphasize the influence of his Virginia experience." He also informs us that "French romantic philosophy was a commonplace in Virginia libraries." Aside from the fact that "French romantic philosophy" is left persistently undefined, not a shadow of proof is offered that it was a "commonplace in Virginia libraries." Although it is true that Channing read Mary Wollstonecraft, Godwin, and Rousseau in Richmond (see *Memoir of William Ellery Channing*, 6th ed., 1854, I, 101, 102), none of these represents "French romantic philosophy" in the sense in which Parrington seems elsewhere to use the term; and the only other French authors mentioned by Channing in his Virginia period are Voltaire, Sully (p. 99), and Fénelon (p. 107)!
In fact, the more one studies the very full *Memoir*, the more one is convinced that Parrington did not read it. In revulsion from the enthusiasm at Harvard for the French Revolution at its beginning, Channing was led to Hutcheson and Ferguson, "the two authors who most served to guide his thought at this period." "It was while reading one day, in the former, some of the various passages in which he asserts man's capacity for disinterested affection, and considers virtue as the sacrifice of private interests and the bearing of private evils for the public good . . . that there suddenly burst upon [Channing's] mind that view of the dignity of human nature, which was ever after to 'uphold and cherish' him. . . . He was, at the time, walking as he read beneath a clump of willows . . . in the meadow a little north of Judge Dana's. . . . It seemed to him, that he then passed through a new spiritual birth, and entered upon the day of eternal peace and joy" (p. 63; and see the confirmation in a letter written in later years, p. 64). The biographer further states: "As Hutcheson was the medium of awakening within him the consciousness of an exhaustless tendency in the human soul to moral perfection, so Ferguson on Civil Society was the means of concentrating his energies upon the thought of social progress. Years afterwards, his remembrance of the enthusiasm in the cause of humanity, first called out in him by this book, was so strong, that he recommended it in terms which would certainly be thought . . . greatly to exaggerate its merits " (pp. 64–65). A third influence was Price, who "saved me from Locke's Philosophy. He gave me the doctrine of ideas, and during my life I have written the words Love, Right, etc., with a capital. That book probably moulded my philosophy into the form it has always retained" (p. 66; see the confirmatory letter from Newport, October 1798, pp. 76–78).
As for Channing's Virginia experiences, he may have dreamed of "*a perfect*

society," but the supposed spread of "French romantic philosophy" among the Virginians had little enough to do with it. "Could I," he wrote, "only take from the Virginians their *sensuality* and their *slaves*, I should think them the greatest people in the world. As it is . . . with a few great virtues, they have innumerable vices" (p. 83; and see also p. 85). He was at the time a strong Federalist (p. 85) and therefore opposed to Jeffersonianism; and though he wrote that "my political opinions have varied a little" (p. 86) in Virginia, they did not veer to the French, for his denunciation of France (pp. 86–95) could hardly be stronger, and he says that he relies "implicitly on the firmness and independence of [President John Adams]" to curb the French, he thought John Marshall "one of the greatest men in the country," and he is "happy to hear that the same odium is everywhere attached to the name of Jacobin." Note his denunciation of French revolutionary thought ("founded in infidelity, Impiety and atheism") in 1810 (p. 333).

30 Trent, p. 302.

31 Clark, p. xlii.

32 Listing the qualities of American romanticism, Kaufman says that "primitivism is omitted because of its conspicuous absence in American literature" (in Foerster, p. 120). Contrast Clark, who argues at some length (pp. xl–xliii) that Freneau's primitivistic theories underlie his radicalism and his romanticism.

33 Thus Walter Just, who seems to have been the first to discover a romantic movement as such in American literature (*Die Romantische Bewegung in der Amerikanischen Literatur: Brown, Poe, Hawthorne*, 1910), confines his exemplars to those who develop aimlessness in life! "Zu einem der wesentlichen Punkte, die sich in den Lebensläufen aller Romantiker finden, rechnet Ricarda Huch die Beruflosigkeit" (p. 8), and following this guide he discusses only Brown, Poe, and Hawthorne. "In der Beziehung waren alle drei . . . echte Romantiker, sie lebten ausser in der realen Welt in einer Welt der Phantasie, die sie in sich aufbauten" (p. 13), cultivated the inner life, and were impractical in the outer. Taylor, however, says that "in America, the romantic movement was both held in check and outfitted with new materials by a number of distinctly American factors," which he lists as the prior achievement of democracy, the frontier, evangelical religion, American, rather than European, nature, the American, rather than the European, past, the national ideals, an agrarian economic structure, an immature, oversentimental, and self-conscious society, certain sectional divergencies, and certain conditions of publication (p. 91). For Leisy the qualities of American romanticism are the cultivation of the sense of wonder, the grotesque, and the ego, an interest in the Middle Ages, the discipline of nature, enthusiasm for social reform, interest in the national past, humanitarianism, etc. (pp. 67–68). Even if all three writers are correct, one's knowledge of the American romantic movement as such is not clarified.

34 Parrington, *The Romantic Revolution*, p. iii.

35 Blankenship, p. 195.

36 Clark, *Poems of Freneau*, p. xxxv.

37 Gilbert Chinard, *Thomas Jefferson: The Apostle of Americanism* (1929), p. 87. For Chinard, Jefferson was a Christian stoic, whose attitude slowly changed while he was still a young man in Virginia. "What brought a change . . . is

certainly not the influence of the 'infidel French philosophers.' The volume of extracts which I published under the title of 'The Literary Bible of Thomas Jefferson' [i.e., Jefferson's commonplace book] does not contain a single quotation from Voltaire, Diderot, or Rousseau, and French literature is represented only by a few insignificant lines from Racine. It is more likely that the first doubts were injected into his mind by the reading of Boling-broke" (p. 21). Jefferson's political philosophy rested primarily on Hooker and Locke. "Can any one imagine anything farther from the universal humanitarianism of the French philosophers?" (pp. 52–53). "Jefferson proposed a definition of liberty entirely different from the French conception as found in Rousseau and reproduced in the 'Déclaration des droits de l'homme' of May 29, 1793" (p. 84). Jefferson's "great ambition at that time was to promote a renaissance of Anglo-Saxon primitive institutions on the new continent" (p. 86). See also pp. 121; 122–123; 127; 130; 173 ff.; 204–205; 215 ff.; 328 ff.; 471; 493; 495; 496; 498–499; 522–524 for further explicit denials by this writer that Jefferson was importantly indebted to "French romantic philosophy."

38 But see in this connection the striking article by Chester E. Jorgenson, "Emerson's Paradise under the Shadow of Swords," *Philological Quarterly*, XI (1932), 274–292, especially section iii.

39 By Clark especially. See, in addition to his *Poems of Freneau*, such an article as his "Toward a Reinterpretation of Thomas Paine," *American Literature*, V (1934–35), 133–145.

40 Clark, *Poems of Freneau*, pp. xxxvi–xxxvii. "Nature is herself rational. Lands, seas, flowers, trees, beasts, and man are

> But thoughts on Reason's scale combin'd,
> Ideas of the Almighty mind.

Since the Creator — who is 'the First Spring of Reason,' an 'Intellectual Flame' — has revealed His Reason in nature and natural laws, the study of these laws in science, which 'stands firm on Reason,' enables man (in Paine's words) to 'see God, as it were, face to face.'" See also his article, "What Made Freneau the Father of American Poetry?" already cited.

41 Clark, *loc. cit.*

42 The general acceptance of the theory that the universe is in Calvinist doctrine "bad" seems to be due to the prestige of I. W. Riley, who in his *American Thought from Puritanism to Pragmatism and Beyond* (2d ed., 1923) rather unfortunately remarks that "as a theory of the cosmos, Calvinism teaches that the world is under the curse of the divine displeasure; that it conceals rather than displays its creator; that it is created from nothing and is destined to return to nothing; that the evil in it is a permissive act of God." If the universe was thus cursed, and if it conceals rather than reveals its creator, Jonathan Edwards fell into dreadful heresy when he wrote that "all beauty consists in similarness or identity of relation," and that "the Equalities in a beauty . . . are so numerous, that it would be a most tedious piece of work to enumerate them. There are millions of these Equalities. Of these consist the beautiful shape of flowers, the beauty of the body of man, and of the bodies of other animals. That sort of beauty which is called Natural, as of vines, plants, trees, etc., consists of a very complicated harmony; and all the natural mo-

tions, and tendencies, and figures of bodies in the Universe are done according to proportion, and therein is their beauty." "For Being, if we examine narrowly, is nothing else but Proportion. When one being is inconsistent with another being, then Being is contradicted." ("Notes on the Mind," pp. 34 ff., in Clarence H. Faust and Thomas H. Johnson, *Jonathan Edwards*, 1935.) And cf. "Dissertation concerning the End for which God Created the World" (*op. cit.*, p. 343), in which the student will learn that God created the world for his glory, that "light is the external expression, exhibition and manifestation of the excellency of the luminary, of the sun, for instance," and "by a participation of this communication from the sun . . . surrounding objects receive all their lustre, beauty and brightness. It is by this that *all nature is quickened and receives life, comfort and joy*" (my italics).

43 *Institutes of the Christian Religion* (trans. by John Allen, 2 vols. in one, 1841, 3d Am. ed.), II, i, 5, p. 225.

44 *Op. cit.*, pp. 58–59 (I, v, 2).

45 Benjamin B. Warfield, *Calvin and Calvinism* (1931), p. 44; and see chap. V.

46 Cf. the "deistic" Franklin: ". . . I imagine it great Vanity in me to suppose, that the *Supremely Perfect* does in the least regard such an inconsiderable Nothing as Man. More especially, since it is impossible for me to have any positive clear idea of that which is infinite and incomprehensible. I cannot conceive otherwise than that He, the *Infinite Father*, expects or requires no Worship or Praise from us, but that he is even infinitely above it." — "Articles of Belief and Acts of Religion" (1728).

47 Cf. Franklin, *loc. cit:* "Also when I stretch my imagination through and beyond our system of planets, beyond the visible fixed stars themselves, into that space which is every way infinite, and conceive it filled with suns like ours, each with a chorus of worlds for ever moving round him; then this little ball on which we move, seems, even in my narrow imagination, to be almost nothing, and myself less than nothing, and of no sort of consequence."

48 Benjamin Colman, *A Humble Discourse of the Incomprehensibleness of God, In Four Sermons* (Boston, 1715), pp. 17, 27 ff., 32, 34, 47.

49 C. A. Moore, "The Return to Nature in English Poetry of the Eighteenth Century," *Studies in Philology*, XIV (1917), 243–291. Moore says that "there is ample evidence to confirm Biese's remark that 'to Judaism and Christianity, Nature was a fallen angel, separated as far as possible from her God'" (p. 290). This may, indeed, be true of early Christian literature and of medieval theology in part, but I am unable to see that it is true of Calvinism.

50 Clark, "What Made Freneau the Father of American Poetry?" *op. cit.*, p. 3.

51 Walter C. Bronson, *American Poems* (1912), pp. 1, 4–19, 37. Nathaniel Evans, *Poems on Several Occasions* (Philadelphia, 1722), p. 33; Bronson, pp. 45–46.

52 Francis Higginson reports on his voyage to New England in 1629: "Fourthly, our passage was both pleasurable and profitable. For we received instruction and delight in beholding the wonders of the Lord in deep waters, and sometimes seeing the sea round us appearing with a terrible countenance, and, as it were, full of high hills and deep valleys; and sometimes it appeared as a most plain and even meadow. And ever and anon we saw divers kinds of fishes sporting in the great waters, great grampuses and huge whales, going by

companies, and puffing up water streams. Those that love their own chim-ney-corner, and dare not go far beyond their own town's end, shall never have the honor to see these wonderful works of Almighty God" (Stedman and Hutchinson, *A Library of American Literature*, I, 1887, p. 141). I am unable to see why this is less "concrete" than Freneau's ocean poetry; e.g., "Hat-teras," in which the poet writes:

> In fathoms five the anchor gone;
> While here we furl the sail,
> No longer vainly labouring on
> Against the western gale:
> While here thy bare and barren cliffs,
> O HATTERAS, I survey,
> And shallow grounds and broken reefs —
> What shall console my stay!

> The dangerous shoal, that breaks the wave
> In columns to the sky;
> The tempests black, that hourly rave,
> Portend all danger nigh:
> Sad are my dreams on ocean's verge!
> The Atlantic round me flows,
> Upon whose ancient angry surge
> No traveller finds repose!

The poem goes on to refer to a pilot who, "with busy hands, Employs both oar and sail" (a phrase that would have drawn a smile from Cooper), and who has "in depths of woods his hut" where lives "a wedded nymph"; the pilot's hopes are, in the best manner of eighteenth-century diction, "in yonder flock, Or some few hives of bees"; in the sixth stanza he has become a "com-modore" who "spreads his tottering sails," while the "fond nymph" is ad-jured to "restrain those idle fears" in the seventh stanza. I may add that Hatteras, a low sandy island, has no cliffs, and that tempests black do not hourly rave around it. And if I seem to have chosen a peculiarly apt poem for this comparison, reminding the reader that Freneau spent many years on the sea, I refer him to the diction of "St. Catherine's," "Neversink," "On Arriving in South Carolina, 1798," "The Hurricane," and other poetical ex-pressions of a maritime existence.

53 Cotton Mather, *Coheleth: A Soul Upon Reflection* (Boston, 1720), p. 5; Jonathan Edwards, "Notes on the Mind," in Faust and Johnson, *op. cit.*, pp. 29-30; Ralph Waldo Emerson, chap. VII ("Spirit") of *Nature*, fifth and eighth paragraphs.

54 "Our first literary period . . . fills the larger part of that century in which American civilization had its planting; even as its training into some ma-turity and power has been the business of the eighteenth and nineteenth cen-turies. . . . [The colonial writers] founded that literature; they are its Fathers; they stamped their spiritual lineaments upon it; and we shall never deeply enter into the meanings of American literature in its later forms without tracing it back, affectionately, to its beginnings with them" (*A History of American Literature during the Colonial Period*, student ed., 2 vols. in one,

1909, pp. 6–7). "The entire body of American writings, from 1763 to 1783 . . . is here delineated in its most characteristic examples, for the purpose of exhibiting the several stages of thought and emotion through which the American people passed during the two decades of the struggle which resulted in our national Independence" (*The Literary History of the American Revolution*, student ed., 2 vols. in one, n.d., p. vi). It is improbable that these two great works will ever be wholly superseded. When Tyler wrote, however, he necessarily lacked the richer interpretation which subsequent scholarship has brought to the movement of thought in the seventeenth and eighteenth centuries.

55 The anti-Catholic literature of the colonial period (and later) is enormous; and the fear and hatred of Catholicism, from the beginnings through the defeat of Al Smith, though politely ignored by literary and philosophic historians, is one of the dominant facts in American intellectual development.

56 Thus, until late in the nineteenth century, the United States has been on the whole relatively poor in abstract speculation, in metaphysical thought for its own sake, in aesthetic theory, in pure science, and other branches of thought which do not appeal directly to conscience; and relatively rich in didactic literature, in moral reform movements, in ethical speculation, and in the ethical interpretation of religious experience.

57 William Charvat, *The Origins of American Critical Thought: 1810–1835* (1936). This excellent study should be carefully read by all students of American romantic literature. In these years the American mind winnowed out romantic elements not acceptable to the national temperament. Thus Byron was banished before the period closed; Keats and Shelley were neglected; Wordsworth and Coleridge accepted with reservations; Hazlitt was attacked; and Scott welcomed. Freneau was ignored largely because of the general disgust with his politics. Criticism was "preoccupied with the social implications of literature, and . . . questions of art and technique were too often neglected" (p. 6).

58 Charvat, p. 7. On the general teleology of the American view see my "Influence of European Ideas in Nineteenth-Century America," *American Literature*, VII (1935–36), 241–273.

59 G. Adolf Koch, *Republican Religion: The American Revolution and the Cult of Reason* (1933). "Our story is thus of the rise, the short-lived triumph, and the collapse of an intellectual movement reflected on this side of the Atlantic in the last three decades of the eighteenth century" (p. 292).

60 I here find myself in sharp contrast to Norman Foerster, who writes that "what we lacked in this country was not, certainly, a Romantic Movement, but a Victorian era at all comparable with England's. Our Victorianism was both brief and undistinguished" (*op. cit.*, p. 34). On the contrary, I should say that in the field of ideas the most striking parallel to the development of American thought in the nineteenth century is that in Victorian England.

61 Allen Porterfield, in his *Outline of German Romanticism* (1914), has conveniently assembled (pp. 177 ff.) some characteristic "definitions" of German romanticism. Some of these naturally approximate to a statement of the American movement in sense four (above), but I believe the candid student will be impressed by the total inapplicability of most of these statements to the aims and accomplishments of American romantic writers. Even when

the words apply, the whole tone and feeling of these statements belong in a world alien to America.

62 I suppose that Thoreau's "Civil Disobedience" comes the closest to philosophic anarchy of all of the important "romantic" documents in the movement. But though Thoreau desires to refuse taxes to a government which upholds slavery, note that his appeal is to the "higher law": "For eighteen hundred years, though perchance I have no right to say it, the New Testament has been written; yet where is the legislator who has wisdom and practical talent enough to avail himself of the light which it sheds on the science of legislation? The authority of government, even such as I am willing to submit to, — for I will cheerfully obey those who know and can do better than I, and in many things even those who neither know nor can do so well, —is still an impure one: to be strictly just, it must have the sanction and consent of the governed. . . . I please myself with imagining a State at last which can afford to be just to all men, and to treat the individual with respect as a neighbor; which even would not think it inconsistent with its own repose if a few were to live aloof from it, not meddling with it, nor embraced by it, who fulfilled all the duties of neighbors and fellow-men" (last paragraph). The ethical "tone" here is that of Robert Frost, and not, shall I say, of Hart Crane. And in this connection it is well to remember the scepticism with which Emerson, Thoreau, Hawthorne, Melville, and Poe regarded most of the reformers of their time — scepticism springing from a distrust of the capacity of average human nature released from customary ethical sanctions. Because of the weakness of human nature, moral law is necessary for control; they did not share Shelley's flaming enthusiasm for philosophical anarchy, and consequently did not, like him, throw themselves enthusiastically into practical reform movements.

63 Attacks on the study of Latin and Greek are among the standard themes of American educational theory in the eighteenth century. Cotton Mather, though he wanted "*Castalio* for the Latin Tongue, and *Posselius* for the Greek," wanted also to substitute "profitable sentences" for the "Vain Fictions and Filthy Stories" of antiquity — scarcely a classical ideal! (See *Bonifacius*, 1710, pp. 109 ff.; and cf. the eulogy of Cheever, in *Corderius Americanus*, 1708, as a grammar-master.) In *The Present State of Virginia* (1724) Hugh Jones says that Virginia children found "*Grammar* Learning taught after the common round-about Way . . . not much beneficial nor delightful," and thought that "without going directly to *Rome* and *Athens*," "all the Arts, Sciences, and learned Accomplishments of the Antients and Moderns" can be "conveyed" in English "without the Fatigue and Expence of another Language for which few of them have little Use or Necessity" (p. 46). In 1751 Richard Peters in a *Sermon on Education*, though he paid lip service to the classical languages, thought them but "a small Part of Education" and chiefly useful "to correct, refine and beautify" English, on the study of which he lays much stress (pp. 22–24). Franklin's plea for an English academy is, of course, well known. *The Independent Reflector* of Livingston and Smith declared the study of Greek and Latin in the main "perfectly idle and insignificant." Classical learning, though it may "perhaps procure its Possessor the Name of a Scholar . . . is in Reality no more than a specious Kind of Ignorance" (no. XVII, March 22, 1753). Though

William Smith in *A General Idea of the College of Mirania* (1753) sets up a "Latin School" as part of his ideal curriculum, he satirizes classical scholarship and condemns "the Practice of neglecting the Mother-Tongue, and embarrassing a young Student, by obliging him to speak or compose in a dead Language" (pp. 36–37). To omit much else, note the attack on classical learning and the plea for a study of English in Trumbull's *The Progress of Dulness* (1772), especially in the opening pages.

64 I follow Lovejoy in referring deism to the classical world-order. See his "Parallel of Deism and Classicism," *Modern Philology*, XXIX (1931–32), 281–299, in which he points out that deism shares with the Enlightenment the doctrines of uniformitarianism, rationalistic individualism, the appeal to the *consensus gentium*, cosmopolitanism (*natura* as opposed to *natio*), an antipathy to "enthusiasm" and "originality," intellectual equalitarianism, etc. See also his "Optimism and Romanticism," pp. 921–945.

65 A great deal of evidence could be assembled to show that for European romantics the new nation represented the ideal to which they were striving as a political concept. See, for example, Walter Graham, "Politics of the Greater Romantic Poets," *PMLA*, XXXVI (1921), 60–78, in which he notes that for Byron America is the home of true political freedom ("Ode to Venice"; "Ode to Napoleon"; *Childe Harold*, IV: xcvi; etc.). Shelley hailed the republic as the "Eagle" among nations (*Revolt of Islam*, XI: xii ff.). The Americans were conscious of their romantic destiny, as appears in patriotic poetry from the days of the Hartford Wits.

THE HISTORICAL APPROACH
TO MUSIC

Edward Joseph Dent, Mus.D.

Professor of Music, University of Cambridge

WITHIN the last few years a new word has made itself manifest, the name, it would seem, of a new science — Musicology. This word "musicology" was first coined, I fancy, in France, and was imported thence to America; in England it is not very willingly accepted, in spite of the fact that it is derived from Greek origins no less honorable than those of theology or physiology. When the Société Internationale de Musicologie was founded at Basle in 1927 the question arose what the society was to be called in English, and I found that such English people as were interested in its aims preferred to call it the Society for Musical Research. English people are notoriously illogical; I think their underlying reason for rejecting the word "musicology" was that, however keenly interested they might be in musical research, they refused to lose sight of the principle that music was an art.

When I was invited to give this lecture I asked the advice of some of my American friends as to a choice of subject; and I was urged with some insistence to defend the dignity of music as a subject of university study. With this honorable task in view, I was preparing to address you on the desirability of historical studies in music, when I received the first number of the Bulletin of the American Musicological Society. It was this bulletin, I need hardly say, which drew my attention to the inward significance of that new and rather frightening word "musicology." The bulletin consists of no more than sixteen pages, containing condensed abstracts of as many learned papers, but it made me realize how little I knew about this new science, which I was simple-minded enough to think had been pursued in one way or another since the days of Pythagoras. And I began to understand more clearly, too, why a learned German professor wrote to me only a few months ago to tell me that he disapproved of my attitude towards musicology. At that moment I was not even conscious of having any defined attitude towards it; I could only say that I was interested in it. I have to thank an American musicologist, Mr. Charles Seeger, for making matters clearer to me, and I will read you his wise words on the subject:

To attain its proper place among the advanced studies of today, musicology must achieve and affirm its own unity. Both the historical and the comparative musicologist should tackle the musical present in which they themselves exist, and no longer stand aside from it as mere spectators or attempt to ignore it. To connect the past with the present and to show how both lead into the future should be the main task of both historical and systematic work.

Mr. Seeger's paper and one immediately preceding it in the bulletin, by Professor Láng of Columbia University, both point out what a vast amount of musical research work has been done in the direction of what I should call mere excavation. We seem at the present day to be living in a museum; never since the early Renaissance has there been such a universal passion for archaeology. All over the world buried cities are being unearthed; in architecture, sculpture, and painting an ever-remoter past is being investigated; furniture and every conceivable object of antiquity are eagerly collected; and surely there never was an age in which so much old music was deciphered, reprinted, and performed. As far as the plastic arts are concerned, there is of course a very sound reason for all this antiquarianism; it is a lucrative business, and every object concerned has its definite value in the auction room. Even musical archaeology is not without its profits; autograph manuscripts of great composers, even if their price is paltry as compared to paintings and drawings, are at least valuable enough to be worth forging. All the same, the old music business is a negligible matter compared with the financial values of living performers, and indeed of a few composers whose works are still copyright. I wish it were possible to present statistics that would compare three factors in musical archaeology — the amount of labor spent on research, the amount of performance resulting therefrom, and the financial profits derived from it. I can only ask you to consider the question yourselves, and to make your own guesses.

I invite you to consider this problem, because I am convinced that all of us, music-lovers, musicians, or musical researchers, ought to ask ourselves — our own selves, and not other people — what is the ultimate use of all this musical archaeology. I was asked the question myself when I first began to pursue research in music, nearly forty years ago, and I have been asked it again many times since then; I have felt it my duty to search for an answer. It is on this fundamental question, no doubt, that I part company from my learned German friend who told me that he disapproved of my attitude to musicology, and I know that he is not alone in his disapproval.

Old Dr. Burney seems to have asked himself much the same question when he set out to write his great history of music in the eighteenth century.

After reading, or at least consulting, an almost innumerable quantity of old and scarce books on the subject, of which the dullness and pedantry were almost petrific, and among which, where I hoped to find the most information, I found but little, and where I expected but little, I was seldom disappointed; at length, wearied and disgusted at the small success of my researches, I shut my books, and began to examine myself as to my musical principles; hoping that the good I had met with in the course of my reading was by this time digested and incorporated in my own ideas; and that the many years I had spent in practice, theory and meditation, might entitle me to some freedom of thought, unshackled by the trammels of authority.

Considering the period at which he wrote, and the materials accessible to him, Burney was a remarkably learned musician. It is only natural, however, that a great deal more excavational work should have been done since then. Burney is often held up to ridicule nowadays for his critical judgments, but this is hardly just. He was a man of his own time. About some composers excavation has taught us more than he could possibly have known; there are others whose works he knew adequately, but whom he judged from the standpoint of his day. In this respect Burney is no more to be blamed than Hugo Riemann, whose archaeological knowledge was far greater, but who judged all music from the standpoint of the nineteenth century, a standpoint which to us of the twentieth is perhaps even more absurd than that of the eighteenth. And indeed if we narrow our field of observation to the music of the eighteenth century alone, Burney's criticism can teach us far more than Riemann's can. He is a document for the taste of his time; so is Riemann; and that is about as much as any of us researchers of today can hope to be for the readers of the future. More important, I think, is the question of what use our work ought to be for those of our own day.

We must follow Dr. Burney's example and examine ourselves as to our musical principles. We must ask ourselves what is the use of musicological research, and before we can answer that question, we must ask ourselves what is the use of music, or at any rate, what is music, what does it signify to us, and what do we expect from it. Questions of this type are very embarrassing, but all investigation of musical aesthetics will inevitably bring us down to them, sooner or later. We may even have to ask ourselves, "What is art?" "What is life?" and in cultivated societies there is a sort of tacit agreement that questions of that kind are not to be mentioned.

If we turn back once more to the pages of Dr. Burney, we shall find that in his preface, as well as in his dedication to Queen Charlotte, he is concerned not so much to defend the dignity of musical studies as to offer excuses for pursuing them. "What is Music?" he asks: "An innocent luxury, unnecessary, indeed, to our existence, but a great improvement and gratification of the sense of hearing." He is indeed not far removed from that old Cambridge character of the 1850's who observed to an undergraduate that music was "a very harmless amusement for a man who could not afford to hunt." To us of the present day, and perhaps more to amateurs than to professional musicians, music has become almost a religion, or a substitute for religion. We recognize in all seriousness that it demands what is called "a dedicated life." This religious outlook on music — an outlook, I must insist, that has little or no association with any form of orthodox religion — is a thing which has grown up gradually during the latter half of the past century. It would be interesting to trace the origins and the gradual growth of this "religion of music"; but here I must limit myself to suggesting that we owe this outlook mainly to the influence of Richard Wagner, who in his turn derived it from Beethoven; and before Beethoven we must go back to Handel, who definitely asserted his desire to make his audiences morally better through his music.

Another modern doctrine which the religious outlook on music has brought us — a doctrine which in these days has become something of a nuisance — is "reverence for the classics." Reverence for the classics was a thing which simply did not exist in the days of Dr. Burney, though it was perhaps due to the influence of his great history that the doctrine came into being. In the days of Handel and Mozart nobody wanted old music; all audiences demanded the newest opera or the newest concerto, as we now naturally demand the newest play and the newest novel. If in those two branches of imaginative production we habitually demand the newest and latest, why is it that in music we almost invariably demand what is old-fashioned and out of date, while the music of the present day is often received with positive hostility? I suspect that reverence for the classics began in England under orthodox religious influences, and that it began at the Handel Commemoration of 1784. The Romantic Movement brought a revival of Palestrina and sixteenth-century church music; it also discovered John Sebastian Bach. We must further remember that in the course of the nineteenth century music became accessible to ever-widening social circles. In Handel's day there was in all European countries an inner ring of cultivated connoisseurs who were the direct patrons of the composers. All music, even church music, was "utility music," music for the particular moment. There was nothing undignified about this; why should not a gentleman desire to hear a new mass, a new symphony, or a new opera every week, just as he might order a new suit of clothes? Whether it was clothes or music, he was determined to have nothing but the very best, and he could afford it. The bourgeois public of the nineteenth century — and indeed

this bourgeois public was developing rapidly in the eighteenth — had no tradition of connoisseurship. It wanted to be startled and amused rather than to experience intellectual enjoyment. And it had no sense of patronage. The great people knew that they wanted great art and knew that they had to pay a great price for it; the small people wanted to get their great art without paying for it, or at least without paying more than the absolute minimum. This is the spirit at the base of most entertainments today; the film cost a million to produce, and you and I can see it for sixpence. For that hour we, too, are millionaires.

The religious outlook on music is an affair of business as well as of devotion; that need not surprise us. It has given us also its own theology and its own antiquarianism; and the curious thing is that these — perhaps they are so in other faculties besides that of music — are subject to the caprice of fashion. We can many of us remember how the primitive Italian painters were discovered, and with what horror persons of taste regarded the baroque; and just in the same way our musicologists have recently rediscovered the baroque opera, and also the primitives of the fourteenth and thirteenth centuries, two periods of musical history which the nineteenth century regarded as respectively degraded and barbarous.

To persons of taste, persons who approach all music in a spirit of reverence for the great masters, all this musical antiquarianism is dangerous and unsettling. The fact is that early medieval music has a strange affinity to that of the present day, and persons of taste do not feel safe outside the limits of that period which begins with John Sebastian Bach and ends with Brahms — the only exception admitted being a little Palestrina on Sunday. It is not surprising that some of the younger generation, as well as one or two of the older, are inclined to throw the classics

and all old music overboard, and maintain that no music is worth listening to except that which is hot from the composer's brain. There, at any rate, is a thoroughly logical and reasonable doctrine: music, the music of today for those who today are themselves alive, and antiquarianism for those who are spiritually dead. If we could only accept it wholeheartedly, we should feel like new beings; we should have escaped for ever from that atmosphere of the museum which is not much better than that of a prison.

Music, according to some of the modern prophets, ought to revert to what it was in the earlier centuries — utility music, composed for the moment, and not expected to last longer than the dinner which was cooked for the day. We want a fresh dinner every day, and a fresh song; but I fear that in some households we may have to put up with cold remains. For it is an economic problem as well as an artistic one. There is a keen movement in some quarters for teaching children in ordinary schools to compose their own music; this is all part of the movement — an economic movement at bottom — to bring music, modern music, that is, into the life of the people. There is too wide a gulf, we are told, between the artist and the people; Schönberg's music is not as popular with the multitude as that of Bach, to say nothing of some other composers. But was there ever a time when pioneer music — the music which we now say made history — was popular with the multitude? Monteverdi, Handel, Beethoven, all composed for an inner ring of connoisseurs; the only difference was that in their day nobody cared about the taste of the multitude, or about educating it to something higher. And the music that they composed for their patrons was "utility music" for the day's consumption, nothing more; why cannot our modern composers follow their example? The patrons have ceased to exist, and the multitude is not educated enough

to demand what the composers want to write. They may
say that they want to write "utility music," but secretly
they hanker after immortality — immortality of a strictly
practical kind. They are very properly jealous of the dead,
and what they really desire is that their own symphonies
should be performed as often as Beethoven's. The obvious
answer to that is that the modern symphonies are not as
good as Beethoven's; but this is a cheap fallacy. Beethoven's symphonies have had the benefit of that unearned
increment which we call a century's reverence; they are
also outside the copyright act. There is yet another reason: the composer being gone to his grave, the modern
conductor can do what he likes with them, whereas in the
case of a modern symphony the conductor has to share the
glory with the composer, even if he does not condescend to
carry out the composer's own intentions.

Herein lies the iniquity of the virtuoso conductor, or of
any virtuoso interpreter: he trades upon our childlike
reverence for the classics in order to get some of that reverence transferred to his own person. It is our own fault;
reverence is merely a self-deceptive mask for ignorance and
lazy-mindedness. If we are still to go on listening to the
classics, we must cease to reverence them: we must set to
work to understand them. It is here that the work of the
musicologists becomes necessary to us; we have to grasp
the fact that all music which is not of the immediate present is "old music," whether it belongs to the current reper-
tory of concert-rooms or not. Sentimental people, especially in Germany, are often inclined to maintain that
certain masterpieces are "timeless," possessions for ever, independent of any historical associations. This is unscien-
tific and absurd; it merely means that these works happen
to be popular at the present moment, whereas many works
contemporary with these favorites have fallen into obliv-

ion — an oblivion from which chance may at any moment
rescue them, as we have recently had occasion enough to
observe.

It is easy to make fun of the pure musicologist, the man
of learning who spends his whole life in libraries, decipher-
ing mediaeval manuscripts, with the occasional relief of
quarreling with some rival palaeographer over what to us
may seem a negligible detail. But he is necessary to our
own studies and indeed to our own enjoyment and pleasure. Half a century ago, England was regarded by all
other nations as "the land without music"; worse than
that, there were many Englishmen who cheerfully accepted this description as true and thought their country
none the worse for it. At the present moment, it can at any
rate be said that Continental opinion has shown signs of
conversion; what is really more important is that the
people of England seem themselves to have been converted.
There exists now a definite belief in England that we are a
musical nation, and that we possess a national music of
which we may feel proud. That belief is for the most part
the creation of the musicologists; it owes something to the
modern composers, but far more — considered as a popular belief — to the historical researchers and to the students of folklore. Consider what has happened in Europe
during recent years; a number of new states have been
formed, and a number of small nations have obtained new
independence. In almost every case the movement towards independence was initiated by men of learning who
collected and wrote down the songs and legends of the
peasant classes. The native language had for centuries
been no more than a dialect spoken only by the illiterate;
the learned classes had spoken and written Latin, the
higher social classes one of the greater modern languages.
During the nineteenth century the native dialect was

gradually and deliberately developed into a literary language by men of learning; whether the ultimate result has been conducive to peace and happiness we must ask the professional historians to decide. I mention this phenomenon merely to show what vast forces can be set in motion by the scholars and the antiquaries.

To return to the world of music and musical research — the problem which is now before us is to direct this research and the forces released by it into such channels as will bring the greatest benefit to musical and general education. The pure musicologist will go his own way; it is impossible to make him submit to direction. Sometimes the best thing that he can do will be to make a dictionary of some sort; fortunately many of them are quite ready to make dictionaries of their own free will.

It is more urgent to consider the direction of research studies for the benefit of two different classes of people: for the ordinary music-loving public, which will certainly not engage in any form of research itself, but which may be induced to read books about music; and for the university-trained musician, who may well be given some training in research methods, even though he prefers in after life to devote himself to more practical aspects of his art.

It is a fundamental principle of all educationalists, I hope, that music, especially for children and young people, should be a source of pleasure and enjoyment. However much they may hate their other lessons — and all of us have hated them in our time — we want to be sure that the music-lesson is a period of happiness. But we must not lose sight of the fact that education is not limited to childhood; if we have been properly started as children, we ought to go on educating ourselves all our lives. One of the main doctrines of modern education is that it is to teach us to make a right use of leisure; and obviously music is here a

factor of the greatest importance, and all the more important to what are called the leisured classes, if they still exist.
We forget, perhaps, when we are comparatively young,
that we ought to prepare for our old age, for a period of life
when emotion plays a diminishing part in our experience,
and when the perceptive and appreciative faculties tend to
become gradually more and more dulled. Our happiness at
that moment, as far as musical enjoyment is concerned,
will depend on how much we have stored up in what I like
to call the "museum of memory" — that section of our
brain in which we have put away our most carefully
selected and treasured recollections of beauty. It is melancholy to renew acquaintance with people whom we remembered as ardent music-lovers at twenty or twenty-five, and
find that at fifty they have almost ceased to care about
music at all. One can often understand that they have had
to give up singing or playing an instrument, and in older
days one could understand that some were cut off against
their will from any sort of cultivated musical intercourse;
but in these days, thanks to wireless, everybody can be a
listener to serious music, and lack of appreciation means
simply that the listener has never accustomed himself in
youth to meet the composer halfway, whether the composer be of modern times or of the past.

There are many people who are positively frightened of
any sort of analytical or historical approach to music, because they are convinced that it would destroy all their
pleasure in the art. There is a saying of some famous scientist that in the field of science chance favors only those
minds which are prepared to benefit by it, and it is a saying which we can apply equally well to every department
of life. None the less — as that scientist knew well —
most people are gamblers by nature; even if they are not
gamblers in finance, they trust to luck for all their emo-

tional experiences, and they even believe that the value of such experience is definitely dependent on its being unexpected. It is a curious thing that even highly cultivated people, who are fully prepared to recognize and to value the intellectual qualities in poetry or in painting, will regard the word "intellectual" as a positive condemnation when applied to music, either to a composition or to its interpretation. It is these people who with their purely instinctive and emotional reactions to music will find themselves left musically bankrupt in old age. We must teach them when young, if we can, that the intellectual appreciation of music immensely widens the powers of enjoyment. What is called good taste generally means submission to reactions that are not analyzed; if we had the courage and the patience to analyze them, we should probably find that they were unreasonable, a hindrance to enjoyment rather than a help.

The historical outlook on music can be cultivated with profit and interest even by the type of amateur who refuses to attempt the most elementary studies in analysis. We must make him see that every piece of music belongs to its own period of history. It is not merely that it expresses the ideas current at a particular epoch; indeed, interpretation of this kind may often become completely misleading, for we are easily tempted to read into a piece of music a subjective interpretation for which there is no real evidence. But we can certainly reconstruct the external conditions under which music was performed at any given period, and they may often help us to a new understanding. All music is movement, and thus associated to a large extent with the movements of the human body. This is most clearly apparent in dance music, but it affects other types of music as well, because so much music of any period is derived in some degree from the rhythms of contemporary dances,

and rhythm is the factor which chiefly defines the characteristics of a period or indeed of a musical nationality. The
music of Handel at once gives us moderns an impression of
stateliness; but why were the movements of Handel's listeners stately? They were obliged to be stately, because
their clothes were so bulky, heavy, and cumbrous; and they
wore heavy clothes because they had such very inadequate
means of warming their houses. Let me give you another
momentary glimpse of those days — this time from Fran-
çois Couperin. "One should always appear to be at one's
ease," he says, "when playing the harpsichord," and to
that purpose he advises the pupil to put a looking-glass on
the desk while he practices, so as to make sure of a pleasing
expression of countenance. We have only to look at the
faces of our modern pianists while playing to see how far
removed we are from the days of Couperin.

I have begun with examples of things one might say to
children or to classes of quite unsophisticated pupils. If we
are considering university students preparing for a musical degree, we shall naturally go far deeper into the subject. The misfortune is that the usual popular handbooks
of musical history and biography are often out of date and
completely misleading. In teaching children, it is no doubt
stimulating to repeat the conventional anecdotes about
the great musicians, if only to impress something on their
memories which will help them to visualize these great
composers as individual human beings in some sort of historical environment. Most of the well-known anecdotes
have now been proved to be untrue; and in any case the
personal biographies of a few selected masters do not constitute the history of music. It is obvious that we must
study the history of the whole technique of composition;
we must analyze the forms in which music is written, and
trace their development. Here again the standard text-

books are hopelessly inadequate. There still remains an enormous amount of scientific research to be done on the history and development of musical forms, and it must be done in conjunction with the history of musical expression, for what the authors of textbooks never seem to make clear to the reader is that the main function of musical form is to intensify expression, that what we call "form" is in fact simply the putting of the expressive climax in exactly the most expressive place.

There are many more things than these which I should wish to include under the historical approach to music, and perhaps I can illustrate them best by taking a single composer as an example, and pointing out some, at any rate, of the lines on which we ought to investigate. Let us consider the case of Handel — I choose him because he is familiar to you all. His period is remote, but at any rate near enough to be well documented. There is still much work on Handel for the pure musicologist to undertake, but at the same time so much information is easily accessible that any ordinary music-lover ought to be able to pursue various aspects of Handel for himself.

Handel's place in the history of oratorio, of opera, of instrumental music — these are all well-worn lecture-subjects, though there is a great deal that is new to be said about them. But I would rather set you thinking about Handel's own personality and how it was formed. One of the favorite methods of modern biographers is to deduce a composer's private life from his music; the result may be an entertaining piece of fiction, but it will have no claim to scientific consideration. We can, however, try to build up Handel's musical personality by studying the music which he himself was certain, or at any rate likely, to have heard in the various phases of his existence. A large quantity of this music has been systematically reprinted in modern times; all we have to do is to go to the library and read it. But we ought to perform some of it too, if we can; it will take a little trouble, for we shall probably have to write out our own orchestral and vocal parts, and perhaps make our own translation into English. There is the old German church music of his days at Halle; there is the German opera of his days at Hamburg. When we follow him to Italy, it will be a little more difficult to reconstruct his environment. Quite early in his Italian tour we shall hear old Corelli say to him that his music is in the French style. So it is; but how did he come to acquire that style without going to France? A little further investigation will show us that French music was well known in Germany in Handel's boyhood, though Handel's German admirers have not drawn too much attention to the fact.

But there is much more to find out about Handel's musical experiences. The poet Brockes tells us in his memoirs that students of the University of Halle used to meet in each other's rooms to practice music. Brockes does not mention Handel by name among his student friends, but it is hardly possible that he should not have come across him. What was the music that those students used to play? Frankly, I do not know; but somebody ought to be able to tell us. And we want to know, too, not only what the serious music was that Handel had to play in church or in the opera house at Hamburg; we want to know what he heard in the streets, what the music was that he heard by accident, perhaps hardly conscious of it, for all this music must have sunk into his brain, just as street music sank into the brain of Bach or Schubert. Handel did hear it, and sometimes he *was* conscious of it, for he pulled a pencil and a piece of music paper out of his pocket and wrote it down; we have evidence of that in some of the Handel manuscripts at the Fitzwilliam Museum in Cambridge. The history of music cannot be limited only to the works of the outstanding men of genius, any more than general history can be limited to that of the kings and queens, or even of the generals and ministers. The political historians many years ago began to give us the history of peoples; and we musical historians must endeavor to reconstruct the history of popular music, even the history of bad music, for that is the inevitable background against which all the great figures stand out, and it is only through a knowledge of the bad music that they can be properly connected with each other and with the social life of their periods.

Handel will furnish us with a good illustration of the vagaries of fashion in musical history. Half a century ago Handel was regarded as pre-eminently a religious composer, the composer not only of *Messiah* and other sacred oratorios, but also of the Chandos anthems. Apart from a few popular favorite songs, such as "Where'er you walk," his secular oratorios were little known, and his operas were so completely forgotten that many ordinary people were quite unaware that he had ever composed any. There was a sort of tacit conspiracy among the learned to suppress all knowledge of them; the admirers of *Messiah* felt positively ashamed of them, and they were considered to be among the things that were not generally talked about. Thanks to a German amateur, now resident in the United States, a professor of fine art and certainly not a musicologist, the world has been made aware during the last few years of these marvelously beautiful dramas. They have opened our ears to a new conception of musical expression, a new association of passion and beauty. Through the study of these works and of other works for the stage which preceded and followed them throughout the course of the eighteenth century we are now gradually finding our way to a new understanding of that whole period, towards a

new appreciation of such composers as Haydn, Mozart, and
Beethoven, whom we thought we had understood for a
hundred years.

But I feel it my duty to warn you against one danger of
modern historical research. I invited you to investigate
the history of the frivolous music of the past; but in doing
so you must not lose sight of its essential frivolity. So
habitual, if not indeed so profound, is our reverence for the
classics, that almost any music seems to acquire the rank
of classicality by the mere passage of time. The comic
operas of Offenbach, when they first came out in Paris
seventy years ago, were regarded as decidedly scandalous;
the public enjoyed them, but serious musicians disapproved of them, as much on technical as on moral grounds.
Now, they are respected classics and are the mainstay of
state-subsidized theatres which thirty years ago would
never have admitted them within their doors. In the same
way we talk reverently of such writers as Galuppi and
Pergolesi — though we do not make much effort to revive
their works on the stage — and we entirely forget that in
their own day they were just providers of popular entertainment, so popular, in fact, that their style was imitated
north of the Alps and eventually became the style of serious symphonic music. It is right that we should study
these forgotten operas in a scientific spirit, but we have to
admit that there is very little use in trying to put them on
the modern stage, except as academic demonstrations.
The learned may be amused by them, but the frivolous
public of today will not. Age has given them respectabil-
ity, and that is fatal to enjoyment.

Ephemeral music of the past teaches us inexorably that
music is of its essence a transitory art. It is made for the
moment, and if it survives for longer, it is only by some
extraneous accident. A piece of music composed yesterday

may be a success today, and if so, the owner of the copy-right will naturally do his best to keep that reputation going as long as he possibly can, in order to make a profit on it. But it is a mistake to think of this as artistic im-mortality; it is a commercial transaction, and artistically speaking, an extraneous accident. What happens today happened in the past as well; the doctrine of artistic immortality has been invented by the museum directors and still more by the art dealers in order to enhance the financial values of paintings and sculptures.

Yet the practical study of musical history has its value — its value, I mean, as a part of the education of young musicians who are eventually going out into the practical world of music. The value of that education does not lie in the memorizing of dates of great composers' births and deaths, or anything of that sort. The real value of histori-cal studies lies in their being made a training of the im-agination. A modern conductor, faced by a score, whether modern or classical, has to be able to read it to himself; more than that, he ought to be able to imagine to himself not merely the pitch and quality of the notes represented, but also their emotional effect. We take all this for granted, and really the task is not such a very difficult one, because the sort of score which a conductor is most likely to have to study will be already more or less familiar to him. Even if he has never heard the work, he may well have heard other works by the same composer or in the same sort of style, so that he is already some way towards imagining the emotional thrill of the one in front of him. But with music of a remoter period, the imaginative act may be much more difficult. There are plenty of conduct-ors who can read a score of Handel or Purcell, and when they come to rehearse it, correct the actual mistakes of their orchestra or chorus. They know quite well how the music will sound when it is played. But there is something missing, and it is the most important thing: they do not know — before they begin the rehearsal — how they *want* this music to sound. The historical student ought to be able to look at a manuscript in a library and be able not only to decipher it and read it, but to read it imaginatively, to read it with the sympathetic knowledge and understanding that comes of learning and scholarship. Nor is this enough. What I want to insist upon is that the reader must consciously and deliberately evoke for himself the complete emotional effect of the work, the emotional effect which the original composer intended; by an act of will and intense self-concentration he must call up and experience in imagination all the emotions which that piece of music evoked in the first audience that ever heard it hundreds of years ago. This act of concentration is a difficult and a very fatiguing experience, but it is well worth while attempting. We are all of us inclined to leave too much to chance in music, whether in listening, in performing, or in composing; even professional musicians, who know the risks they are running, are still liable to leave certain details unanalyzed, especially those details which they suppose to be a matter of what is called temperament or inspiration. It is exactly these mental and emotional problems which really require the most searching analysis. People shirk this emotional analysis not so much from laziness of mind as from a certain sense of fear. They are still haunted by the remains of that futile sense of reverence; they experience an emotion, and like to think that it is a mysterious inspiration direct from heaven. It may be, but even if it is, that is no reason for not analyzing it.

A teacher of music — I speak as a teacher of university students — has to bear two things in mind: he has to encourage his pupils to look at music technically, scientifi-

cally, and analytically; and at the same time he has to encourage them by every means in his power to experience
music emotionally, and to widen their emotional range and
intensify that experience to the utmost. Pupils have to be
considered individually, because every one has his own
peculiarities of temperament; some incline naturally to the
analytical outlook, others to the emotional. The teacher's
difficulty is to persuade them, whichever be their type,
that these two outlooks are not in the least incompatible;
they are only the front and back, the outside and inside, of
the same thing. The trouble with English pupils is that
they have been brought up from infancy to maltreat their
emotions — to conceal them, to suppress them, and even
to ignore them: the result is that even when they have very
deep emotional reactions to music, they do not know what
to do with them. It is curiously difficult to induce them to
practice self-analysis and at the same time self-intensifica-
tion on the emotional plane. They regard self-intensifi-
cation, perhaps not unreasonably, as dangerous or im-
moral, perhaps as mere foolishness; and emotional analysis
seems cold-blooded and possibly even devilish. The study
of old music, like the study of a dead language, has the
advantage that it removes these emotional problems on to
what one might call an academic plane. It is easier to perform an anatomical demonstration on the dead than on the
living.

The professional musician — by which I mean the man
who takes upon himself the dedicated life of music — has
to realize that what distinguishes him from the amateur is
that he is perpetually under contract to his public; that he
makes music, not for his own pleasure, but to give pleasure
to others. Like the actor on the stage, the musician has to
stir and control the emotions of his audience, not his own.
He can do this only if he has himself experienced the emo-

tions which he wishes to produce: that is, if he has experienced them at some former time, analyzed them and stored them up in his memory, knowing exactly how to find them when required, like a book in a well-ordered library, knowing exactly how to reproduce the actions which will induce them in his listeners. This process is the same always, whether it be applied to composition or to interpretation.

Historical studies in music are a valuable aid to the training of the mind in this analysis and conscious synthesis of emotional understanding. Music is a language which changes much more rapidly in the course of time than any of our literary languages. Ordinary languages are obliged to retain a certain number of words which hardly ever change, because they express things which have remained the same for centuries — human relationships such as "father" and "mother," human necessities such as "bread" and "cheese." It is the poetic element in language which changes more rapidly, because poetry is halfway from speech to music. It is this part of language which becomes obsolete and even dead, in the sense in which we talk of dead languages; and just as we have to set to work to learn these dead languages systematically, so we have to learn the dead languages and dialects of music. They are the foundation of our own, as Greek and Latin are of the languages of speech. It is on these principles that we must train up the coming generations of musicians. To walk through a picture-gallery, verifying the titles and numbers in the guide-book, noting perhaps industriously the features and characteristics therein summarily mentioned, without receiving or even seeking any emotional artistic experience, is a waste of time. The study of musical history is equally a waste of time unless we perform the old music that we excavate and hear it with our own ears. It